New Perspectives on Human Resource Management

The idea of Human Resource Management has become topical and controversial. The term suggests that people in any organization are an asset to be upgraded and fully utilized rather than merely a variable cost to be minimized. This in turn implies that the way in which people are managed is a matter of crucial strategic concern.

Increased international competition has produced various initiatives world-wide for new approaches to management, in particular human resource management. Despite growing interest among both practitioners and observers, serious, considered and informed literature on the topic has lagged far behind the demand for knowledge. There has been a lack of theoretical analysis and of hard empirical data. This volume seeks to correct the neglect on both fronts, with important new contributions from leading teachers and researchers in the field.

This new and searching set of interpretations will be of interest to serious practitioners and students alike. General managers and line managers, as well as those in personnel specialist positions, will find the book of use. The different perspectives provided by individual chapters will be necessary reading for students of management at second and third year level and those taking MBA courses.

The Editor

John Storey is a Principal Research Fellow in the Industrial Relations Research Unit at the University of Warwick, where he is also the lecturer responsible for the Human Resource Management module on the Consortium MBA.

New Perspectives on Human Resource Management

Edited by
John Storey

R

Routledge
London and New York

ROBERT MANNING
STROZIER LIBRARY

FEB 21 1990

Tallahasse   la

HF
5549
N375
1989

First published 1989 by Routledge
11 New Fetter Lane, London EC4P 4EE
29 West 35th Street, New York, NY 10001

© 1989 John Storey (in the editorial material and in his own contributions).
Chapter 2 © Karen Legge; Chapter 3 © David E. Guest; Chapter 4 ©
Derek Torrington; Chapter 5 © John Purcell; Chapter 6 © Barbara
Townley; Chapter 7 © Ewart Keep; Chapter 8 © Tom Schuller; Chapter 9
© Nicholas Kinnie; Chapter 10 © Peter Armstrong; Chapter 11 © John
Storey and Keith Sisson.

Phototypeset in 10pt Times by
Mews Photosetting, Beckenham, Kent
Printed and bound in Great Britain by
Biddles Ltd, Guildford and King's Lynn

All rights reserved. No part of this book may be reprinted or reproduced or
utilized in any form or by any electronic, mechanical, or other means, now
known or hereafter invented, including photocopying and recording, or in
any information storage or retrieval system, without permission in writing
from the publishers.

British Library Cataloguing in Publication Data

New perspectives on human resource management.
  1. Personnel management
  I. Storey, John, *1947–*
  658.3

ISBN 0-415-01040-3
    0-415-01041-1 (pbk)

Library of Congress Cataloging-in-Publication Data

New perspectives on human resource management / edited by John Storey.
     p.   cm.
  Bibliography: p.
  Includes index.
    ISBN 0-415-01040-3 (U.S.). — ISBN 0-415-01041-1 (U.S.: pbk.)
    1. Personnel management. I. Storey, John.
  HF5549.N375 1989
  658.3—dc20   89-33067
                                      CIP

Contents

Contents

Tables

Figures

Contributors

Peter Armstrong, Lecturer, University of East Anglia

David Guest, Senior Lecturer in Industrial Relations, London School of Economics

Ewart Keep, Research Fellow, Industrial Relations Research Unit, University of Warwick

Nicholas Kinnie, Lecturer in Industrial Relations, University of Bath

Karen Legge, Reader in Personnel Management, Imperial College, London

John Purcell, Fellow, Templeton College, Oxford

Tom Schuller, Senior Lecturer, University of Warwick

Keith Sisson, Professor of Industrial Relations and Director of the Industrial Relations Research Unit, University of Warwick

John Storey, Principal Research Fellow, Industrial Relations Research Unit, University of Warwick

Derek Torrington, Senior Lecturer in Personnel Management, University of Manchester Institute of Science and Technology

Barbara Townley, Lecturer in Industrial Relations, Industrial Relations Research Unit, University of Warwick

Preface

The idea for a book of this kind was conceived during the early stages of a major research project upon which I was engaged from January 1986. But there is also a more general and a more immediate background to the volume. The former is the coordinated programme of research in the IRRU at the University of Warwick directed at assessing 'the managerial role in industrial relations' broadly defined. A number of interlinked projects, most of them funded by the ESRC, were launched around three years ago. They include wide-scale survey work (Edwards 1987; Marginson et al. 1988); analysis of public policy regarding the management of training (Keep 1987); the management of collective bargaining (Sisson 1988); theoretical and historical analysis of the divisions within and the competition between managerial professions (Armstrong 1988); assessment of flexible employment strategies (Pollert 1988); and case-study work on changes in the management of the employment relationship with particular emphasis on the developing role of general and line managers (Storey 1987a and b and forthcoming). Also part of the general background has been the ferment in the whole area of management in recent years and a growing awareness of the urgent need to pull many of the separate strands together in order to begin a reasoned assessment of the meaning and significance of these developments.

The more immediate trigger to this particular collection of chapters has been the organization of Warwick conferences and short courses on the themes discussed herein. For example, in conjunction with the Department of Continuing Education, the IRRU is running a series of workshops for lecturers in higher education; the one on human resource management has now run twice and has been oversubscribed. New modules in such courses as BTEC probably represent one explanation for the level of current demand for knowledge in this area. But it is by no means the only one. At a time when it was often thought that hard-pressed MBA students would flock mainly to electives such as accounting and marketing which at the moment command high currency in the jobs' market, the human resource management electives on the various versions of the MBA at Warwick and elsewhere, have in fact been enjoying popular support and acclaim. Noticeably the demand comes not only from students but from their employing organizations. Moreover, if we move beyond the MBA, it is also apparent that senior management from a wide spectrum of organizations are keen to develop their understanding in this area and this is amply demonstrated by the take-up of places at workshops and conferences which have been offered in recent months. In Britain there are plans for two new journals on human resource management and at Warwick there have been proposals for a distance learning master's degree with the same title – moreover, there is much institutional support from the major professional bodies for such initiatives.

From these few examples it may be gauged that the subject (or field of enquiry) is burgeoning. But what is remarkable is that there is very little rigorous academic research to underpin the debate. There was, in consequence, an evident gap and so, in addition to preparing a research monograph which would report on recent field work in the area (Storey, forthcoming), it seemed sensible to bring together a number of key contributors whose work would bring a variety of perspectives to bear. The final trigger to the actual production of this book was a researchers' workshop at the University of Warwick in January 1988. Invited guests from most of the major business schools and industrial-relations and management departments gathered together to assess the kind of issues addressed in this book. The workshop was novel in a number of respects and the production of formal papers, for example, was discouraged; the intention was to examine these important issues without the constraints of 'defending' prepared positions. Hence the chapters in this book are decidedly not an edited collection of conference papers. Rather, they are especially commissioned papers on themes which the contributors have all had a chance to debate collectively before even drafting their chapters.

The intended audience for this book includes anyone who is seriously interested in making sense of what can fairly be described, without overstatement, as 'the HRM phenomenon'. It would be tedious to go through the routine of elaborating a list of types of potential readers; suffice it to say that our experience of managerial practitioners and trade-union representatives through our conference programme and through our research activity, leads us to emphasize the point that in addition to the students from a range of academic disciplines who are likely to find this book of use there will also be a considerable number of other readers. For example, moves towards devolved budgeting, new forms of appraisal and performance-linked pay in such diverse settings as health care and education as well as the private-sector services and manufacturing, suggest that a wide range of general readers may also find the commentaries in this book to be of interest. By no means, therefore, will it be personnel specialists alone who will be looking to a book of this type to cut through the pieties and the 'motherhoods' on communications, 'walking the job', and the like. General managers and line managers from all sectors may be expected to look to it in order to gain access to the less prescriptive but, we trust, the more enduringly useful forms of searching analysis and informed commentary which we have striven to produce here.

Acknowledgements are due to the ESRC for funding much of the work upon which many of the ensuing analyses draw. In addition I would like to thank all the people who devoted their time and energy in cooperating in the project on the management of human resources on which I have been engaged since 1986. Thanks are also due to colleagues within the IRRU who continue, in multifarious ways, to recreate it as a unique institution.

Abbreviations

ACAS	Advisory, Conciliation and Arbitration Service
BSC	British Steel Corporation
CBI	Confederation of British Industry
DE	Department of Employment
EETPU	Electrical, Electronic, Telecommunications and Plumbing Union
ESRC	Economic and Social Research Council
FT	The Financial Times
GNP	Gross National Product
HMSO	Her Majesty's Stationery Office
HRD	Human Resource Development
HRM	Human Resource Management
IBM	International Business Machines
IDS	Incomes Data Services
IPM	Institute of Personnel Management
IRRR	Industrial Relations Review and Report
IRRU	Industrial Relations Research Unit
MBA	Master of Business Administration
MSC	Manpower Services Commission
NEDO	National Economic Development Office
OD	Organizational Development
QWL	Quality of Working Life
SAYE	Save As You Earn
TUC	Trades Union Congress
TVEI	Technical and Vocational Educational Initiative
WIRS1	Workplace Industrial Relations Survey, Number 1
WIRS2	Workplace Industrial Relations Survey, Number 2

Chapter one

Introduction: from personnel management to human resource management

John Storey

It seems hard to deny that there is a highly charged atmosphere surrounding the discussion of management at the present time. Fuelled by such best-selling books as *In Search of Excellence*, *The Change Masters* and *Iacocca*, the cult of the manager appears, if anything, to have been never so entrenched. At the same time, the idea of 'the management of change' has come to assume a place which is part and parcel of the everyday job responsibility of the manager. It is no longer a special sub-routine only brought out for special occasions such as the opening of a new facility or a corporate merger. There would appear to be a plethora of initiatives, programmes and innovations of all kinds. From the financial and management pages and from such sources as IDS and IRS, examples assail us of moves to introduce total quality, to re-differentiate organizations into strategic business units, to enhance flexibility, to install performance-related pay, to institute novel forms of employment contract, and the launch is announced of many other such initiatives. The image is of restlessness and organizational innovation. The frequently heralded displacement, or at least modification, of bureaucracy as the dominant organizational form seems belatedly to be taking place.

One cannot help but be impressed by the widespread awareness among practitioners of such experimentation; meetings with managers at all levels even in conventional, mainstream organizations soon reveal the fact that current 'flavours' have permeated the managerial consciousness and imagination in a way that was never the case with, for example, OD, job enrichment, QWL and other much-vaunted 'movements' of previous decades which some critics cite as equivalents.

There is some prima facie evidence that in response to conditions of heightened competition and a range of other environmental changes, many if not most of the organizations which survived the severe recession of the early 1980s have initiated changes of one sort or another in order to improve their viability. These have included structural changes such as a move beyond divisionalisation into strategic business units (SBUs). The underlying idea here is to promote and exploit entrepreneurial behaviour. Hence, even in single-business and single-product organizations which have lent themselves to neither divisionalization nor SBUs, the cognate tendency has manifested itself in attempts to generate the idea that

1

separate units, departments, areas or zones could and should be treated as if they were 'mini-businesses'.

On the face of it these sorts of changes have been associated with, and possibly underpinned by, accompanying cultural changes. Notable here has been the attention given to in-company campaigns (usually steered by management consultants) to establish a culture of 'total quality' and to give renewed emphasis to customer-orientation, innovation, enterprise and competitiveness. Developments of this kind have given rise to, and in turn been fuelled by, an influential literature on 'excellence' and 'corporate culture'.

For those interested in the management of the employment relationship, two questions immediately arise even from such a brief sketch of recent business initiatives. First, to what extent do they mark a paradigmatic break with a previously predominating form? Second, what association do they have with the way labour is managed?

The latter issue is considered first. Clearly, the battery of changes indicated above cannot, in themselves, be thought of as necessarily coterminous with the phrase 'human resource management' – no matter how widely that concept is stretched. But they might suggest a set of circumstances which impel senior managers who used to take little interest in 'industrial relations' (see Winkler 1974) to identify the people factor as peculiarly critical in successfully managing the transformations outlined. This may in part derive simply because respected sources continually emphasize the apparently trite message that 'people are the key' (to success). But prescription and exhortation rarely seem to have been influential in the past with British managers (witness the subject of training). In addition therefore, one has to look also to the kind of context which seemingly generates a more receptive climate for ideas which spell a change in direction. A classic example is the case of British Airways which, in the early 1980s, faced a dire situation and where the strategy chosen to achieve competitiveness – namely an enhanced form of customer-care – clearly depended critically upon the behaviour of employees at many points across the operation.

The dramatic turnaround of BA (though by no means solely attributable to its training programme) and the publicity given to similar cases, added another ingredient to the climate of change: a highly visible group of 'role-models'. Of greater importance, however, has probably been the infiltration of these ideas into the not inconsiderable network of personal contacts at senior echelons of corporate Britain. 'Significant others' were beginning to treat the people question as crucial. But in what way?

A key tendency appears to be the increased emphasis that is being placed upon 'individual' as opposed to 'collective' relations. Accordingly, there is the recent upsurge of interest in direct forms of communication and involvement – often taking the form of team briefings, quality circles and the like. Commensurate with this are the developments in integrated reward systems, and the linking of remuneration to performance. The renewed interest in harmonization can also be seen as a logical extension of such initiatives. There is also some evidence of new patterns of working – perhaps the most notable theme here being the attention given to various forms of flexibility. In a number of organizations these kinds of development are symbolized by the change in terminology from 'industrial relations' to 'employee relations' and from 'personnel management' to 'human resource management'.

This notion of 'human resource management' has become very topical. As a set of interrelated practices with an ideological and philosophical underpinning, it appears to align closely with prevailing ideas of enterprise, and the freeing-up of managerial initiative. There is tremendous interest in the phenomenon from both practitioners and observers alike but, as yet, the literature has by no means caught up with the demand for knowledge. Knowledge, that is, both in the sense of 'facts' and informed analysis. There is a lacuna in theoretical and conceptual discussion (for example, on the meaning, distinctiveness and significance of HRM) and hard empirical data (e.g. on the extent of its application across organizations and its pervasiveness and impact in those organizations which profess to practise it). This book seeks to correct for the neglect of information on both fronts. It brings together some of the country's foremost teachers and researchers on the management of personnel and industrial relations. They bring to bear a variety of disciplines (economics, sociology and psychology to name just the most basic) and a variety of perspectives (empirical, theoretical, practical and critical).

There is another distinctive feature to this book: the contributions herein are all British. Previously, nearly all of the available material on the topic was American and in consequence it was such corporations as IBM, Hewlett Packard, and General Motors which loomed large in most case-study discussion. Moreover, American perspectives differ and the language, assumptions, and so much else are at a sufficient distance from their British counterparts that it has been very difficult to make sensible interpretations of the relevance of this literature to the British and European employment scene. Thus, for example, the figure of one Irving Bluestone, the United Auto Workers' Vice President, who cuts such a dash in many American accounts of 'transformations' to labour relations in the United States, would seem to have no counterpart in Britain. Despite the diversity in the stances taken by the contributors to this volume, none adopts quite the same kind of effusiveness which is often encountered in American commentaries and which strikes such a discordant note in the British context. There are of course certain instances where British literature appears to ape the prescriptive American style (see for example, Goldsmith and Clutterbuck 1984; Lessom 1986; Martin and Nicholls 1987) but, in the main, academics and practitioners alike tend to remain sceptical. And rightly so, for, despite certain undoubted similarities in particular practices, the British work context is very different and it is only sensible to expect that any 'take-up' of American-style/Japanese-style 'human resource management' will involve, at best, some considerable adaptation. It is the precise nature of this which has so far failed adequately to be considered.

The various chapters in this book examine the phenomenon of human resource management both in toto and in its various parts. Given that the intention was to promote a searching *analysis* of the concept, it was inevitable that certain contrasts and disagreements would emerge between the contributors. This is to be welcomed. The reader has the opportunity to engage with, and to assess, the topic at different levels ranging from the overview – as in Legge's chapter – to the more specific, where the implications for practice in selection, appraisal, training and involvement are addressed. It would not be appropriate in this introductory chapter to attempt to 'resolve' aspects of the ensuing debate. The main strands are, however, pulled together in the concluding chapter. But it may be helpful here if a backcloth to the discussion, a framework and an overview of the contributions were to be sketched out. These then will be the aims of the remainder of this introduction.

The backcloth

Within the academic as opposed to the 'managerial' literature, there is – despite an earlier period of caution – an increasing recognition that something significant may be happening in the management of the employment relationship. The landmark and relatively sober contribution by Kochan, Katz and McKersie (1986) has charted and interpreted the changes in the United States, but as noted, there has, as yet, been no British equivalent. Debates have raged none the less about 'the new industrial relations' and about a possible shift from the management of collective relations to the management of human resources.

For some readers, of course, the term 'human resource management' can be expected to carry no particular connotation or convey any particular distinctive meaning when placed alongside such terms as 'personnel management', 'employee relations' or indeed simply 'the management of people'. Yet, to an astonishing degree for an increasing number of managers and students of management, the term 'human resource management' – usually somewhat grandiloquently abbreviated into the capitalized 'HRM' – has recently come to take on a quite extraordinary significance. Whether to be applauded or derided, the concept has come to represent one of the most controversial signifiers in managerial debate in the 1980s. So much so indeed that, for example, even the house journal of the Institute of Personnel Management experienced a period of dispute over the proposal to change its title from 'Personnel Management' to 'Human Resource Management'. The journal now carries, as a compromise solution, the subtitle 'The Magazine for Human Resource Professionals'. The IPM has also sponsored a Chair at Strathclyde University, notably not in personnel management but in human resource management.

The term itself is in fact not new: one can find examples of its use nearly 40 years ago, especially in North America. But for many years the term carried no special significance and it tended to be used more or less interchangeably with a whole host of alternative formulations to signal what most would understand as personnel management. In the 1980s it has, however, come to denote a radically different philosophy and approach to the management of people at work – applicable alike to manual workers, staff and managerial grades. In its reworked usage it often purports to signal the interweaving of a number of elements which, in sum, demarcate it sharply *from* personnel management as commonly understood.

Arguably even 20 or 30 years ago, commentators using this term were wanting to signal the possibility of a more 'sophisticated' alternative approach to labour management. Hence what is different about the 1980s is not so much that the message itself has changed but that it is being received more seriously.

Personnel management has long been dogged by problems of credibility, marginality, ambiguity and a 'trash-can' labelling which has relegated it to a relatively disconnected set of duties – many of them tainted with a low-status 'welfare' connotation. The classic analysis of such power and credibility issues is to be found in Legge (1978) and she updates her analysis in Chapter 2 of this book. She raises the key question concerning whether HRM and personnel management are in fact so different after all when both are compared at the normative (i.e. 'this is how the practice *should* be') level.

For a brief interlude, a new era for personnel specialists seemed to have arrived in the 1970s when trade-union power had to be accommodated and a new body of employment legislation had to be absorbed. In the 1980s, however, employers have taken a relatively more relaxed attitude to both of these forces and personnel management has accordingly been re-exposed to traditional uncertainties. Purcell (1985), for example, raised doubts about the future survival of personnel at the corporate level. (He, in fact, records a major reappraisal of his thinking on this issue in Chapter 5 of this book.)

At this juncture, HRM might appear to offer timely salvation to a specialism which has been diagnosed as highly vulnerable. To use Tyson's terminology, the 'contracts manager' – the collective bargaining expert whose skills were so valued in the 1970s – has come to seem a threatened species in the 1980s. The IPM is trying to reorientate the profession so that its members become identified not so much with trade-union relations and with 'over-bureaucratic departments isolated from the main priorities of the business' but instead they become associated with 'positive images' such as imaginative pay schemes, profit-sharing arrangements, flexibility and training, and management development. To a large extent, the IPM will be pushing against an open door with this campaign, for it is remarkable to encounter so many senior personnel practitioners today who profess to have 'always believed' that personnel work was really about training and development and the like. HRM now seems to promise a board-level or at the very least a senior-executive-level presence for the people-management specialist (M. Armstrong 1987; Miller 1987). But there still seems to be considerable uncertainty as to whether HRM represents a threat or an opportunity to personnel management (for example, see Torrington and Hall 1987). There remains contention about the extent to which personnel specialists are in control of, or can even influence the course of the phenomenon (Storey 1987a and b).

Each of these themes will be found to figure prominently in the ensuing chapters.

Concepts and frameworks

In spite of the flurry of activity noted above, the concept at the centre of it remains problematical. In stereotyped form it appears capable of making good each of the main shortcomings of personnel management. Thus, far from being marginalized, the human resource management function becomes recognized as a central business concern; its performance and delivery are integrated into line management; the aim shifts from merely securing compliance to the more ambitious one of winning commitment. The employee resource, therefore, becomes worth investing in, and training and development thus assume a higher profile. These initiatives are associated with, and maybe are even predicated upon, a tendency to shift from a collective orientation to the management of the workforce to an individualistic one. Accordingly, management looks for 'flexibility' and seeks to reward differential performance in a differential way. Communication of managerial objectives and aspirations takes on a whole new importance; it is not undertaken because the EEC, the government, the trade unions, or even a section of the workforce want it to be done, or because it sounds like a laudable and 'fair' thing to do, but because it is regarded as necessary if the workforce is to be effectively *utilized*. When trying to communicate, for example, managers are increasingly unwilling to submit to the erstwhile convention of transmitting messages via the trade unions. In sum, through a range of such *mutually reinforcing* initiatives, management may, it is thought, be able to effect a step-change in its dealings with employees.

The attribute of HRM which perhaps excites the most intense interest is that which allegedly locates HRM policy formulation firmly at the *strategic* level (Beer *et al*. 1985). But this raises the question as to whether the strategic link is a sine qua non of HRM. There has been considerable discussion of the concept of 'strategic human resource management' (e.g. Fombrun, Tichy, and Devanna 1984; Hendry and Pettigrew 1986; Foulkes 1986). By implication this would seemingly allow for the possibility of *operational* HRM at a more routine level. Such a usage would also mean that the viability of HRM is not totally dependent on the 'strategic' link and attempts to define HRM in terms of the strategic connection would likewise be invalidated. It would follow therefore that there are variants of HRM.

Interpretations of either type tend, however, to insist that a characteristic of HRM lies in its internally coherent approach. That is, there is a suggested alignment between each of the main 'people-management' interventions. This is classically expressed by Devanna, Fombrun, and Tichy (1984: 41) as illustrated in Figure 1.1.

Empirical research (Storey 1987; and forthcoming), does indeed reveal a considerable degree of revitalized attention in many of Britain's major companies to each of these four key constituent elements of selection, appraisal, rewards, and development. Hence, the increase in experimentation with psychological testing for managers, staff and manual workers (e.g. at Austin Rover, Jaguar and Peugeot) is some indication of how selection procedures are being tackled

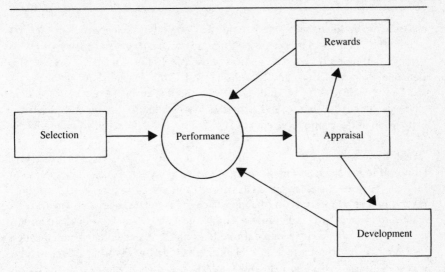

Figure 1.1 The human resource management cycle

more seriously. In the area of rewards, there is heightened interest in installing performance-linked pay (as, for example, for NHS managers and managers in the major clearing banks). Appraisal systems are being dusted down (in the wake of a flurry of activity built around the concept of 'competencies' following the American work by Boyatzis (1982) and others. Hence, many big companies in Britain such as Shell, National Westminster Bank, BP and Whitbread are now moving with alacrity towards delineating managerial 'competencies' and key skills. Perhaps most controversially, the whole area of training and development has been bathed in limelight. A host of reports have catalogued the lack of serious attention to training in this country (see, for example, Coopers and Lybrand 1985; NEDO/MSC 1984) and a host more have made the same point about management education, training and development (Constable and McCormick 1987; Handy 1987). Certain companies seem on the face of it to be attending to this area with renewed vigour and commitment. Thus one could instance Jaguar's open learning programme; the investment made in training by Lucas (NEDO 1987); the well-publicized case of British Airways, and the less-publicized case of British Steel. A climate of official blessing for this kind of activity is generated by the work of the Training Commission. What may be significant, however, is that while reports lamenting the under-provision of training in this country are not new (see, for example, NEDO 1965), the head of steam built up around the Management Charter Group Initiative – despite certain internal conflicts – suggests that the climate of receptivity may be very different. It would of course be premature to speculate about the future of this specific initiative.

Faced with such a catalogue of developments, some observers are persuaded of the idea of a sea-change while others remain deeply sceptical. At bottom there are two arenas for debate; one is empirical, the other conceptual. On the first it has to be said that, remarkable as it may seem, and despite a number of major surveys that touch on cognate matters (Edwards 1987; Marginson *et al.* 1988; Batstone 1984; Millward and Stevens 1986; or, for a synopsis of the surveys, see Legge 1988), there is, quite simply, a marked insufficiency of *systematic* evidence about the nature and extent of change in the practices which give expression to the central concepts of HRM. This issue is examined more closely in the final chapter.

On the second area for debate, the conceptual, it is also evident that interpretations of found changes vary because of the elasticity in the meaning of the term 'human resource management'. Clearly, it can be used in a restricted sense so reserving it as a label only for that approach to labour management which treats labour as a valued asset rather than a variable cost and which accordingly counsels investment in the labour resource through training and development and through measures designed to attract and retain a committed workforce. Alternatively, it is sometimes used in an extended way so as to refer a whole array of recent managerial initiatives including measures to increase the flexible utilization of the labour resource and other measures which are largely directed at the individual employee. But another distinction can also be drawn. This directs attention to the 'hard' and 'soft' versions of HRM. The hard one emphasizes the quantitative, calculative and business-strategic aspects of managing the headcounts resource in as 'rational' a way as for any other economic factor. By contrast, the 'soft' version traces its roots to the human-relations school; it emphasizes communication, motivation, and leadership.

These two types of distinctions do not correspond, but it is possible to consider the implications of different combinations of them. For example, under the restricted and the soft versions, HRM is to be regarded as *one* type of strategy chosen in preference to a range of others. The agenda for research and debate naturally turns to the question of which employment sectors and which types of organizations opt for this sort of approach. With the extended and hard versions, however, the assumption tends to be that this usage is so expansive it becomes simply a generic term to substitute for labour management in all of its forms. But thinking about the issue in this way may lead us to miss an important point: namely, what is significant about 'human resource management' – and the factor that could explain the remarkable level of interest in it – is that it *marks a departure* from a largely prevailing orthodoxy, it promises an alternative (or more accurately and significantly) a *set* of alternatives to what might be described as the 'Donovan' model. Hence, 20 years after the Royal Commission's Report was published (Donovan 1968) it is becoming clear that the fragile consensus built around formalization of procedures and around juridification as a means of handling employment relations and of propitiating labour, has come under severe strain. In this sense, HRM is a near-equivalent in the labour sphere, of the currently popular idea of 'the management of change'. If this interpretation has any validity it would remain the case that the meaning of the term is still much wider than the 'investment in a valued resource' version which some commentators will undoubtedly wish to retain as their preferred version. But it does narrow the concept to something far more distinctive than a simple catch-all which has usually been thought to be the only alternative meaning to the narrow one.

What is crucial is that HRM in either of the two senses sketched here is to be seen as an 'emergent' phenomenon and relatedly, therefore, it implies something different from the proceduralized approach to handling labour. The classic definitions of industrial relations refer to it as 'the making and administering of rules which regulate employment relationships' (Bain and Clegg 1974) and declare the focus of its study to be 'the institutions of job regulation' (Flanders 1965: 10); but what is distinctive about HRM, in both the hard and soft versions, is that it eschews the joint regulative approach – and even more so the craft regulative approach. It is impatient of custom and practice, of the going rate, of parity, mutuality, of rule-books and procedure manuals, of deferring to personnel and IR specialists. In their place the various initiatives which might, for convenience sake, be denoted as HRM, place emphasis on utilizing labour to its full capacity or potential. HRM is therefore about (and the term is used neutrally here) *exploiting* the labour resource more fully. This may be by upgrading it through training or by job redesign so that labour is deployed more flexibly across tasks, it may also mean, however, de-manning so that the remaining labour time is simply used more intensively. Whether labelled as 'sophisticated managerialism' or in some other way, it has to be remembered therefore that, at its most basic, HRM represents a set of managerial initiatives. But this is only the beginning not the end of the story, for there are many interesting questions relating to the nature and composition of these initiatives, the circumstances of their formulation, and the drama of their attempted implementation.

Naturally, depending upon the particular interests to be defended, reactions to each approach will differ markedly. The TUC has expressed profound concern about the perceived spread of HRM not least because of its association in the United States with non-unionism. Largely for this reason NEDO has judiciously opted for the term 'human resource development' (HRD). Meanwhile, for their part, personnel professionals may take up Torrington's suggestion in this book that they stake out clearly the sort of distinctive contribution which they can make. For Torrington this would be an expertise based on a melding of a range of earlier approaches and dispensed (using a medical analogy) in the manner of the general practitioner. But if Armstrong in Chapter 10 is correct, their chances of success in marking out a distinct contribution will be slim so long as they remain in thrall to the parameters laid down by management accountants.

If HRM is seen to cover both the hard and soft versions, one final question remains and this relates to the issue of 'integration'. As we have seen, this is one of the most often-cited criteria of HRM. Despite the host of examples of take-up of appraisal, development, and the like, there is still almost no evidence available about the extent to which organizations have in fact managed to *interlink* these in a mutually supportive way. (Though many organizations have certainly embraced the idea as a priority aspiration.) This is an issue that should be borne in mind therefore when reading this book and related works. There is also the question of integration with wider corporate strategy. Here the renewed recognition of the potentially vital role played by the people-element in delivering a successful business strategy is illustrated in the MSC/NEDO (1987) package put together by the consultants Peat Marwick McLintock, entitled 'People: The Key to Success' and subtitled 'Strategic Planning, Performance, and People'. The package includes a demonstration video, an 'action pack' and a pre-prepared model 'presentation'. Significantly this is all aimed not at personnel specialists but at the chief executive – indeed the slide presentation is actually headed 'Chief Executive's Presentation to the Board'. The contents are broadly familiar; the idea that competitive advantage is gained through people; that this therefore requires a competent and committed workforce; and that the business plan must itself embrace the people aspects. The case examples of 'good practice' furnished in the accompanying video make clear that the preferred model is built centrally around the upfront 'soft' dimensions of HRM though, as is so often the case, the 'hard' elements are there in the background.

Such instances of top policy-level prescription serve to raise in sharp form the urgent issue of the theoretical coherence of the model and a need to have available sound and rigorous academic research, analysis, and comment. Regrettably it has to be said that, so far, the academic community has not responded to the challenge. Remarkable though it may seem, there is simply no serious extended treatment available on this potentially crucial set of developments. There are of course numerous textbooks on personnel management and a still-thriving prescriptive stream. But, until now, it has been very hard to locate material which attends to these issues in a searching and critical fashion.

Chapters in this volume: rationale and overview

In selecting the range of topics and contributions to be found in this book three criteria were uppermost. First, the broad field of human resource management had to be given a reasonable coverage. Hence the contributions range from conceptual and theoretical analysis, through corporate strategic issues, trade unions and industrial relations, divisions within management, the relationship between HRM and managerial control systems, and on to particular aspects of HRM practice focusing especially on training, selection, appraisal, and involvement.

Second, in addition to an extensive coverage we also looked for depth of analysis. All of the contributors are experienced researchers whose past work has demonstrated a rigour and substance which eschews superficial 'flavour of the month' reportage. Thus the aim under this heading was to ensure that each of the contributory themes would be tackled with this kind of serious rigour.

Third, without imagining that it would be possible to achieve a precise 'balance' of perspectives, it was nevertheless intended to encourage a plurality of approaches. There has been no attempt to find a 'party line' or to disguise disagreement: it is from these areas of uncertainty that we expect to gain guidance in identifying the issues requiring the most urgent attention by researchers and policy-makers.

In Chapter 2 Karen Legge opens up the debate with a closely-reasoned critique of the ideas behind the term. She begins with a distinction between normative and descriptive meanings of HRM. At the normative level she judges that there is, in fact, very little difference between HRM and personnel management; after all it is not difficult to find idealized models of the supposed integrative and strategic nature of personnel work and such books date back many years.

But it is interesting to note that while she says there are *few* differences, she nevertheless finds that there are *some*. Three key ones are discussed. These are, first, that HRM focuses on what is done to managers whereas personnel implies that managers do things to other employees. Secondly, HRM casts line managers in a far more proactive role. They are to be held accountable for the way in which they handle labour – measured now not by how punctilious they have been in following the personnel manual but in terms of utilization as measured by bottom-line results. Thirdly, HRM emphasizes top management's responsibility for 'managing culture'.

Having isolated these, Legge demonstrates how each of them is beset by contradictions of an external and internal character. For example, the adoption of business portfolio management techniques by multi-business companies presents attendant problems of engendering a coherent corporate culture. Withdrawing from certain markets or even simply reducing exposure within them is likely to entail a number of human casualties and these she suggests are not likely to be rationalized away with the notions which have so far been canvassed – such as that of 'tough love'. As regards internal contradictions, these can be seen, for example, in the clash between individualism and team working – both of which are central values to HRM. Similarly, Legge detects tensions in trying to develop certain forms of commitment – such as commitment to skill – when the organization also seeks to persuade employees to be flexible. Though perhaps a more obvious tension is between commitment and lack of job security.

A different approach is taken by David Guest in Chapter 3. The analysis begins with the useful observation that the nature of HRM can be derived empirically or conceptually and that either approach carries the risk of tautology. The escape from the dilemma is made by developing instead a set of testable propositions. Here Guest develops a model which draws connections between HRM aims, policies, and outcomes. The basis of the idea is indicated by Table 1.1.

Table 1.1 A human resource management framework

HRM aims	HRM policies	HRM outcomes
For example: *high commitment *quality *flexible working	For example: 'selection will be on the basis of specific criteria using sophisticated tests'	For example: *low labour turnover *allegiance to company

Turning to the implications of such an approach for trade unions and industrial relations, Guest distinguishes between the circumstances of the greenfield sites and the established plants. He observes that HRM though unitarist and individualist in character is not necessarily overtly anti-union and he warns against conflating non-unionism and HRM. It is also stressed that HRM is only one of a range of possible options available to management.

He suggests that there is an incompatibility between HRM and IR; in consequence, if HRM policies are pursued something has to give. At 'a significant proportion of foreign-owned greenfield sites management is pursuing some of the central features of HRM' (p. 50). In these cases there tends, at best, to be only a limited role for trade unions. For established plants, Guest turns to the major surveys for evidence about the extent of HRM-type initiatives. He finds a mixed picture but on the whole draws the lesson that HRM in these situations has made limited progress. Using the examples of Tioxide and Norsk Hydro, however, he draws the interim conclusion that there are particular examples of far-reaching change. On the broader front, the evidence is noted which suggests that IR institutions remain essentially intact; yet if HRM and IR are incompatible how can these findings be explained? A number of possibilities are advanced: the assumed incompatibility could be incorrect; dual systems may operate; the extent of HRM has been exaggerated by head office management; or significant productivity improvement could have been made as of late within the existing IR machinery. Guest's preferred explanation is that while HRM has been in the ascendant on greenfield sites and on certain other locations, in the majority of established plants, attempts to move towards HRM have not as yet made much impact.

But Guest concludes on a distinctive note. He argues that the British economy still lags behind its major competitors and 'for further catching up to occur, it seems likely that a fuller use of human resources will be necessary. This is likely to require a shift in emphasis away from the industrial relations system towards HRM policies as the main path to improved performance. In the absence of a radical shift in the relationship between unions and the employers, if this shift occurs it is likely to do so at the expense of the trade unions' (p. 55).

In Chapter 4, Derek Torrington shifts the focus to the implications of HRM for personnel management. In this chapter also, another new perspective is adopted. He views HRM as potentially a threat to personnel management; indeed, the chapter is in many respects a spirited defence of the distinctive contribution and value of personnel management as a specialism. At the same time, he also wants to claim that in any case HRM is but the latest 'addition' which takes its place in a long line of similar innovations and new beginnings which personnel management has successfully absorbed.

This chapter is thus useful in locating the emergence of HRM in a broader historical perspective by tracing earlier realignments and readjustments in the evolution of personnel. Six characterizations of successive models capturing the essence of what personnel was primarily thought to be at different periods are reviewed, ranging, for example, from the 'social reformer' role through 'welfare' to the 'computer-assisted manpower analyst'. The contemporary model is a complex blend containing elements of each.

In this chapter Torrington updates his earlier work and significantly, he argues 'it would be unrealistic' to suggest that the findings from his mid 1980s survey would be replicated today. HRM at that time was 'not liked' by personnel managers whereas now he judges, HRM has been 'assimilated' (p. 61).

Torrington draws on a medical analogy to illustrate the nature of this new role. He sees the modern personnel manager as like a general practitioner respected for possessing a 'rich combination of expertise', a professional who mediates between the patient and the consultants whom he or she selects and monitors. Thus the personnel manager is again cast as a person-in-the-middle but now 'not between management and employees but between managers and the host of external resources now available' (p. 66). Hence, for Torrington, HRM clearly represents an important development but it is not so much a revolution more a 'further embellishment' of a developing role.

In Chapter 5, John Purcell analyses the way in which different corporate strategies and structures influence the shape of human resource management practices. His focus is on the large multi-divisional companies which on many measures dominate the economic and employment scene in the advanced economies. Indeed, this chapter makes a valuable contribution to this book by profiling the corporate composition of British industry and employment.

His analysis of corporate strategy is built on the distinction between 'upstream' and 'downstream' types of strategic decision. The chapter assesses the way in which developments in business policy decision making (i.e. upstream decisions) impact upon human resource management strategic decisions. In the course of his review, Purcell takes us through portfolio planning theory and reveals how its increasing usage impels companies to abandon administrative control systems with their characteristic personnel manuals in favour of control built on financial performance targets. In turn this shift encourages decentralization in employee relations. The varied circumstances of the constituent businesses in the portfolio have been linked to different requirements in terms of types of business manager and their associated modes of management.

Differentiation, and in particular decentralization, is a key theme of this chapter. But, following Goold and Campbell (1986), Purcell notes that not all multi-divisional companies are alike – thus the degree of a head office involvement in strategic business unit activities, for example, can vary significantly. Hence, a sharp contrast is drawn between strategic-*planning* companies (which do seek to stamp a corporate character on their constituent businesses) and financial-*control* companies which mainly do not. Periods of financial stringency tend to impel companies towards the latter mode and City preferences further reinforce this drift.

In consequence, it is argued that business units in Britain are being driven towards short-termism and these trends are inimicable to the fostering of human resource management 'ideals' – by which Purcell means the narrower version of HRM entailing investment in resourceful humans. The implication of this chapter is that, however persuaded many managers may be by the logic, morality, or good sense of HRM, there are structural tendencies at play which will, for the foreseeable future, constrain such aspirations from being implemented – at least in those large multi-divisional companies which opt for the financial-control model.

Chapters 6 to 8 shift focus and turn our attention to some of the main constituent elements and techniques which are normally seen as characterizing HRM. Thus in Chapter 6, Barbara Townley examines selection and appraisal. She suggests that what evidence there is points towards the use of more systematic procedures in these areas. The chapter is largely concerned to interpret the meaning and significance of this. The central thrust is that these moves represent not a mere technical readjustment reflecting the upgrading of personnel capabilities but are part of the wider human resource management trend. The aim of the more sophisticated selection and appraisal techniques is to be able to shape attitudinal and behavioural characteristics. The context is a shift from direct supervision and technical control to production systems predicated on discretion and flexibility; in such circumstances alternative monitoring devices are required.

Developments in selection indicate a greater interest in personality profiling through the use of testing instruments; similarly, initial screening may utilize personal history (or biodata) inventories. Indices of loyalty and appropriate attitude may be more important than technical competence.

Systematic appraisal likewise appears to be spreading out from the managerial grades; hence one survey indicates that the proportion of organizations using it for blue-collar workers increased from 2 per cent to 24 per cent between 1977 and 1985. Townley interprets the increased use of appraisal as associated with a developing tendency to aim to control by communicating 'implicit expectations'. The interesting point is made that what is sought is compliance though not compliance with bureaucratic rules but rather with the more 'nebulous construct of norms'. In this regard use is made by Townley of Offe's framework of three types of norms – in particular with the third of these, the 'extra functional norms' which underpin authority in the organization. But in the conclusion some reservations with the model are expressed. Appraisal is seen as essentially an exercise in personal power. It elevates the role of the supervisor by emphasizing individualism and obscuring the social nature of work.

The selection and appraisal techniques discussed in this chapter may be seen therefore as 'natural accompaniments'. They express a trend towards control through shaping normative orientations. Although these developments may, to a degree, reduce the amount of subjectivity on the part of selectors and appraisers by systemizing managerial practice it is suggested that they court the danger of bestowing on these procedures the status of scientific objectivity and therefore lend to them an undeserving measure of technical legitimacy.

Ewart Keep, in Chapter 7, analyses another main pillar of human resource management – indeed one which has sometimes been claimed as *the* vital component: training. Keep uses the notion of HRM to highlight the key idea of investing in and developing an organization's human assets. Used in this sense, training's place within HRM is, quite simply, central. The existence of policies and practices designed to realize the latent potential of the workforce at all levels becomes the litmus test of an organization's orientation. Using this test, Keep casts a sceptical eye across the British employment scene.

At the macro level, he notes the overwhelming survey evidence which places Britain at or near the bottom of the international league of training provision. Yet a number of positive indicators are educed at the organizational level, including, for example, a measure of change in company training strategies. Some senior managers of leading British companies appear to have been convinced of the rationality of taking training seriously. The possibility of 'a step-change' is further suggested by the degree to which training has been integrated with wider business planning and has been further integrated with selection, appraisal, quality movements, and communication programmes – i.e. the two types of integration (vertical and horizontal) outlined above.

Keep argues, however, that such developments have occurred in only a few exceptional cases in Britain. The main weight of his argument is devoted to a searching and wide-ranging analysis of the factors which inhibit the extension of HRM and training in this country. The problem areas are numerous. They find expression in statistics which indicate, for example, that while leading employers in West Germany, Japan, and the USA spend up to 3 per cent of turnover per annum on training, on average employers in Britain spend only 0.15 per cent (p. 117). Keep exposes a number of 'barriers' which impede progress in the British context. Managers in Britain, he observes, have themselves had comparatively low levels of formal education and training. He suggests that as a consequence they are likely, in turn, to accord a low priority to the training and education of their subordinates. It is even possible, he further contends, that such managers may even regard an educated workforce as a threat. One reason for this is that a more self-reliant workforce would be incompatible with traditional styles of management. At a more fundamental level, Keep traces a range of underlying *structural* factors which militate against training and human resource management in this country. British employers have found it easier to follow other avenues such as overseas acquisitions and investment, these being devices whereby ready-trained workforces can quite simply be bought in. At home, far too many organizations still pursue a standardized mass volume/low skill product-market strategy – examples are cited from such sectors as clothing, kitchen furniture, and retailing. The organization of capital markets in Britain and the takeover/divestment cycle hardly induce unit managers to strive for long-term upgrading and commitment.

Hence, Keep concludes that, while there is increasing evidence at the level of rhetoric of a growing enthusiasm for human resource management, the analysis of the prospects for this one key element of it reveals so many deep-seated barriers to change that he remains highly pessimistic. Unfortunately, 'in a world where international competitive advantage is increasingly likely to turn upon the skills, knowledge and commitment of an enterprise's employees', the economic consequences of this failure to invest in the human resource are deemed to be dire. There are echoes here of Guest's conclusion.

In Chapter 8, Tom Schuller turns to the topic of employee involvement. This may be considered as potentially an important path towards the key HRM concept of 'commitment'. It is worthwhile therefore to take a closer look at the contemporary forms of involvement – forms which have distanced themselves from the Bullock-style blueprints of the 1970s.

As Schuller observes, a distinctive feature of contemporary forms of employee participation is the shift from collectivist to individualistic modes. Using these as polar opposites and focusing specifically upon financial participation, he draws a continuum along which a range of different possibilities can be located. Using this, the main forms of financial participation are briefly reviewed before closer analysis is made of two approaches – profit sharing and employee involvement in pension fund management. On profit sharing, it is reported that while the search for commitment has indeed been revealed as one important reason for introducing it, this was nevertheless secondary to tax efficiency in reward packages. Moreover such schemes were normally introduced unilaterally, and there seems to be little evidence that they are integrated with other managerial initiatives. Pension-fund participation is likewise viewed as an outcome not so much of HRM-style strategy but as a result of threatened legislation. In the 1980s the unexpected growth of the funds tended to bring pension administration closer to corporate decision-making but member trustee involvement tended still to be peripheral to such key issues.

Overall, despite the apparently high level of interest in forms of involvement (notably, from employers in the 1980s) the results of Schuller's investigations into financial involvement suggest that its linkages with HRM are, in practice, only tenuous.

Another aspect and another perspective on HRM are added by Nicholas Kinnie in Chapter 9. Kinnie's distinctive contribution is to examine the potential links with new financial and production-control systems. In particular this chapter sheds light on the extent to which HRM may contribute to the effectiveness of management-control systems, the basic link being the expanded role and responsibility of line managers for the utilization of financial, material, informational, and human resources.

The analysis is grounded on case study research in four manufacturing plants. Regarding financial control, the problems of implementing delegated budgets and profit-centre devices are discussed. In relation to production control, innovations such as just-in-time, and the use of computer-based material resources planning, are examined. The underlying feature common to both is the increasing responsibility and accountability of line managers and therefore the accompanying increase in skill requirements on their part in a range of human resource aspects.

Kinnie notes the lack of support from HR departments which was evident in his case companies, but he also emphasizes the potential importance of HRM in terms of training, reward and selection. He takes each of these three areas in turn and gives instances. As with a number of the other contributors to this book, Kinnie notes the limited take-up of HRM techniques to date, but he tends to go a step further by examining just how human resource management might play a part under the revised production systems. The precise reasons why these opportunities have, in the main, not been taken up, are also explored.

In Chapter 10, Peter Armstrong contrasts the strategic aspirations surrounding HRM with the cold facts of its current subjugation to management accountancy. Armstrong sees the personnel profession as the group most likely to sponsor HRM and sets out to examine the extent to which personnel will be able to progress through the means of such sponsorship.

Limits and possibilities are traced. In the first place the current state of affairs for personnel is viewed as giving far less ground for complacency than a superficial reading of much of the survey evidence would suggest. On present trends, he discerns a further removal of most personnel specialists from the centres of important decision-making. Moreover, he interprets the marginalization of the profession as occurring not because of 'recession' but because the key functions in which personnel could lay claim to have some expertise have already been captured by management accountants.

Personnel specialists, while they may be tempted to draw upon HRM as a means of hoisting themselves into areas of key strategic decision-making, will have to recognize that in so doing they will inevitably be *competing* with other managerial professions. Thus HRM as a phenomenon will not simply be judged 'on its merits' by a notionally undifferentiated group known as management. It is argued that no matter how successfully accomplished, acquiescence to simply meeting the demands for 'data' from accountants offers no satisfactory way forward for personnel as a specialism. Nor will the rationale for personnel, deriving from a claimed people-expertise, cut much ice if, as seems likely, it entails simply operating within the 'given' framework of budgeting, planning, and control.

The potentialities lie in personnel developing sufficient awareness, expertise and confidence to be able to mount a reasonable critique of the shortcomings of management accounting itself. There are parallels here with the work of Ewart Keep and his analysis of the structural limits to the spread of HRM.

Any managerial group seeking to champion HRM which wanted to make progress would first have to come to terms with 'the enduring fact of accounting controls' and secondly have the wherewithal to appreciate and exploit their problematical aspects. On the face of it, some progress on both of these could at least be commenced, for example, by leading practitioners familiarizing themselves with the kind of contributions to be found in such learned journals as *Accounting, Organizations and Society*. But Armstrong is, in the final analysis, doubtful of much change; he finds 'little awareness that today's personnel function operates within a managerial culture which is increasingly dominated by the language and structures of management accounting' (p. 166). It is this which, perhaps most of all, places the most insurmountable barrier to the extensive and successful implementation of HRM.

In the final chapter entitled 'Looking to the future', Sisson and Storey tackle four tasks. They pull the main strands together; they take an overview of the evidence and the arguments by constructing a 'balance sheet' for and against the proposition that HRM has made a significant impact on employment practices; thirdly, they assess some of the main implications for practitioners; and fourthly, they identify what they see as the most pressing future research needs.

Chapter two

Human resource management: a critical analysis

Karen Legge

Introduction

In recent years, in both the UK and USA, as companies have been confronted by Japanese competition and employment stereotypes, struggled with recession and searched for excellence, so the vocabulary for managing their workforces has tended to change. 'Personnel management' is giving way to 'human resource management' or, better still to '*strategic* human resource management'. Nor is this shift exclusively confined to those followers of fashion, the commercial management consultants. It may be charted first in the writings of US academics and managers (e.g. Beer *et al*. 1985; Foulkes 1986; Tichy *et al*. 1982; Walton and Lawrence 1985) but has now been recognized by both managers (e.g. Armstrong 1987; Fowler 1987) and academics (e.g. Guest 1987; Hendry and Pettigrew 1986; Miller 1987; Storey 1987b; Torrington and Hall 1987) in the UK. Of course this is hardly the first time that the language of management has changed: the shift over the years away from traditional manufacturing industries towards process industry, high-tech manufacturing and service sectors, with accompanying changes in occupational and employment structures had already been mirrored in managers' increasing tendency to refer to 'employee' rather than 'industrial' – let alone 'labour' – relations, well before the perceived slackening in trade-union pressure in the politico-economic environment of the 1980s. But whereas that shift reflected some changes in the practice of management (e.g. moves towards staff status in process industries) can the same be said of this latest shift in vocabulary? Is HRM different in substance or emphasis from personnel management? If so, in what ways and what might such a shift signify?

In this chapter I propose critically to consider this question. In doing so I wish to examine not only the similarities and differences between 'personnel management' and 'human resource management' but to explore the potential contradictions and paradoxes that might be embedded in both approaches. The question will also be posed as to whether HRM offers a new approach that might resolve the contradictions embedded in personnel management (Watson 1977, 1983) or whether it is merely a new rhetoric aimed at masking old contradictions in the language of today.

Personnel management and HRM: is there a difference?

Both managers and academics, particularly in the UK, have recognized the problem of identifying clear differences between personnel management and HRM. Fowler (1987: 3), for example, argues that substantively there is little new in HRM:

> What's new [personnel managers will ask] about the concept that 'the business of personnel is the business' (to quote the theme of a Personnel Management essay competition of yesteryear). What is new about the view that employees give of their best when they are treated as responsible adults? Haven't these been at the heart of good personnel practice for decades? To which the answer is, of course, yes.

Such words are echoed by Armstrong's (1987: 32) comment that:

> It could indeed be no more and no less than another name for personnel management, but, as usually perceived, at least it has the virtue of emphasising the need to treat people as a key resource, the management of which is the direct concern of top management as part of the strategic planning processes of the enterprise. Although there is nothing new in the idea, insufficient attention has been paid to it in many organisations. The new bottle or label can help to overcome this deficiency.

Nor is Armstrong alone in suggesting a re-labelling process. Guest (1987: 506) points out that a number of personnel departments have become 'human resource departments' without any obvious change in roles, just as the new editions of several long-standing textbooks have changed title but little else. Scepticism about there being little substantive difference betwen 'human resource management' and traditional personnel management is further reinforced by the practice, particularly in the US, of using 'human resource management' as a generic term and one interchangeable with 'personnel management'.

In order to identify possible differences between personnel management and human resource management, we can take two approaches. First, we can ask whether their normative models differ; secondly, whether descriptively their respective practices differ. As Guest (1987: 507) suggests, we cannot really ask what human resource management looks like in practice unless we have a model about what it should constitute. Otherwise we run the danger of accepting as HRM any practices so labelled, even if indistinguishable from what a few years ago we would have termed 'personnel management'. In theory, once a normative model of HRM is established and empirical research undertaken, several outcomes are logically possible: the normative models of personnel management and HRM might be similar but their practices differ; their normative models might differ, but their practices be similar; both their respective normative models and respective practices might be similar, or both, respectively might differ. It is in the final case that we might be most confident that HRM and personnel management really are different approaches to managing employees.

Examining the normative models is amenable to conceptual analysis of published statements, but identifying similarities or differences in the practice of personnel management and HRM is a matter of empirical observation. Unfortunately at the time of writing, while empirical research is being conducted, notably by researchers in the School of Industrial and Business Studies, University of Warwick, and at Templeton College, Oxford, few *detailed* published studies exist, particularly in regard to the UK context. This has given rise to the danger that some commentators may be comparing like with unlike – that is, comparing descriptive, empirically grounded models of personnel management (such as those of Legge 1978; Mackay and Torrington 1986; Tyson and Fell 1986; Watson 1977) with normative models (e.g. Walton 1985) of HRM (Guest 1987: 507). In the light of these considerations, it seems sensible initially to focus on a comparison of the *normative* models of personnel management and HRM.

Normative models of personnel management

It may be useful to start with several conventional definitions of what the function of personnel management ideally should be. (Relatively lengthy quotations defining personnel management and HRM from a normative perspective are presented here in order to provide a data base to support and illustrate subsequent observations. I should add, though, that the majority of the definitions of personnel management appear in a 1978 publication (see Legge 1978) and were not chosen 'selectively' for the purposes of this chapter alone!)

First some American definitions:

> Since management aims at getting effective results *with people*, personnel administration is a basic management function or activity permeating all levels of management in any organization. Personnel administration is . . . organizing and treating individuals at work so that they will get the greatest possible realization of their intrinsic abilities, thus attaining maximum efficiency for themselves and their group, and thereby giving the enterprise of which they are a part its determining competitive advantage and its optimum results.
>
> (Pigors and Myers 1969)

> It is believed that the most significant aspect of personnel management is to be found through the direction and control of the human resources of an organization in its daily operations . . . the successful performance of the personnel function necessitates that each manager orient himself within his total business environment in order to help achieve the various organizational programs and objectives.
>
> (Megginson 1972)

> Basically personnel is concerned with the matching of people to the jobs that must be done to achieve the organization's goals.
>
> (Glueck 1974)

> Personnel management is defined here as follows: The field of management

which has to do with planning, organizing, directing and controlling the functions of procuring, developing, maintaining and utilizing a labor force, such that the

(a) Objectives for which the company is established are attained economically and effectively.
(b) Objectives of all levels of personnel are served to the highest possible degree.
(c) Objectives of society are duly considered and served.

(Jucius 1975)

These may be contrasted with some British definitions:

Personnel management is a responsibility of all those who manage people, as well as being a description of the work of those who are employed as specialists. It is that part of management which is concerned with people at work and with their relationships within an enterprise. Personnel management aims to achieve both efficiency and justice, neither of which can be pursued successfully without the other. It seeks to bring together and develop in an effective organization the men and women who make up an enterprise, enabling each to make his own best contribution to its success both as an individual and as a member of a working group. It seeks to provide fair terms and conditions of employment, and satisfying work for those employed.

(IPM 1963)

Personnel management is concerned with obtaining the best possible staff for an organization and, having got them, looking after them so that they will want to stay and give of their best to their jobs.

(Cuming 1975)

Personnel management is a series of activities which: first enable working people and their employing organisations to agree about the objectives and nature of their working relationship and, secondly, ensures that the agreement is fulfilled.

(Torrington and Hall 1987)

Analysing these statements, some common themes emerge. It would appear that personnel management is about selecting, developing, rewarding, and directing employees in such a way that not only will they achieve satisfaction and 'give of their best' at work, but by so doing enable the employing organization to achieve its goals. Furthermore, personnel management is the task of all managers, not just of personnel specialists alone. If these are common themes some differences are implicit when comparing the American and British definitions. The American definitions clearly assume a unitary frame of reference: achieving the 'greatest possible realization of [employees'] intrinsic abilities' is assumed to be not only perfectly compatible with 'attaining the maximum efficiency for themselves and their group', but a precondition of the organization's achieving its 'optimum results'. The British definitions, in contrast, adopt a pluralist perspective:

efficiency and justice are contrasted in the IPM definition, although their ultimate reconciliation is assumed possible; Cuming's definition recognizes that employees' loyalty and commitment is problematic and conditional; above all, Torrington and Hall assert that the employment relationship should be rightly the subject of joint negotiation, agreement and regulation.

Normative models of human resource management

How do such definitions of personnel management differ from normative statements about HRM? Again, let us start with some American definitions:

> We have come to believe that the transformation we are observing amounts to more than a subtle shift in the traditional practices of personnel or the substitution of new terms for unchanging practices. Instead the transformation amounts to a new model regarding the management of human resources in organizations. Although the model is still emerging, and inconsistencies in its practice are often seen, we believe that a set of basic assumptions can be identified that underlie the policies that we have observed to be part of the HRM transformation. The new assumptions are:
>
> • proactive, system-wide interventions, with emphasis on fit, linking HRM with strategic planning and cultural change (c.f. old assumption: reactive, piecemeal interventions in response to specific problems).
> • people are social capital capable of development (c.f. people as variable cost).
> • coincidence of interest between stakeholders can be developed (c.f. self-interest dominates, conflict between stakeholders).
> • seeks power equalization for trust and collaboration (c.f. seeks power advantages for bargaining and confrontation).
> • open channels of communication to build trust, commitment (c.f. control of information flow to enhance efficiency, power).
> • goal orientation (c.f. relationship orientation).
> • participation and informed choice (c.f. control from top).
>
> (Beer and Spector 1985)

> The new HRM model is composed of policies that promote mutuality – mutual goals, mutual influence, mutual respect, mutual rewards, mutual responsibility. The theory is that policies of mutuality will elicit commitment which in turn will yield both better economic performance and greater human development.
>
> (Walton 1985)

> Effective human resources management does not exist in a vacuum but must be related to the overall strategy of the organization . . . . Too many

23

personnel managers have a tendency to create and function in their own little worlds, forgetting that their primary value is helping to realize top and line management goals.

(Foulkes 1986)

The British definitions again may be contrasted with the American:

What, from a review of the existing literature does 'strategic HRM' appear to mean?
    We start out by noting that there are two themes which overlap one another: the first contained in the term 'strategic', the second in the idea, or philosophy, of 'human resources'. The latter suggests people are a valued resource, a critical investment in an organisation's current performance and future growth. The term 'strategic' . . . in this context has both established and new connotations [these are]
1. the use of planning;
2. a coherent approach to the design and management of personnel systems based on an employment policy and manpower strategy, and often underpinned by a 'philosophy';
3. matching HRM activities and policies to some explicit business strategy; and
4. seeing the people of the organization as a 'strategic resource' for achieving 'competitive advantage'.

(Hendry and Pettigrew 1986)

The main dimensions of HRM [involve] the goal of integration [i.e. if human resources can be integrated into strategic plans, if human resource policies cohere, if line managers have internalized the importance of human resources and this is reflected in their behaviour and if employees identify with the company, then the company's strategic plans are likely to be more successfully implemented], the goal of employee commitment, the goal of flexibility/ adaptability [i.e. organic structures, functional flexibility], the goal of quality [i.e. quality of staff, performance, standards and public image].

(Guest 1987)

Human resources management is directed mainly at management needs for human resources (not necessarily employees) to be provided and deployed. There is greater emphasis on planning, monitoring, and control, rather than on problem-solving and mediation. It is totally identified with management interests, being a general management activity and is relatively distant from the workforce as a whole.
    Underpinning personnel management are the twin ideas that people have a right to proper treatment as dignified human beings while at work, and that they are only effective as employees when their job-related personal needs

are met. Underpinning human resources management is the idea that management of human resources is much the same as any other aspect of management, and getting the deployment of right numbers and skills at the right place is more important than interfering with people's personal affairs.

(Torrington and Hall 1987)

In the majority of these definitions several common themes stand out: that human resources policies should be integrated with strategic business planning and used to reinforce an appropriate (or change an inappropriate) organizational culture, that human resources are valuable and a source of competitive advantage, that they may be tapped most effectively by mutually consistent policies that promote commitment and which, as a consequence, foster a willingness in employees to act flexibly in the interests of the 'adaptive organisation's pursuit of excellence'. However, again, some differences may be observed between the American and British models. The American models of HRM, in a similar manner to their models of personnel management, assume a unitary frame of reference: that 'there is a long-run coincidence of interests between all the various stakeholders of the organization', as Beer and Spector (1985: 283) would put it. Even where potential union problems are recognized, co-optation is identified as the way forward: 'other managers have decided to actively promote more co-operative relations with their existing unions . . . [concluding] that they could not successfully transform their workforce management strategy without the active support of the unions' (Walton 1985: 61). The British models adopt a rather different position. While Armstrong's 'revised' model (1987) merely makes some gestures in the direction of a pluralistic stance, other commentators, in recognizing that the HRM model is essentially unitaristic, and marginalizes the role that trade unions might play in organizations, find this a source either of logical inconsistency within the model or of practical infeasibility in its execution. Thus, on the one hand, Fowler (1987: 3) asks 'Is it really possible to claim full mutuality when at the end of the day the employer can decide unilaterally to close the company or sell it to someone else?', while, on the other, Guest (1987: 520) suggests that 'for many, the unitaristic implications of human resource management could only begin to have an appeal following a much more radical shift of ownership and control in industry'.

Most HRM models, whether British or American, assert that employees are valued assets and, with the emphasis on commitment, adaptability and employees as a source of competitive advantage, the image might equally be presented as 'resourceful' humans. But as Tyson and Fell (1986: 135) point out, 'human resource' may be understood in a completely different sense, as a factor of production, along with land and capital, and an 'expense of doing business' rather than 'the only resource capable of turning inanimate factors of production into wealth'. This perception of 'resource' appears to underlie Torrington and Hall's model of HRM, with its emphasis on appropriate factors of production ('numbers' and 'skills') at the 'right' (implicitly the 'lowest possible') price. In their model, too, the human resources appear passive ('to be provided and deployed') rather than (to quote Tyson and Fell) 'the source of creative energy in any direction the organization dictates and fosters'. Indeed Torrington and Hall's description of the conception of employees in a *personnel management* model appears to have far more in common with most models of *HRM*, than their own conception of human resources in their HRM model. It is partly on the basis of these different conceptions of human resources that Storey (1987b: 6) draws a distinction between what he terms the 'hard' and 'soft' versions of HRM. The former emphasizes the 'quantitative, calculative, and business strategic aspects of managing the head-count resource in as "rational" a way as for any other economic factor' and the latter emphasizes 'communication, motivation and leadership'. Put differently the 'hard' version might be said to emphasize the *management* aspect, and the soft version, the *human resource* aspect of HRM. This distinction may also be seen as echoing an earlier one made by Legge (1978) between the conformist ('management') and 'deviant' ('human resource') innovation in personnel management.

The normative models compared

A close examination of commentators' normative statements about personnel management and HRM suggest there are clear similarities between the two.

1 Both models emphasize the importance of integrating personnel/HRM practices with organizational goals. Particularly in the case of the American commentators, it cannot even be said that the language has changed – Pigors and Myers (1969) speak of 'determining competitive advantage' and Megginson (1972) of 'orienting to the total business environment'.

2 Both models vest personnel/HRM firmly in line management.

3 Both models, in the majority of instances, emphasize the importance of individuals fully developing their abilities for their own personal satisfaction and to make their 'best contribution' to organizational success. The similarity of the two models in this respect is underlined when comparing Torrington and Hall's model of personnel management with the other commentators' models of HRM. For their conception of the ideas underlying *personnel management* 'that people have a right to proper treatment as dignified human beings while at work, and they are only effective as employees when their job-related personal needs are met' is identical to the values underlying all the 'soft' version *HRM* models. Furthermore, their statement elaborating this position, that speaks of the desirability of 'mutuality' and 'reciprocal dependence' between employer and employee in order for the employer to obtain 'commitment to organizational objectives that is needed for organisational success' (Torrington and Hall 1987: 11) uses the same language as Walton's (1985: 36) *HRM* model: 'the new management strategy involves policies that promote mutuality in order to elicit commitment, which in turn can generate increased economic effectiveness and human development'.

4 Both models identify placing the 'right' people into the 'right' jobs as an

important means of integrating personnel/HRM practice with organizational goals, including individual development. Glueck's (1974) and Cuming's (1975) statements about *personnel management's* function in this respect are virtually identical to that of Tichy *et al.* (1982: 51) that an 'essential process' of strategic *human resource management* 'is one of matching available human resources to jobs in the organization'. The recognition that this matching process is nevertheless a dynamic one given the rate of environmental and organizational change, and that employees really should be selected and developed in ways that enhance their adaptability and flexibility is common to both HRM models and to what might be termed the 'deviant innovation' model of personnel management as embracing OD value systems and practice (c.f. Guest 1987: 514–15; Legge 1978: 87–9).

So, is there any difference between the normative models of HRM and those of personnel management? One is tempted to say 'not a lot'. And, indeed, the sharp contrasts that Guest (1987: Table I) elicits in his comparison of what he terms personnel management and human resource management 'stereotypes', in spite of his disclaimers, appear to owe much to an implicit comparison of the descriptive practice of personnel management with the normative aspirations of HRM, rather than comparing like with like. However, both stark comparisons *and* assumptions of similarities should be treated with caution. Even at the level of normative analysis – let alone empirical observation – neither personnel management nor HRM is a singular model, but each is conceptualized in a variety of guises. Perhaps the sharpest contrasts may be found in comparing British personnel management models with US HRM models, or paradoxically, the 'hard' and 'soft' versions of the HRM model. However, I think some general differences can be detected, even if these are largely of meaning and emphasis rather than substance.

First, many statements about personnel management, when placed in the context of the texts from which they are derived, seem to see it as a management activity which is largely aimed at non-managers. Apart from management development (often treated as a separate activity or function) personnel management appears to be something performed on subordinates by managers rather than something that the latter experience themselves – other than as a set of rules and procedures that may constrain their freedom in managing their subordinates as they think fit. HRM, on the other hand, not only emphasizes the importance of employee development, but focuses particularly on development of 'the management team' (see, for example, the interviews with Bob Beck, Alan Lafley and Clifford J. Erlich in Foulkes 1986). This shift of emphasis appears related to two other differences.

The second is that while both personnel management and HRM highlight the role of line management, the focus is different. In the personnel management models, line's role is very much an expression of the view that all managers manage people, so all managers in a sense carry out 'personnel management'. It also carries the recognition that most specialist personnel work still has to be implemented within line management's departments where the workforce is physically located (see for example Legge 1978: 22–3). In the HRM models, HRM is vested in line management as business managers responsible for co-ordinating and directing *all* resources in the business unit in pursuit of bottom-line results. Not only does the bottom-line appear to be specified more precisely than in the personnel-management models, with much emphasis on quality of product or service (see for example, Storey 1987b: 16; Upton 1987), but a clear relationship is drawn between the achievement of these results and the line's appropriate and proactive use of the human resources in the business unit. Personnel policies are not passively integrated with business strategy, in the sense of flowing from it, but are an integral part of strategy in the sense that they underlie and facilitate the pursuit of a desired strategy.

The third difference is that most HRM models emphasize the management of the organization's culture as the central activity for senior management. Although the OD models of the 1970s proclaimed a similar message, these were not fully integrated with the run-of-the-mill normative personnel management models of the 1970s. OD was always seen as standing slightly apart from 'mainstream' personnel management and, in fact, was generally kept separate in a formal institutional sense, with separate OD consultants, not always with a background in, or located within the personnel department (see Pettigrew 1985). Above all, it was often presented as a fringe activity, an initiative that was 'nice to have' but essentially the gilt on the gingerbread, to be dispensed with at the first hint of financial cutbacks (along with training!). Peters and Waterman's (1982) link-ing of 'strong cultures' with financial success (however spurious), along with American management's fascination with the linkages between a stereotyped 'Japanese' employment culture and Japanese economic strength, has raised the development and management of an appropriate culture as *the* strategic or 'transformational' leadership activity, that gives direction, a sense of purpose and involvement to all organizational members. It is through an integrated and internally consistent set of HR policies in relation to recruitment, selection, training, development, rewarding and communications, that the organization's core values can best be conveyed, according to the normative HRM models. Integration, therefore, is a doubly important issue – not just integration of HRM policies with strategy, but the internal integration and consistency of HRM policies themselves to enact a coherent 'strong' culture. The normative personnel manage-ment models do not present personnel policies as senior management's instru-ment for reinforcing or changing organizational values in a manner consistent with preferred business strategy.

These three differences in emphasis all point to HRM, in theory, being essen-tially a more central strategic management task than personnel management in that it is experienced by managers, as the most valued company resource to be managed, it concerns them in the achievement of business goals and it expresses senior management's preferred organizational values. From this perspective it is not surprising that Fowler (1987: 3) identifies the real difference between HRM and personnel management as 'not what it is, but who is saying it. In a nutshell

HRM represents the discovery of personnel management by chief executives'. If this is so, what are the problematic issues in its enactment?

Contradictions in human resource management

It will be argued here that HRM is problematic at two levels. First, at the surface level, the value of integration that it promotes contains a logical contradiction, given the dual usage of the concept of 'integration'. 'Integration' appears to have two meanings: integration or 'fit' with business strategy and the integration or complementarity and consistency of 'mutuality' employment policies aimed at generating employee commitment, flexibility, quality, and the like. This double meaning of integration has been referred to also as the 'external' and 'internal' fit of HRM policies (Baird and Meshoulam 1988). The problem is that while 'fit' with strategy would argue a contingent design of HRM policy, internal consistency – at least with the 'soft' human resource values associated with 'mutuality' – would argue an absolutist approach to the design of employment policy. Can this contradiction be reconciled without stretching to the limit the meaning of HRM as a distinct approach to managing employees? Secondly, at a deeper level, it may be suggested that HRM, no less than personnel management, is confronted by a contradiction of capitalism: that is, responsibility for accommodating the dilemma that, although the 'labour commodity' is a major means to further the interests of dominant groups in capitalist society, it is liable to subvert those interests (Watson 1977). Does HRM have the potential to cope more effectively with this tension than traditional approaches to personnel management?

The problem of integration

A characteristic of HRM is to argue for the matching, even the tight meshing, of HRM policies with business strategy. Various approaches have been proposed. Perhaps the most popular is to suggest that HRM policies – in particular those related to recruitment and selection, training and development, appraisal and rewards – should 'fit' the stage of development at which the organization has arrived in pursuing growth. Typically the organization's stage of development is characterized in terms of product or geographical diversity (e.g. single product; single product, vertically integrated; growth by acquisition of unrelated businesses; related diversification of product lines through internal growth and acquisition; multiple products in multiple countries) and by the associated organizational form (e.g. owner manager/agency; functional; separate self-contained businesses; multi-divisional; mixed forms; global organization). See, for example, Purcell (this volume), but also Baird and Meshoulam (1988), Smith (1982), Tichy *et al.* (1982).

A similar approach, but leaving aside explicit assumptions about organizational growth, is Miles and Snow's (1984) identification of three basic types of strategic behaviour and supporting organizational characteristics, which they term 'defender', 'prospector' and 'analyzer'. A 'defender' strategy is characterized by a narrow and relatively stable product-market domain, single, capital-intensive technology; a functional structure; and skills in production efficiency, process engineering and cost control. Miles and Snow cite Lincoln Electric as a typical example. A 'prospector' strategy is typified by the continual search for new product and market opportunities and experimentation with potential responses to emerging environmental trends. 'Prospector' characteristics include a diverse product line; multiple technologies; a product or geographically divisionalized structure, and skills in product research and development, market research and development engineering. Hewlett Packard is identified as a typical 'prospector'. Analyzers, according to Miles and Snow (1984) operate in two differing types of product market domains – one relatively stable, the other changing. Given different market demands 'analyzers' enact a diversity of behaviours. Thus they are characterized by a limited basic product line; search for a small number of related product and/or market opportunities; cost-efficient technology for stable products and project technologies for new products; mixed (frequently matrix) structure; and skills in production efficiency, process engineering and marketing. Miles and Snow (1984) identify Texas Instruments as a typical 'analyzer'. The logic of these different strategies is that the organizations' HRM policies should differ, depending on strategy. For example, Miles and Snow (1984) suggest that the basic HRM strategy of 'defenders' will be to 'build' human resources, that of 'prospectors' to 'acquire' human resources and that of 'analyzers' to 'allocate' human resources.

These different approaches to HRM in theory have very different implications for choice of policy. If we take the examples of selection and development, for instance, Miles and Snow (1984) suggest that a 'defender' company should typically engage in little recruiting above entry level, with selection based on 'weeding out undesirable employees', while training and development should involve extensive, formal skills-building programmes (i.e. the 'make' approach). In contrast, 'prospectors' should seek to 'buy in' talent – a strategy that should involve sophisticated recruiting at all levels, with selection involving pre-employment psychological testing, training being limited, the emphasis being on skills-requirements identification and their acquisition in the labour market. By implication Miles and Snow suggest that 'analyzer' companies should match recruitment, selection, and development strategies to the nature of the product (stable, innovative) and the stage of the product life-cycle and thus engage in 'make' (stable product, 'cash cow') or 'buy' HRM policies (innovative product, 'rising star') as appropriate to the different market domains.

Miles and Snow's (1984) analysis raises two potentially problematic issues, when attempting to achieve 'external fit' or the integration of HRM policies with business strategy. First, is it possible to have a corporation-wide, mutually reinforcing set of HRM policies, if the organization operates in highly diversified product markets, and, if not, does it matter in terms of organizational effectiveness? Second, if business strategy should dictate the choice of HRM policies, will some strategies dictate policies that – unlike most normative HRM models – fail to emphasize commitment, flexibility and quality? If these questions are relevant to an organization with market diversity in Miles and Snow's terms, they are writ large for conglomerates operating not only in different markets in one industry, but in a range of industries.

Taking the first point, if a highly diversified corporation is to match its HRM policies to a wide range of very different product-market requirements then clearly the logic of such a position is that different policies would emerge in different divisions or subsidiaries. Indeed, conversely, Miller (1987) does well to draw to our attention that many of the companies generally recognized as pursuing company-wide, internally consistent HRM policies – for example, Hewlett Packard or Marks and Spencer – are notable for low levels of business, (as opposed to product) diversification, of 'sticking to the knitting'. However, whether the pursuit of different sets of HRM policy in a diversified corporation 'matters' is another question, assuming such an organization sought integration only at the financial level and allowed its business units a high level of autonomy. All that would then be required for congruence would be that each unit adopt policies that were consistent with its own business strategy and mutually reinforcing – irrespective of the extent to which they contradicted HRM policies pursued in other business units elsewhere in the corporation. While, as a consequence, no organization-wide 'strong' culture would be likely to develop, arguably this would not be necessary as integration, other than financial, would not be sought either. (I say 'arguably' as some commentators maintain that stock-market confusion over a clear corporate image can lower share prices) (Ahlstrand and Purcell 1988).

Against this, strong unit sub-cultures, a claimed ingredient of competitive advantage, might well develop. A problem would only arise if there developed a perceived requirement to integrate two or more sub-units in a manner that required integration at operating level and, hence, of personnel. Then not only would the difficulty of merging distinct sub-cultures be likely, but perceptions of potential inequalities and inconsistencies between erstwhile autonomous units' HRM policies might undermine the trust and commitment that is supposed to develop from perceptions of congruence.

In relation to this question Miller (1987) makes a further interesting observation. To suggest that to achieve competitive advantage each business unit in a diversified corporation should tailor its HRM policy to its own product-market conditions, irrespective of potential inconsistencies with HRM policies being pursued elsewhere in the corporation, is to assume that the business units are market driven. While this may be true of individual units within the corporation, it is not necessarily so of the corporation as a whole. As Miller points out, the success criteria of diversified conglomerates are defined in financial terms and largely sought through the manipulation of corporate assets. 'The success of Hanson Trust will depend not on building competitive advantage in the businesses within the portfolio . . . but by acquired growth' (Miller 1987: 359–60). Such a corporate strategy though may not lead to organizational effectiveness as broadly understood 'and, indeed, there is a creeping criticism that these businesses, as a result of their failure to engage world markets, are bad for the economy' (Miller 1987: 359).

If a multi-business conglomerate's success is sought through acquisition, asset stripping and attention to its price-earnings ratio on the stock markets, its HRM 'policies' – if not entirely pragmatic –may logically call for actions (e.g. compulsory redundancy, reward based on short-term performance results) which, although consistent with business strategy, are unlikely to generate employee commitment. Even where a company does seek competitive advantage in the market for its products or services, patterns of demand and cost structures may argue that, at least at the level of non-managerial employees, flexibility is more effectively achieved through Tayloristic work organization, treating labour as a variable input, and exploiting the secondary labour market rather than through enhancing the skills and quality of the workforce. This would appear to be the chosen strategy of much of the High Street, whether fast food chains or a large part of the retail sector. In cases such as these, the 'hard' version of human resource *management* appears more relevant than the soft version of *human resource* management. In other words, matching HRM policies to business strategy calls for minimizing labour costs, rather than treating employees as a resource whose value may be enhanced, in terms of Guest's model, by increasing their commitment, functional flexibility, and quality. Furthermore where such cost-minimization policies are pursued in relation to direct employees, lack of integration may occur at another level. It may be in such companies that 'soft' version HRM policies are followed for *managerial* staff, resulting in a lack of internal consistency which may further undermine the commitment of direct employees.

Attempts to reconcile this contradiction – that matching HRM policy to business strategy ('external fit') may involve the denial of 'internal fit' with core 'soft' HRM values – have taken two forms. First is the argument that the lack of consistency in the two forms of integration is illusory. Actions that may appear to epitomize the treatment of individuals as a variable cost, rather than resource, in the interests of business strategy e.g. chopping out dead wood whose performance is not up to standard, tying rewards closely to individual performance, transferring employees to other jobs and parts of the organization in the light of business requirements, is in fact providing an opportunity for employees to develop their resourcefulness and competences. If some employees prove unequal to the challenge and have to 'be dispensed with' or if business circumstances dictate that some have to be sacrificed in the interests of the organization as a whole, this is really an example of 'tough love', or 'care which does not shy away from tough decisions' (Barham *et al*. 1988: 28; Peters and Waterman 1982: 96, 240).

The use of 'tough love' as a rhetorical device to mediate this contradiction may be illustrated by quotations from two managers, cited in Barham *et al*. (1988) and Foulkes (1986) respectively. First, in a booklet setting out its management principles, an insurance company's chief executive asserts:

The needs of our business will be most effectively attained if the needs of people for fulfillment, success, and meaning, are met. If people are in poor shape, the company's objectives are unlikely to be achieved. Yet the needs of the business still come first. People need to be developed, but this will not be achieved by treating them with soft 'care', by allowing issues to be smoothed over without being properly addressed. To treat people without care will cause them and, therefore the business, to diminish. Experience suggests that the needs of people and the business will be best met if we treat ourselves with 'tough love' . . . . This is very different from 'macho' management, which basically does not involve care. Tough love requires courage. Respect for the individual does not mean pandering to the individual's weaknesses or even wishes. Involving people through tough love to secure both their development and good performance requires managers to take initiatives . . . .

People, of course, are far and away the most important resource in any company. But they are not more than that. It is very easy to forget when endeavouring to develop people and to care for them, and even to love them, that the needs of the business must come first. Without that, there can be no lasting security. A fool's paradise in which effort is concentrated only on the present well-being of the staff, without regard for the future, will eventually disintegrate and it may well be the staff that suffer most.

(Barham *et al.* 1988: 28)

Note here that 'putting the needs of the business first', is presented as an intrinsic part of 'tough love', and that 'love', as opposed to 'soft care' – or even 'pandering to the individual's wishes', is a question of sometimes being 'cruel to be kind'. Without toughness the staff may be the ones to 'suffer most'. 'Care' for the individual appears essentially as respect for employees' ability to be 'developed' in ways that the organization deems appropriate and, implicitly, to be 'man (or woman) enough to take it' if personal sacrifice for the good of the organization is required. Indeed the very denial that 'tough love' is at all like 'macho' management only serves to reinforce the suspicion that in its manifestation to unfortunate employees exhibiting 'individual weaknesses' it may appear indistinguishable.

The assumptions of paternalism and a unitary frame of reference which pervade the quotation above are echoed in the words of a vice-president of ITT, cited in Foulkes (1986: 382):

The positive fact is that the removal of a marginal, unproductive or unnecessary surplus employee, provided it's legally and ethically handled, almost always *improves* the morale of the average and above-average employees, who are, after all, the people the company most wants to retain. It is demoralising to a good, productive employee to observe a fellow worker who is consistently dogging it – and getting away with it.

It is the personnel manager's responsibility to see that the level of employee performance and productivity is always as high as possible, even when the achievement of that objective requires the unilateral removal of unsatisfactory employees.

'Tough love', then, possibly in substance, and certainly in rhetoric, glosses the potential tensions between 'external fit' and commitment to 'soft' HRM values. Development, flexibility and adaptability are defined by the organization and in its own interests. The company's interests and those of its employees are equated. If an individual's abilities and performance are defined as inappropriate by the company, given the identification of employee and organizational interests, that person must inevitably be redefined as no longer an employee, and a tough decision may have to be made in loving concern for the employees the company wishes to retain, who depend on its survival and growth.

An alternative approach to reconciling these potential contradictions is to point to changes in business strategy. Thus, the argument has been presented that even in sectors where, traditionally, cost-minimization has been the order of the day (e.g. in mass production, supermarket retailing), given the levels of cost-effectiveness achieved in the early 1980s, competitive advantage can now best be achieved by enhancing the quality of the product or service. Hence commitment must be generated in employees directly manufacturing the product or at the customer interface – whether through participative structures and policies of employee involvement or through training and development. Austin Rover's 'Working with Pride' programme of quality circles and employee involvement (Storey 1987b) and Bejam's training programmes (Upton 1987) have been cited as typical senior management initiatives to improve quality, although we await systematic research on the workings of these policies in practice. Again it is difficult to know where rhetoric ends and the extent to which compliance with the normative 'soft' version HRM model is really sought or achieved on the shop floor. Certainly the managers Storey (1987b: 17) cites, suggest a gap between 'espoused theory' and 'theory in use'. Furthermore, this line of argument comes close to suggesting a higher degree of homogeneity in business strategy among organizations than the commentators cited earlier perhaps would suggest.

Is the HRM model internally consistent?

Leaving aside potential contradictions between integration of HRM policy with business strategy and the ability to achieve an integrated company-wide HRM policy; between policy matched to business strategy and the 'soft' HRM model, indeed between the 'hard' and 'soft' versions of the model itself, contradictions may be found in the goals of commitment, flexibility and quality, and of 'strong' culture sought by the 'soft' version of the model.

First, there seems to be some confusion over the concept of commitment. Guest (1987: 513) in querying 'commitment to what?', identifies 'multiple and perhaps competing commitments' to organization, career, job, union, work group, and family. If we assume that HRM emphasizes high standards of performance – 'the excellent companies are measurement-happy and performance-oriented . . . borne of mutually high expectations and peer review' (Peters and Waterman 1982: 240) – and quality of product/service, individuals' job commitment would seem important, along with their desire to develop their skills and competences. But the higher the level of commitment to a particular set of skills, arguably, there may occur a decrease in an employee's preparedness to be flexible as between jobs, or willing to accept a redefinition of a job that might diminish elements to which a commitment has been made.

Hendry and Pettigrew (1988: 43) suggest an interesting sidelight on this potential conflict in their discussion of multi-skilling at Hardy Spicer:

> Retraining itself has unforeseen consequences. One effect is the belief that it adversely changes attitudes to production. Learning to overcome equipment faults means that the particular interest then lies in the exercise of these skills, and the job is only really interesting when the machine breaks down. As the managing director put it: 'we taught them everything but the importance of the production ethic. You could almost hear them saying to the machine "break down, break down" '.

Secondly, HRM appears torn between preaching the virtues of individualism and collectivism. At first sight most commentators, observing its backgrounding of collective, union-based employee relations and its highlighting of individual skills and development, assert that it is individualistic rather than collectivist in orientation (see, for example, Guest 1987; Storey 1987). In this they are supported by much management rhetoric. For example, according to a manager at BMW:

> At BMW there is a new concentration on the individual. We have got to achieve as far as we can a self-organizing company and this means that there has to be much more individual responsibility.
>
> (Barham *et al.* 1988: 54)

But, at the same time, there is a parallel emphasis on team work, whether in the form of quality circles or functional flexibility, and above all, on the individual's commitment to the organization, represented not just as the sum of the individuals in it, but rather as an organic entity with an interest in survival. The potential conflict between emphasizing the importance of the individual on the one hand, and the desirability of cooperative team work and employee commitment to the organization on the other, is glossed over through the general assumption of unitaristic values. For example, from Norsk Data comes the observation:

> Norsk Data is made up of individuals like yourself. We have the 'Norsk Data Spirit'. If you'll be yourself, and use your whole personality in your job, the rest of the team will stand behind you and your efforts.
>
> (Barham *et al.* 1988: 30)

This quotation also points to why HRM stresses the development of a strong corporate culture – not only does it give direction to an organization, but it mediates the tension between individualism and collectivism, as individuals socialized into a strong culture are subject to unobtrusive collective controls on attitudes and behaviour.

However, thirdly, there exists a potential tension between the development of a strong corporate culture and employees' ability to respond flexibly and adaptively. Following Brunsson's (1982) arguments, 'objective' ideologies (defined as ideas shared by all organizational members), when 'conclusive' (that is, clear, narrow and consistent) in one sense – speed of response – can promote adaptability. This is because decisions can be made quickly as the conclusive ideology – read 'strong' culture – acts as an effective filter on the acceptability of an action, eliminating lengthy discussion while generating commitment to implementing it. But this 'adaptability' is only when the action required involves no radical departure from the tenets of the 'strong' culture, as conclusive ideologies rule out changes that challenge their assumptions. Leaving aside the strong bureaucratic cultures that inhibit risk-taking and innovation *per se* (Golzen 1988), the development of a culture congruent with and supportive of a particular business strategy can act as a block to employees adopting different behaviours in response to changing market demand. A much-quoted example is that of IBM whose narrow ideology of 'IBM is service' contained particular assumptions about the nature of product and service (mainframe, customized systems, salesmen as management consultants to customer-as-end-user, seeking quality of product and service) which were inappropriate when strategy dictated an entry into the personal computers market (standardized product, cost competition, dealer as customer) (Mercer 1987). The very success of the IBM service ethic in its traditional markets inhibited an adaptive response from employees to a new market.

Yet conclusive ideologies, reflecting strong cultures, Brunsson argues, in the long term may be more amenable to radical shifts than the broad, ambiguous ideologies, often taken as symptomatic of a 'weak' culture. Superficially, while the latter might appear to allow more flexible responses on the part of the employee, their very vagueness fails to generate the necessary commitment for effective action. Nevertheless, such ideologies tend to survive as they are difficult to disconfirm, being apparently applicable to a wide range of situations. In contrast the very precision of conclusive ideologies allows their disconfirmation as individuals' own experience of changed circumstances cannot be reconciled with their unequivocal prescriptions and justifications. In these circumstances the ideology (culture) is likely to be questioned and replaced. Until a new ideology is in place, Brunsson suggests, it will be impossible for the organization to take effective action as the period of transition will be marked by conflicts and uncertainties that will inhibit individuals' willingness to make a commitment to any one course of action and hinder coordination.

Hence it could be said that the relationship between 'strong' cultures, employee commitment, and adaptability contains a series of paradoxes. Strong cultures allow for a rapid response to familiar conditions, but inhibit immediate flexibility in response to the unfamiliar, because of the commitment generated to a (now) inappropriate ideology. 'Weak' cultures, in contrast, when equated with ambiguous ideologies, allow flexibility in response to the unfamiliar, but cannot generate commitment to action. Yet strong cultures, through disconfirmation and eventual ideological shift may prove ultimately more adaptive to change, assuming the emergence of a new strong yet appropriate culture. This may be at the cost of a transitional period when ability to generate commitment to any course of action – new or old – is minimal.

HRM and the 'contradictions of capitalism'

Underlying the contradictions in HRM outlined above is, of course, the major contradiction embedded in the management of employees in capitalist systems committed to the production, realization, and accumulation of surplus value. As Watson (1983: 25) points out, industrial capitalism depends 'on the institution of the employment and rational organisation of free labour'. But while the principle of control of employees is implicit in ideas of employment and rational organization, that of freedom and autonomy is implied in the notion of formally free labour. In buying employees' capacity to work, organizations are buying the rights to control people's work, but in return they have to cope with the consequence of employees developing a 'calculative' orientation to their effort–reward bargain. This 'calculative' orientation is equally a product of the 'freedom' of labour to 'think for themselves' and to move between employers, a requisite of notionally unconstrained labour markets. Although buying the right to control employees' work, employers cannot prescribe tasks in detail, particularly when highly complex. Furthermore, in the interests of flexible response to variances in day-to-day operational processes, neither would they wish to. Employers may buy the right to control their employees' work, but because in practice they must surrender on a daily basis the means of production to the 'control' of workers for their use in the production process, they must also seek their employees' cooperation to ensure that their discretion is exercised for rather than against the employers' interests.

Hence as Buroway (1979), put it, there exists the need on the part of the employer to achieve control by 'manufacturing consent', rather than by exclusively exercising coercion. But, as already discussed, while the exercise of control through coercion carries the problem of provoking employee non-cooperation and resistance, the creation of commitment to the job carries the potential danger of generating employee inflexibility and conservatism. Furthermore, as Hyman (1987: 43–4) points out, in attempting to walk this tightrope, employers are faced with another dilemma. Efficient labour and administrative processes often call for cohesive relations within a workforce and standardization of their terms and conditions of employment, negotiated through representatives accountable to and for groups of employees. Yet such cohesion and standardization is likely to generate a collective solidarity which employees may use against the employer's interests.

Following Hyman's (1987: 42–3) argument, it might be suggested that HRM just as much as traditional personnel management is confronted by the problem of mediating these contradictions. But the logic of the 'soft' version HRM model would argue a rather different approach to traditional personnel management. Traditional personnel management emerged at a time when most direct labour was treated as a variable rather than fixed cost. The consequent frequent hiring and firing not only made it sensible to have a specialist function perform this and related 'terms and conditions of employment' activities, but by doing so, enabled a dissociation between the sale of labour power and the performance of the labour process, thereby obscuring the commodity status of labour. Apart from performing this function, personnel specialists also had to cope with and ameliorate the consequences of coercive direct control, often employing the masking activities of 'welfare' to disguise the application of rational techniques to counter the problems created by other rational techniques. Not surprisingly, then, the personnel specialist traditionally has been identified as the 'man in the middle', a buffer and potential scapegoat for the actions of the rest of management (Watson 1977: 175–7; Watson 1983: 34). (In a similar vein Purcell in Marginson *et al.* (1988) interprets correlational evidence from the Warwick Company Level Survey to suggest that large corporate personnel departments perform a gatekeeper function to divorce trade unions from strategic management considerations – but at the cost of becoming isolated from strategic decision making.

'Soft' version HRM, on the other hand, insofar as it advocates the treating of labour as a fixed cost, has less need to separate the sale of labour power from its application in production into different management activities. Instead 'terms and conditions of employment' can be linked to work organization as part of an integrated management responsibility. For, in emphasizing the importance of quality (skills), flexibility (with its potential implication for the need to exercise discretion) and commitment in employees, it has opted to obscure the commodity status of labour by adopting strategies of co-optation through the development of 'responsible autonomy' rather than attempting to exercise 'direct control' (Friedman 1977).

Furthermore, in its emphasis on 'strong culture', in theory HRM is able to achieve a cohesive workforce but without the attendant dilemma of creating potentially dysfunctional solidarity. For a 'strong culture' is aimed at uniting employees through a shared set of managerially sanctioned values ('quality', 'service', 'innovation' etc.), that assume an identification of employee and employer interests. Such co-optation – through cultural management, of course – reinforces the intention that autonomy will be exercised 'responsibly', i.e. in management's interests.

If it was possible to apply consistently the 'soft' version HRM model, it might well be argued that it mediates the contradictions of capitalism more effectively than traditional personnel management, as the implied rejection of 'direct control' strategies allows a more complete 'securing and obscuring of the commodity status of labour' (Hyman 1987: 42). But, as argued earlier, if HRM, in theory, demands the integration of employment policies with business strategy, and hence, in some circumstances, to treat labour as a variable input, consistent adherence to the 'soft' version model will come under pressure as 'employers require workers to be *both* dependable *and* disposable' (Hyman 1987: 42). The tensions this may cause are illustrated by the problems that face computer companies when simultaneously confronted by recession and growing market maturity. Companies such as IBM and Hewlett Packard were caught between commitment to 'no redundancy' in the light of their very public adherence to the 'soft' version HRM model and the need for fewer people and different skills. While the adoption of retraining strategies was consistent with the model, the problem in achieving a lower headcount overall is illustrated by the dubious masking strategies of compulsory unpaid leave days and offers of 'early' retirement incentives – no doubt illustrations of 'tough love' in action (Sparrow and Pettigrew 1988).

Conclusions

This chapter has argued that while normative models of personnel and human resource management are not dissimilar, some significant differences in focus exist. While these differences point to HRM being a more central management task than personnel management, at least in theory, the contradictions embedded within the 'mutuality' model and the tensions between the 'hard' and 'soft' versions of the model, call into question whether its enactment will realize its aspirations. Furthermore, the model's contradictions both reflect and are reinforced by the deeper contradictions of capitalism.

It will be most interesting to identify from presently on-going empirical research the extent to which companies are able to enact the 'soft' version mutuality model and, at the same time, achieve 'external fit' with business strategy. It will be interesting too to discover whether even the most 'transformational' leader attempts to do so. Indeed, how often, and in what circumstances was the normative model of personnel management ever fully enacted? Clearly, we need to know more about the organizational and market circumstances that facilitate the adoption of the mutuality model, and how widely within an organization it can be applied. Are there circumstances in which the 'soft' version model is applied to managerial and specialist staff, but the 'hard' version to direct employees? Are there situations where the application of the 'soft' version model to direct employees on a greenfield site, goes hand in hand with the implementation of a 'hard' version on traditional sites? Is such 'soft' version implementation often preceded by a 'hard' version plant closure programme and enforced redundancies? Certainly, reading between the lines, this seems to have been the case at Norsk Hydro (Fox 1988).

It may be suggested that the tensions generated by the potentially conflicting requirements of 'external fit' (for a contingent approach) and of 'internal fit' (for an absolutist approach to HRM) will inevitably give rise to a pragmatism which contradicts its avowedly strategic approach. It is not surprising then that recent research by Purcell and Ahlstrand in multi-divisional companies suggests that there is often a lack of fit between strategic restructuring and employee-relations practice as different managerial groups pursue their own interests and protect their own domains (Ahlstrand and Purcell 1988; Purcell and Ahlstrand 1987). It may well be that some of the apparent implementations of HRM involve the adoption of particular 'Japanese' techniques, but opportunistically rather than strategically.

Given these problems it might well be asked why the language of HRM has gained the currency it appears to have – not least among management groups themselves. After all, as has been argued, there is little real difference between normative HRM and personnel–management models and, in practice, it is probable that managing employee relations in the vast majority of companies remains a pragmatic activity, whether labelled personnel management or HRM. Furthermore, many of the techniques of HRM can be found in any personnel management textbook of a decade ago.

I would suggest that, in many cases, the use of the 'new label' is no more or less than a reflection of the rise of the 'new right' – whether in the UK or USA. In Britain 'personnel management' evokes images of do-gooding specialists trying to constrain line managers, of weakly kowtowing to militant unions, of both lacking power and possessing too much power. Our new enterprise culture demands a different language, one that asserts management's right to manipulate, *and* ability to generate and develop resources. The dual usage of the concept 'resource', with its simultaneous passive and proactive connotations, and its 'hard' and 'soft' version HRM models, is very useful here. While the language and policies of the 'hard' version model can be used on employees peripheral to the organization, those of the 'soft' version model can be used to reassure and secure 'core' employees whose resourcefulness is deemed essential for the achievement of competitive advantage. The language of 'tough love' seeks to co-opt the assent of both those who may suffer as well as those who may benefit from its effects. Ironically, it is the contradictions embedded in HRM that have facilitated the development of this rhetoric even if they simultaneously render strategic action problematic.

Chapter three

Human resource management: its implications for industrial relations and trade unions

David E. Guest

Introduction

The aim of this chapter is to explore the link between human resource management (HRM), industrial relations and trade unions. Inevitably this must be a somewhat speculative venture. By imposing a particular definition of HRM, it is possible to make out a case for the incompatibility between HRM and the traditional pluralist form of industrial-relations and trade-union activity which predominates in the UK. To seek empirical verification for this is much more difficult, since very little is known about personnel practices in organizations. Any link between HRM, industrial relations, and organizational performance must therefore rely either on a limited amount of case material with all the attendant risks of unrepresentativeness; or it must be based on inference from a range of indirect sources of evidence.

The chapter is divided into four main sections. The first examines the nature of HRM and its implications for industrial relations. The second explores the link between HRM and what is sometimes called 'the new industrial relations'. The third considers industrial relations in organizations where HRM or something close to it is practised. This section will draw upon American data and upon the experience of green-field sites in the UK. The fourth section explores the implications for industrial relations of attempts to move towards HRM in plants where industrial relations and trade unionism are well established. A short final section reassesses the relationship between HRM, industrial relations and trade unionism.

The implications of human resource management for industrial relations

As it gains wider usage, the term human resource management runs the risk of becoming a catch-all phrase, reflecting general intentions but devoid of specific meaning. It was argued in an earlier paper, (Guest 1987) that any attempt to use the term mainly to revitalize the rather jaded image of personnel management was unlikely to be either operationally or conceptually helpful unless it contained a set of specific policy goals. A second view of HRM is that it can be distinguished from what preceded it by its adoption of a strategic view of personnel issues. This again is unsatisfactory. Personnel management has always espoused the importance of adopting a strategic view. It has been less successful in practice. What is more important is the input to this strategic concern. In other words what is needed is not just a capacity to think strategically but some distinctive view of the strategic direction that should be pursued. It is this direction that constitutes the distinctive feature of HRM.

The nature of HRM can be derived empirically or conceptually. From either approach there are risks of a tautological analysis. An empirically derived view will be based on an assessment of the practices of firms which either claim to practise HRM or have at some point been identified as exemplars of HRM. However, the basis for the initial labelling may reflect a set of biases or values which imply a specific meaning for HRM. In much the same way a conceptual analysis will be based on a set of assumptions about what constitutes appropriate management of human resources.

One way out of this impasse is to develop a set of propositions for testing. Fortunately there is a growing body of research evidence from within the social sciences, and more especially from within what is normally described as organizational behaviour, which can guide the development of propositions. This evidence has been described briefly elsewhere (Guest 1987, 1988). What is proposed is that there is an organizational pay-off in a combination of HRM policies designed to produce strategic integration, high commitment, high quality, and flexibility among employees. Strategic integration refers to the ability of the organization to integrate HRM issues into its strategic plans, to ensure that the various aspects of HRM cohere and for line managers to incorporate an HRM perspective into their decision-making. High commitment is concerned with both behavioural commitment to pursue agreed goals and attitudinal commitment reflected in a strong identification with the enterprise. High quality refers to all aspects of management behaviour, including management of employees and investment in high-quality employees, which in turn will bear directly upon the quality of goods and services provided. Finally, flexibility is primarily concerned with what is sometimes called functional flexibility but also with an adaptable organization structure with the capacity to manage innovation. The link between HRM policies (for example, selection on specific criteria, using advanced selection techniques), HRM goals (for example, high commitment to the company) and organizational outcomes (for example, low labour turnover and allegiance to the company rather than the union) can be developed into a set of propositions for testing. Indeed there is already a significant body of research on each of the four central HRM policy goals within the model.

The empirical derivation of HRM is based on an analysis of the policies and policy goals pursued by successful companies. Put simply, the case is that companies which are successful according to financial criteria (Peters and Waterman 1982; Goldsmith and Clutterbuck 1984), capacity for innovation and turnaround (Kanter 1984; Grinyer et al. 1987) and ability, despite large size, to remain non-union (Foulkes 1980) have adopted HRM policies in pursuit of HRM goals.

The empirical evidence also indicates that the driving force behind the introduction of HRM appears to have little to do with industrial relations; rather, it is the pursuit of competitive advantage in the market place through provision of high-quality goods and services, through competitive pricing linked to high productivity and through the capacity swiftly to innovate and manage change in response to changes in the market place or to breakthroughs in research and development. Nevertheless, if the preceding analysis is valid, HRM has considerable implications for industrial relations. Its underlying values, reflected in HRM policies and practices, would appear to be essentially unitarist and individualistic in contrast to the more pluralist and collective values of traditional industrial relations.

HRM values are unitarist to the extent that they assume no underlying and inevitable differences of interest between management and workers. This does not deny that previous experience might have created considerable distrust and a perception of different interests and priorities. In cases where the levels of distrust are so strongly embedded as to be resistant to change, careful recruitment and selection should be able to filter such individuals out. One obvious way of doing this is to recruit a very young workforce. Of course where such individuals are already employed, the company faces a different set of problems.

HRM values are essentially individualistic in that they emphasize the individual-organization linkage in preference to operating through group and representative systems. Both the formal and the psychological contracts for shop-floor workers are more akin to that typically offered to managers. Analysis of even the large American non-union companies described by Foulkes (1980) reveals very few examples of consultative committees or any other sort of representative system.

These values underpinning HRM leave little scope for collective arrangements and assume little need for collective bargaining. HRM therefore poses a considerable challenge to traditional industrial relations and more particularly to trade unionism. At the same time, HRM is not necessarily anti-union. If the four central components of HRM outlined earlier are considered, then neither strategic integration nor quality is in any sense incompatible with trade-union activity. On the other hand, flexibility is likely to pose a significant challenge to some unions, more particularly at multi-union sites. However, it is an issue on which the unions have shown themselves willing to bargain. The main challenge to the unions is therefore likely to come from the pursuit of employee commitment.

It must be acknowledged that the concept of commitment is highly problematic and appears to be used in a variety of ways. The version of most interest here, attitudinal commitment, is essentially concerned with the strength of the individual-organization linkage. Mowday, Porter, and Steers (1982) identify three key dimensions: identification with the organization's values and goals, a desire to work hard for the organization, and a desire to stay with the organization. This raises the question of whether high company commitment can coexist with commitment to a trade union. Interest in this question has recently led to a resurgence of research into what is commonly termed dual allegiance. The thrust of the research, most of which is American, (see, for example, Angle and Perry 1986) indicates that dual allegiance is possible where a cooperative industrial relations climate exists. In a less cooperative climate, workers may be forced to make a choice.

Since HRM seeks to produce a positive working climate, it need not appear overtly anti-union. However it poses a threat in three ways. Firstly, in organizations where unions are already established HRM goals are likely to be pursued through policies that tend to by-pass the union. For example, management is likely to prefer its own channels of communication, to foster individualized forms of incentive and reward schemes, and to control socialization of new recruits very carefully. Secondly, by practising high-quality management, the need for the union as a protective device against arbitrary management behaviour is likely to be reduced. The industrial relations system will still be used to negotiate annual wages, but if a policy of paying above-average rates is pursued, individualized incentive schemes are increasingly operating and longer-term pay deals are concluded, even this central trade union role may be diminished. The risk is that after a while the union will gradually wither and die. The third threat arises in non-union plants and at new sites where HRM policies should obviate any felt need for a union. It must be emphasized that in the UK much of this analysis is speculative since, as we shall see in a later section, little empirical evidence on the link between HRM and industrial relations exists.

From the foregoing analysis it would appear that HRM poses a challenge to traditional industrial relations and to the trade unions. It also presents a major challenge to management competence and to the ability of management to sustain the quality of performance necessary to prevent issues arising which provide fertile ground for union activity. In many cases, more especially in workplaces where the unions are already well established and the system of management and control is built on more traditional adversarial assumptions about management–employee relations it is likely to prove extremely difficult for management to rise to this challenge. In such cases a more sensible strategy might be to pursue the conventional arrangements based on the Donovan approach which still appears to represent the dominant paradigm within which industrial relations and personnel policy is pursued within the UK. However, it would be wrong to present HRM as the only alternative; recent developments show that the choice is wider than this.

HRM and the new industrial relations

HRM has been closely linked to what is sometimes termed 'the new industrial relations'. This is a loose multi-dimensional term used to describe and explain certain industrial relations developments of the 1980s and sometimes to prescribe policy. One of its starting points is a decline in trade union density in the UK from a high of approximately 58 per cent in 1980 to under 50 per cent in 1987.

These figures have been disputed and some estimates put the level of trade union density much lower. Whatever their level, the decline is used alongside the reduction in days lost through industrial disputes as evidence that we are now in a new era of industrial relations. 'The new industrial relations' has also been used to describe a new set of management practices affecting both collective bargaining arrangements and the management of employees. These practices include a move towards longer-term deals, recognition of only one union or even no unions and attempts to create employee involvement and a more flexible and swiftly adaptable workforce. These innovations have been encouraged by government legislation and by government policy. One consequence of these practices has been a decline in the centrality of industrial relations issues and therefore in the role of trade unions and trade union representatives in the workplace.

What is not in dispute is that the recession of the early 1980s, high unemployment, and the Conservative government's industrial relations legislation have shifted the balance of power away from the unions. The issue in doubt is whether this represents a long-term change or a temporary shift in the balance of power. Some commentators (Bassett 1986; Roberts 1987) believe that we are witnessing the beginning of a long-term trend reflecting a shift in workers' attitudes from a collective to a more individualistic orientation. One outcome will be a long-term decline in the membership of trade unions. Others (e.g. Kelly 1988; MacInnes 1987) are more sceptical. They challenge the extent of the changes and the novelty of the circumstances, suggesting it is possible to be misled by a few well-publicized cases, and pointing to the upsurge in industrial unrest and the increase in the membership of a number of trade unions that was reported in the early months of 1988.

In any analysis of the permanence or otherwise of these changes, much would appear to depend on management policy and practice. It is at this point in the analysis that the role of HRM becomes crucial. The green-field sites of the 1930s and the companies welcoming back workers in the 1940s became susceptible to trade union organization, according to the analysis of Barnett (1986), largely because of the incompetence of management. HRM places a premium upon the competence of management and if the changes associated with the 'new industrial relations' are to persist, then it will be partly because HRM policies provide the basis for management practice. At the same time, pursuit of HRM is not risk-free; but to organizations driven by market pressures to seek improved quality, greater flexibility, and constant innovation, HRM may appear to be an attractive option.

HRM is only one of the policy options which challenges traditional industrial relations and the role of trade unions. Indeed, when the various elements within the 'new industrial relations' are disentangled, there appear to be at least three further approaches which management might pursue within established enterprises. First, there is the possibility of an aggressively anti-union stance, made possible either by union weakness resulting from the recession and government legislation or by opportunities arising in the context of a takeover or relocation. Some cases of derecognition as at Wapping and in a small number of publishing houses fall into this category. The Labour Research Department (1988) found thirty-nine cases since 1984 of either derecognition or a move from multiple- to single-union status. It is possible that the report underestimates both the extent and the seriousness of the problem. Even ACAS (1988) notes the increase in the number of management groups that have ceased to operate under collective arrangements and hints that derecognition is on the increase.

A second possibility is the more positive assertion of traditional management authority within the conventional pluralist perspective, as found in steel, coal, the railways, and in car plants. Two important elements of this approach are firstly cost-cutting and rationalization exercises involving large-scale shedding of labour; and secondly an attempt to raise productivity through a combination of capital investment and the use of various forms of financial incentive. Embarking on this route has often necessitated a challenge to union authority and therefore a phase of industrial conflict.

A final approach within the ambit of the 'new industrial relations', which will be explored in more detail in section three, leaves the industrial relations machinery more or less intact and sets up alongside it a number of initiatives such as employee share ownership, quality circles, improved communication and mechanisms for enhancing flexibility. The research evidence (Batstone 1984; Edwards 1987; Millward and Stevens 1986) suggests that this is probably the most popular path for established companies. The evidence also suggests that it tends to be piecemeal, opportunistic, and limited in its impact (Batstone 1984; Edwards 1987). In short, it lacks any form of strategic integration and therefore falls short of HRM.

Adoption of HRM requires the capacity to think strategically and to manage innovative HRM policies. From existing research, we know that foreign and especially American companies are much more likely than UK companies to adopt innovative HRM practices in the UK (Purcell *et al*. 1987). This at least has the advantage of showing that it can be done. Secondly we know that personnel managers are in general either reluctant to innovate and undertake strategic planning in their area of work or else they are very poor at it. Thirdly we know that the majority of managers are satisfied with the industrial-relations status quo, which contains a collective union voice (Millward and Stevens 1986). This raises the question of how far this reflects a failure to consider alternatives, how far it is a form of satisficing and how far managers genuinely believe in a pluralist view of industrial relations. Or do they share the assumed anti-unionism of many American managers (Kochan, Katz, and McKersie 1986) to the point where they would prefer to manage without trade unions if that were a realistic possibility?

The preceding analysis suggests that HRM is only one of a number of innovative policy choices. The need to consider policy choices is most apparent when setting up green-field sites when the constraints of established practice are largely absent. It may appear equally desirable to those managing existing plants, but it will usually be much more difficult to introduce into a context of established practices.

Human resource management and industrial relations in green-field sites

HRM is an American concept and it finds its fullest expression in a number of well-known and successful American companies. It also overlaps in some respects with the stereotypical view of Japanese management (Ouchi 1981). It is therefore plausible to expect that foreign companies setting up new plants in the UK and bringing with them an established model of HRM are most likely to consider adopting an HRM strategy in the UK.

That model is often of a non-union company. Indeed, many of the best-known American examples are found in Foulkes's (1980) analysis of personnel policies in large non-union companies. He notes that in almost all the companies he looked at the HRM policies came first, often encouraged by the values of a powerful CEO, preceding any considered non-unionism. In many cases, remaining non-union has subsequently become a policy goal. On the basis of the companies he studied, this has a number of cost implications. Personnel policies must be sufficiently good and sufficiently integrated and reinforced by line management practice to avoid giving grounds for union organizing. Foulkes found that most of the companies he studied paid above average rates. They also provided mechanisms for individual expression of grievances and were likely to monitor reactions to personnel policies through the communication systems and the use of attitude surveys. All of these practices are to be found in a company like IBM which provides the best-known model of HRM but which is also what Bassett, who describes their policies at some length, refers to as 'the ultimate non-union company' (Bassett 1986: 170).

Not everyone would agree that HRM is inevitably associated with an absence of trade unions, even in the USA. Perhaps the best defence of a trade union role is presented by Kochan, Katz, and McKersie (1986). They argue that although market forces are driving American companies towards an inevitable embrace of HRM and non-union companies have been at the leading edge of this movement, it can be achieved in collaboration with trade unions. They present case studies, most notably from General Motors and Xerox which illustrate the role of the trade union in facilitating a move towards HRM. This is their 'transformation' of American industrial relations. If a new set of practices can be introduced, it is not clear what role is left for the union. The most likely one is that of policing management practices and dealing with grievances which seem almost inevitable with repetitive production line work and persisting pressures to increase productivity. By implication, management is not practising effective HRM and the door is left open for the unions to play a role.

Companies setting up green-field sites in the UK have an ideal opportunity to consider new initiatives in many aspects of management. Among other things, management must decide what sort of relationship it wishes to foster with its potential workforce and whether or not to adopt HRM. In this context, the company faces explicit choices about the management of industrial relations. These choices can be expressed in terms of trade union recognition. There are four main possibilities:

1. Adopt a unitarist individualistic HRM policy and have no union and no collective arrangements.
2. Adopt a unitarist perspective with no independent trade union, but provide a collective voice through some form of company consultative council.
3. Accept a pluralist perspective, but plan it carefully, seeking a single-union agreement, signed on the company's terms and possibly containing some form of no strike clause linked to pendulum arbitration.
4. Accept the traditional pluralist perspective in the UK and recognize any unions who can demonstrate significant membership.

If the policy alternatives listed above are explicitly considered, a number of factors will help to shape the decision. These include the policy in the home country (which in some cases will be the UK), any established policy in existing plants in the UK, local traditions and union strength, government grants and policies, the advice of professional consultants and the profile of the company and the attendant publicity that this implies.

One indication of HRM practices in green-field sites might therefore be the presence of a trade union. An organization consciously pursuing HRM will almost always prefer the non-union path, emphasizing individual rather than collective arrangements. Unfortunately, for the purposes of the present analysis, a company may pursue non-union policies or remain fortuitously non-union without practising HRM. Therefore such evidence is at best indirect and unreliable. Clearly there is a danger of conflating non-unionism with HRM which must be borne in mind in the following section. On the other hand, success in remaining non-union suggests that the personnel policies being pursued are effective. In practice the picture is further obscured because for various reasons, including a high public profile, a union presence may be seen as inevitable. In this case, a single-union arrangement is likely to be sought, usually with some sort of no-strike deal. Single-union deals have not always stood in the way of HRM; indeed, in cases like Toshiba and Nissan, a union has played a supportive role in instituting HRM policies. One consequence has been that the union has had a marginal role and it is not surprising to find that union density at Nissan is only about 25 per cent, with some estimates placing this figure considerably lower.

It seems plausible to expect that American companies, reflecting their home culture of anti-unionism, individualism, and familiarity with HRM, will generally pursue the non-union path. Japanese companies, used to 'house' unions can be expected to seek either some form of non-union company council or a single-union deal. European companies, more familiar with the pluralist perspective, are the most likely to plan a positive union role, including collective bargaining.

The evidence on the presence of trade unions at green-field sites is sketchy and industrial relations were not always the central focus of the studies from which evidence can be derived. For example, a government survey of 300 foreign companies setting up plants in the UK (quoted on BBC *Newsnight*, 5/4/88) found that 56 per cent had no union, 21 per cent recognized a single union and the remainder were presumably multi union. The Workplace Industrial Relations Survey (WIRS2), which might be expected to be more authoritative, is of little help. The 1984 sampling frame contained only twenty-two private-sector establishments set up within the previous three years. Of these, 43 per cent had manual union members and 19 per cent had non-manual union members compared with 54 per cent and 34 per cent for the private sector as a whole (Millward and Stevens 1986: 52). The results are therefore in the predicted direction, but with the small sample size and the lack of control for size are not very useful.

A Welsh Development Agency survey of foreign-owned companies in Wales (FT 13/10/87) found that 54 per cent of them recognized trade unions. 75 per cent recognized in-house staff associations and 40 per cent were non-union. Among those recognizing trade unions, 46.5 per cent recognized only one. Relations with the unions appeared to be good. 92.5 per cent of the companies recognizing unions said they had a positive or neutral effect on company performance, 58.1 per cent seeing them as helpful; 84.8 per cent had experienced no loss of working days due to disputes since 1980 and a further 14 per cent had lost less than 1 per cent.

Scotland has gained a reputation for hosting large numbers of new high-technology firms which have remained non-union. Indeed the Scottish Development Agency found that none of the American electronics or high-technology firms established in Scotland in the last 10 years has been unionized, while the TUC found that only 6.6 per cent of firms of any sort established in Scotland between 1976 and 1986 recognized trade unions (Bassett 1988).

These types of study suggest a development of non-union and single-union plants among green-field sites. However, they must be treated with caution. We know little about the size and age of the plants and whether there have been changes in union recognition, perhaps as a function of growth. (There is at least one Japanese plant in Wales which invited in the EETPU when expansion made it difficult to communicate effectively with the workforce (Bassett 1986)).

Any HRM policies can only be inferred from union-recognition data and there is no good data on the personnel policies of green-field plants. However, anecdotal support for a link between an absence of unions and HRM can be found in a report on Livingston in Scotland (FT 15/2/1988) where several USA and Japanese companies have established plants in the 1980s. According to the report, their recruitment has been largely restricted to young school leavers or skilled workers. NEC, for example, employs approximately 280 operators with an average age of 18.5 years. Mitsubishi claims that its elected staff consultative committee, which among other things prepares an annual wage claim, obviates the need for a union. At the American company, Unisys, the aim, echoing the US HRM experience, is to do better than any third party for the workforce. They provide free life and private health insurance, five weeks holiday and single status for all employees. These examples indicate that at least some companies are pursuing a careful and deliberate HRM policy, one part of which is to avoid a felt need for unionization.

Some of the best documented cases of an HRM approach come from Japanese companies which have recognized a single union. One example is Toshiba in Plymouth, which started off as an unsatisfactory joint venture with Rank. The plant was closed down and reopened under full Japanese control and, in effect, as a green-field site. This involved much greater care in recruitment and selection, training, socialization and emphasis on targets, quality of work and regular attendance.

The experience at Nissan has been described by its personnel director (Wickens 1987). He reports how the high public profile of the company was perceived as likely to make the plant a target for unions should the company try to pursue a non-union path, with the probable consequence that it would become multi-union. In seeking to manage industrial relations and to integrate it into the wider set of HRM policies and especially single status, the advantages of a single union seemed clear. Nissan therefore followed the path of most Japanese manufacturing plants in the UK and concluded a single-union deal on terms largely determined by management.

One of the advantages for management of non-unionism is the opportunity to pursue total functional flexibility and thereby ensure the fullest and most efficient use of the workforce. Where companies setting up new plants have decided to recognize a union, a central topic for discussion in what is sometimes termed the 'union beauty contest' is the willingness of a union to accept full flexible working, something which is easier to implement where only one union is involved. Both Nissan and Komatsu provide illustrations of the acceptance by the AUEW of agreements involving flexible working.

One of the most interesting studies of personnel policies and non unionism comes from the Republic of Ireland (Toner 1985). He compared perceptions of a variety of policies and practices among a sample of 248 workers from three non-union and four unionized plants. Each plant was foreign owned, drawn from the electronics industry and employed more than 200 workers. All but one had been set up in the late 1960s or the 1970s. Significant differences emerged between the unionized and non-unionized workers on 14 of the 19 items which examined perceptions of personnel policy and practice. In each case attitudes were more positive among the workers from the non-unionized plants. It appears that in these plants management pursued a set of policies which were sufficiently attractive to the workforce to obviate any felt need for a trade union. Although the study was not directly concerned with HRM, the items on which responses were positive in the non-union plants such as management style, communications and grievance handling suggest that something close to HRM was being practised. An important corollary of this finding is that the unions did not appear to be providing the workforce in the unionized plants with a very effective 'voice'.

Despite the poor quality of the evidence, there is some indication that at a significant proportion of foreign-owned green-field sites, management is pursuing some of the central features of HRM. These include flexible working, employee commitment and attention to high quality, which is partly reflected in the investment in careful selection and training. In many cases there are individual contracts and no collective arrangements. There is either no role for trade unions or at best a limited one where unions are allowed to operate but only on management's terms.

Moving towards human resource management in established plants

A series of studies (Brown 1981; Daniel and Millward 1983; Batstone 1984; Millward and Stevens 1986; Edwards 1987) has charted changes in industrial relations and personnel institutions and practices in the UK over the past 10 years. On the basis of these and some related studies, some tentative conclusions can be reached about the changes which have occurred.

1. There have been a variety of initiatives in all sectors of industry to adopt practices to improve flexibility, quality of work and employee commitment among the workforce. For example WIRS2 (Millward and Stevens 1986) noted that 31 per cent of the organizations in the sample had taken some sort of initiative to increase employee involvement, much the most popular initiative being the development of two-way communication. (This compares with 24 per cent in the first workplace industrial relations survey, WIRS1). These initiatives are consistent with moves towards human resource management.

2. Despite considerable improvements in productivity in British industry, there is no convincing evidence of any clear link between these initiatives and productivity improvements (Batstone 1984; Edwards 1987). Since it seems intuitively reasonable that there should be a link if the initiatives are serious, and since there is case material that demonstrates the potential benefits of specific initiatives, this suggests that these new practices are occurring either on a very limited scale or in a very piecemeal fashion. The evidence on the lack of strategic thought that goes into flexibility schemes (Atkinson and Meager 1986; Hakim 1988) would support this interpretation.

3. These practices seem to exist alongside and almost independently of existing industrial relations arrangements (Edwards 1987; Storey 1987b). There is general satisfaction with existing industrial relations institutions and no strong desire to change them (Millward and Stevens 1986). This implies acceptance of an essentially pluralist system in which collective bargaining with trade unions plays a central role.

There are a number of qualifications to this pattern, three of which deserve some attention:

1. Some companies have used the collective bargaining machinery to promote flexibility agreements, flexibility in this context referring to what Atkinson terms functional flexibility and therefore falling within the ambit of HRM.

In general these represent a continuation of the traditional pluralist system within which they were negotiated rather than an attempt to change personnel policies. The evidence (see IDS 1988b) suggests that with a few exceptions these have been enabling agreements which have subsequently encountered considerable worker opposition. There is little evidence to conclude that multi-skilling and the flexible firm are about to become realities in significant sectors of British industry, at least not in unionized plants.

2. There has been a small increase in pay deals extending beyond the dominant 12-month duration. The CBI databank reveals that throughout the 1980s, about 4 per cent of agreements in manufacturing industry have extended beyond a year, though in the year to July 1987 this rose to 7 per cent. A survey of 46 such agreements (Lindopp and Haslett 1988) reveals that they are particularly likely to be linked to change. Indeed, 59 per cent contained provisions for more flexible working and the removal of restrictive practices compared with 11 per cent of all settlements during the relevant period. Thirty-three per cent, compared with 6 per cent, covered the introduction of new technology and 24 per cent, compared with 1.5 per cent, incorporated changes in shift patterns. The most frequently cited 'very important' advantages of these longer-term deals were industrial relations stability (74 per cent), cost stability/predictability (70 per cent), savings in management time (41 per cent) and ability to plan working practice changes (24 per cent). Although the questioning may have confused planning with implementing change, the data do not provide strong support for any link between these deals and an HRM strategy. In this respect they appear to differ from some of the long-term deals concluded in the USA.

3. A number of companies have taken specific initiatives with heavy overtones of HRM which have resulted in the implementation of changes at some cost to union organization and strength. Two examples will serve to illustrate the possibilities.

Tioxide is a heavy chemicals company with its main UK site at Grimsby, where until fairly recently it employed almost 1,000 workers. Following a strategic analysis of its markets and the type of contribution it needed from its workforce, Tioxide embarked upon a long-term policy of implementing a series of HRM initiatives. A feature of their planning was the heavy involvement of line and personnel managers, thereby ensuring a greater likelihood of strategic integration of the initiatives. At a fairly early point it became clear that the traditional divisions based on the categories of worker recognized for collective agreements and associated with the industrial relations arrangements were going to be an obstacle to change. At one of the small plants, management was able to take an initiative which led to de-recognition of the unions. At the main Grimsby plant, the unions took an initiative to press for single status with the particular goal of improving the pension arrangements. Management's response was to offer a package which apparently went ahead with a good measure of local shop steward support. In January 1987, on a 93 per cent turnout, 76 per cent of the workers voted to accept a staff status package which contained a number of features. The five unions were de-recognized for the purposes of collective bargaining. 'Total flexibility' was introduced. The production bonus was replaced by profit sharing. Individuals were to progress within simplified salary bands based on performance appraisal. This in turn was linked to the adoption by a worker of a wider range of activities, following skills training, as part of the flexibility package.

The interesting feature of the Tioxide case is the use of aspects of HRM and most notably strategic integration and attempts through a major communications programme to generate employee commitment to the company, prior to confronting the industrial relations issue. They had also developed a more clearly thought-out industrial relations strategy than often appears to be the case, carefully linked into HRM. The language of the agreement indicates that the company is looking for continuing change; 'The future requirement . . . is *real flexibility* involving a *real* commitment to continual change' (IDS 1988b). The benefits of these changes for the company, according to one report (Kennedy 1987) have not yet filtered through and a third small plant is still unionized. However, at Grimsby there was a 25 per cent increase in output and a net reduction in the workforce in the years from 1984 to 1987 prior to the agreement and a further slimming down of the workforce through natural wastage is anticipated (IDS 1988b).

The second case is that of Norsk Hydro. After taking over Fison's fertilizer division, Norsk Hydro had closed two of the three plants and made an investment of £80 million at Immingham conditional upon acceptance of a 4-year deal. This involved de-recognition of all the unions except the TGWU, single status, team working and the removal of process/maintenance demarcations. The deal was opposed by the unions but accepted by the workforce in a ballot. This is typical of some of the flexibility agreements except that it was more far-reaching and directly tackled the multi-union demarcation issues which have caused many of the other deals to flounder. It was also promoted in the context of changes in the management of the organization leading to the introduction of several aspects of HRM (Fox 1988).

The subjective evidence of those who have been monitoring industrial relations and personnel practices is that there has been a lot of change (Morris and Wood 1988; Storey 1987b). The foregoing analysis challenges the significance of these changes in many, if not most, established plants. Attempts to negotiate flexibility, to operate quality circles, to improve communication systems and to take steps towards single status have been introduced with some fanfare in many companies. Given the poor quality of the available evidence it would be foolish to claim that these initiatives have had no impact. However, much of the impact may be on attitudes rather than behaviour. Programmes of employee involvement through two-way communication and single status may generate increased commitment and satisfaction. But in line with the more carefully researched evidence on organizational commitment (Reichers 1985), when introduced in isolation their impact on performance is likely to be very limited. More direct attempts to confront barriers to productivity improvements through flexibility agreements have often run into union opposition. Only in exceptional cases, such as the two outlined above, where the changes are integrated rather then considered piecemeal, is the impact likely to be greater. It is in these contexts that something closer to HRM is being attempted.

Conclusions: the compatibility of HRM and industrial relations

This paper has presented the view that there is an incompatibility between the essentially unitarist HRM and pluralist tradition of industrial relations in the UK. The best available evidence shows that there has been no collapse of industrial relations institutions in the UK. It is true that the density of trade union membership has steadily declined during the 1980s and this decline is steeper than that found in most other countries. However most of this can be accounted for by the cutback or closure of large plants and sectoral shifts in employment away from traditional, highly unionized sectors of the economy. The important point to note here is that the decline cannot be attributed to any significant employers' offensive against trade unions. Further support for this position can be found in all the main surveys of workplace industrial relations (Millward and Stevens 1986) which show that the central institutions of plant- and company-level industrial relations are still in place and in use.

We also know from the same sources that there have been initiatives in many companies to increase employee involvement and to take other steps on the path towards HRM. Given the assumed incompatibility of these approaches, how can we explain this? One obvious answer is that the underlying assumption of incompatibility is wrong. This is essentially the view of Kochan, Katz, and McKersie (1986). However, their analysis applies to single-union plants in the USA where the challenge to the 'territory' of several potentially competing unions is not an issue. They also do not consider a sufficiently long time scale to analyse the possibility that the unions may be colluding in their own gradual demise. Finally, there must be doubts about whether there are more than a very few cases where the unions have a pivotal role in introducing the type of HRM being discussed in this chapter.

A second possibility, and one for which there is some evidence (Storey 1987b), is that the two systems can coexist. Essentially, what this means is that it is possible to make some progress towards HRM through initiatives in conventional areas such as communication, involvement, and training without posing any challenge to industrial relations institutions. There may come a point where a challenge does exist, more particularly when attempts are made to introduce functional flexibility or job redesign. Few companies seem to have confronted this and where they have the unions have often rebuffed them.

A third overlapping possibility and one which has been supported by some of the research on joint consultation (Marchington and Armstrong 1985; Cressey *et al.* 1985) and quality circles (Bradley and Hill 1987) is that initiatives which appear impressive when described in the company head office become heavily diluted in practice. For example, Bradley and Hill (1987) have compared the impact and sustainability of quality circles in an American and a British plant. At the British plant they found that middle management was opposed in principle to workers' participation and saw little benefit to themselves in the quality circles. Therefore, despite some enthusiasm from senior management and a claim by top management that quality circles were a reflection of their HRM policy, most of the circles soon collapsed. In contrast in the USA company, middle managers had more autonomy to implement suggestions and, since it was linked to their performance appraisal, more reason to make the circles succeed. Predictably, they therefore survived and flourished over a longer period. This type of detailed evidence suggests that the claims made by managements about the initiatives they are taking must be treated with caution. There is often a lack of what we have termed strategic integration, in that those middle managers who are responsible for making the innovations succeed lack either the ability or the commitment to ensure their success.

A fourth and again overlapping possibility is that top management has failed to adopt a strategic view of HRM and industrial relations. (An alternative argument is that managers do have a strategy which centres around the belief that they should not confront the existing industrial relations institutions. This may be an operational rather than an espoused policy.) However, there is evidence that senior managers are increasingly thinking strategically about human resources (Morris and Wood 1988). The problem arises at the point of implementation. Here the approach appears to be essentially opportunistic. As a result, HRM issues are rarely pursued to the point where the industrial relations system is seriously challenged. At some point, any company pursuing HRM will confront the industrial relations institutions in areas like flexibility, job design, and reward systems.

Finally, in many established plants there may be a view that it is not necessary to push ahead very fast or far with HRM because it has been possible to do well enough without it. Throughout the 1980s, British manufacturing industry has been able to obtain major productivity improvements while continuing to operate within the traditional industrial relations system (Metcalf 1988). Perhaps the more robust economic climate has encouraged both sides to make better use of the existing system. Yet despite the improvements in productivity, British industry still lags far behind its main competitors. For further catching up to occur, it seems likely that a fuller use of human resources will be necessary. This is likely to require a shift in emphasis away from the industrial relations system towards HRM policies as the main path to improved performance. In the absence of a radical change in the relationship between unions and employers, if this shift occurs it is likely to do so at the expense of the trade unions.

Chapter four

Human resource management and the personnel function

Derek Torrington

From workforce centredness to resource centredness

Theoretically the concept of human resource management provides a major shift of direction in the employment of people; moving away from the traditional emphasis of personnel management on conciliation, propitiation and motivation of employees as a potentially uncooperative *cost*. The HRM argument is that people need less goading and supervision, but more scope and autonomy. They are not to be seen as a cost, but as an *asset* in which to invest, so adding to their inherent value. A less apparent feature of HRM is that some of those who do the organization's work are regarded as less committed to that organization through being located at the periphery rather than in the core.

Some years ago human-asset accounting (Giles and Robinson 1972) was widely condemned as dehumanizing the process whereby people were employed. In the 1980s we hear from the United States about *strategic management of human resources*, which is human asset accounting reinvented and re-presented as a version of human capital theory (Fombrun *et al.* 1984; Odiorne 1984; Hendry and Pettigrew 1986).

There is now perhaps less scope for the type of scepticism that was voiced in the 1970s. How effective have our 'traditional' human values been in protecting people's jobs? What use has personnel management been (and, for that matter, what use has trade-union organization been?) in the decade of economic recession? Jobs have been an expense to be reduced, training has been a cost to be eliminated and the people who have lost their jobs or who have not been trained have been victims for whose plight there remains no convincing solution.

Slimming of workforces, computerization and the use of numerically controlled machines have all tended to make individual jobs more self-contained, more skilled and more varied, reducing the need for supervision and increasing the degree of workers' control over their own activities (White and Trevor 1983). Patterns of work are becoming more flexible and there is greater scope for self-employment and working (through agencies) for a number of employers (Atkinson 1984; Dobson 1986). These developments make possible the close specification of what is needed from employees and measurement of what is produced. Jobs can be set apart from each other so that the contribution is distinctly that of the job holder. This requires training of the employee, so that the investment can be made worthwhile by increasing the value of the asset.

A shift in emphasis within and around the personnel function of organizations can already be detected, with personnel management tending to decline and for human resource management to increase, but this is often no more than changes of labels and few people have a clear view of what they are doing and of the way in which their situation is changing (Mackay and Torrington 1986: 178).

Researchers continue to point to the ineffectual nature of the personnel contribution to decision-making in organizations, yet current indications are that the personnel profession is thriving. Enrolments for IPM examinations are increasing at between 12 per cent and 15 per cent each year, with a particularly steep rise in 1987–8, and there was a dramatic increase in the number of general personnel and training posts advertised in *Personnel Management* in the first six months of 1987. General personnel posts advertised were 51 per cent higher than in the same period of 1985 while training and development posts were 48 per cent higher.

How the personnel function has developed

If we are to assess the implications of HRM for the personnel function, it helps to review how the function has altered and evolved up to the present day. Although a particular ideology cannot be attributed to a complete group of people at any one time, the development of the personnel function can be traced by suggesting a general self-image for personnel specialists that has been dominant at different periods, with each still remaining as part of a complex of ideas that make personnel management what it now is.

In this section there is a summary of the main stages in development from the nineteenth century to the present, suggesting that a complete preoccupation with employee welfare at the beginning of the period has changed to a current situation where successive waves of management approaches to getting better value for money from employees now dominate personnel thinking, without the initial welfare concern being abandoned.

The social reformer

Before personnel emerged as a specialist management activity at the beginning of the twentieth century, there were those who intervened in industrial affairs to support the severely underprivileged factory workers. Although the Industrial Revolution had initially helped people move away from the poverty and hope-lessness of rural life, the organization of industrial work soon degraded human life. It was the social reformers like Lord Shaftesbury and Robert Owen who brought about some mitigation of this hardship, offering criticism of employer behaviour.

This influence and example enabled personnel managers to be appointed and provided the first frame of reference for the appointees to work within.

The acolyte of benevolence

The first people appointed with specific responsibility for improving the lot of employees were welfare officers who saw their role as dispensing benefits to the deserving and unfortunate employees. The motivation was the Christian charity of the paternalist employer, who provided these comforts, partly because the employees deserved them, but mainly because he was willing to provide them.

The leading examples of this development were the Quaker families of Cadbury and Rowntree, and the Lever brothers, who set up progressive schemes of unemployment benefit, sick pay and subsidized housing for their employees. Cadbury Schweppes and Unilever remain among the most efficient and profitable businesses in the United Kingdom a hundred years after the foundation of the Bournville village and Port Sunlight.

The Institute of Welfare Officers (now the Institute of Personnel Management) was established in 1913 and the welfare tradition remains strong in personnel management, despite the determined attempts of some practitioners to eradicate it.

The humane bureaucrat

The first two phases were concerned predominantly with the physical environment of work and the amelioration of hardship among 'the workers'. As organizations increased their size, specialization was emerging in the management levels as well as on the shop floor. This led to the growth of personnel work on staffing the organization, with great concern about role specification, selection, training and placement. The personnel manager was learning to operate within a bureaucracy, serving organizational rather than paternalist employer objectives. For the first time there was a willingness to look at the social sciences for ideas, with scientific management (Taylor 1911), administrative management (Fayol 1949) and the human-relations movement (Mayo 1933) all finding enthusiastic devotees among personnel managers.

Most of the technology of personnel work was developed in this period and many of these methods remain at the heart of what personnel managers do.

The consensus negotiator

Personnel managers next added expertise in bargaining to their repertoire of skills. After the Second World War there was relatively full employment, labour became a scarce resource and trade unions extended their membership. Where the personnel manager could at best be described as a 'remembrancer' of the employees, the trade-union official could be their accredited representative. Trade-union assertiveness brought a shift towards bargaining by the employer on at least some matters. There was a growth of joint consultation and the establishment of joint production committees and suggestion schemes. Nationalized industries were set up with a statutory duty placed on employers to negotiate with unions representing employees.

The personnel manager acquired bargaining expertise to deploy in search of a lost consensus and the in-between role became less pronounced.

Organization man

Then came a development of the humane bureaucracy phase into a preoccupation with the effectiveness of the organization as a whole, which should have clear objectives and a widespread commitment among organization members to those objectives. The approach was also characterized by candour between members and a form of operation supporting the integrity of the individual and providing opportunities for personal growth.

This development was a major change of focus among personnel specialists away from dealing with the rank-and-file employee on behalf of the management towards dealing with the management and integration of management activity itself. Its most recent manifestation has been in programmes of organization and management development, as companies have sub-contracted much of their routine work to peripheral employees and concentrated on developing and retaining an élite core of people with specialist expertise on whom the business depends for its future.

Manpower analyst

The last distinct historical stereotype is the manpower analyst. The humane bureaucrat was concerned to get a good fit between a particular worker and a particular job: employees were individuals. Trade-union representation required personnel specialists to think more collectively; individuals coalesced into manpower. As the rate of technological change began to accelerate and innovation became more necessary, the forecasting of future needs for manpower was added to the personnel specialist's collection of odd jobs.

The methods were those of manpower planning. Although originally based on an assumption of organizational expansion, manpower planning has been reshaped during organizational contraction to ensure the closest possible fit between the number of people and skills required and what is available. The activity has been boosted by the advent of the computer, which makes possible a range of calculations and measurements that were unrealistic earlier.

These six stereotypes have all blended together to make the complex of contemporary personnel management. Although they have emerged roughly in sequence, all are still present to a varying degree in different types of personnel post and the nature of personnel work today can only be understood by an appreciation of its varied components.

Four other features have emerged but not yet established a lasting place in the complex of personnel work. *Social engineering* is a concern with the potential of the workplace to solve social problems. *Legal wrangling* became dominant in the 1970s, when a plethora of legislation protecting the rights of workers and trade unions gave managers a fright, but managerial concern about legislation has lessened since 1980. There is a move towards a more aggressive use of legislative powers by some employers, which requires detailed work by personnel specialists, but examples are few. *Industrial democracy* has also receded, although there are moves towards greater employee participation. *Labour market analysis* improves the understanding of the economic context in which the business operates. There are questions about the nature of the labour force and the way it is changing, as well as the way in which the employment being offered is changing.

The human resources addition

The nature of human resources management is not yet clear. Like most innovations, it tends to be whatever the person speaking at the time wants it to be. We all have a vested interest in not being obsolescent and therefore tend to create human resource management in our own image, producing a model that will fit what we think we can do, or in the image of our enemies, so that we can deride it and demonstrate its irrelevance. The definition is not made any easier by those who espouse the term 'human resources' only as a way of avoiding the apparent sexism of 'manpower'.

The assumption of this chapter is that personnel management is directed mainly at the employees of the organization; finding and training them, arranging their pay and contracts of employment, explaining what is expected of them, justifying what the management is doing and trying to modify any management action that could produce an unwelcome response from the employees. Personnel management puts a high priority on employee attitude, interest, and response, not only for the sake of the employees, but also because their commitment and cooperation is essential to organizational effectiveness. For this reason personnel managers are never totally identified with management interests, as they become ineffective when not able to understand and articulate the views and values of the employees. To some extent the personnel manager is always a mediator between them and us.

In contrast, the human resources manager starts not from the organization's employees, but from the organization's need for human resources: with the demand rather than the supply. This is little different from the focus of the manpower analyst and, in assessing the impact of human resource management, we should remember that the techniques of manpower planning and human-asset accounting scarcely got beyond the pages of textbooks until very recently. The human resources manager then undertakes a range of actions to ensure that the supply meets the demand and does *not* regard manpower as an inflexible resource. The actions include the generally welcome, such as training (now translated into human resource development), and the generally unwelcome, such as dismissal (which has been euphemized into outplacement). Human resource demands can be met not only by employees, but by sub-contractors, consultants, agencies and so forth. Personnel management is supply-driven; human resources management is demand-driven.

Human resource management seeks to eliminate the mediation role and adopts a generally unitarist perspective. It emphasizes strategy and planning rather than problem-solving and mediation, so that employee cooperation is delivered by programmes of corporate culture, remuneration packaging, team building and management development for core employees, while peripheral employees are kept at arms' length. The concept of core and periphery workforces is an essential feature of human resource management and recent scepticism about the adoption of this idea (Pollert 1988) helps prevent the advocates of human resource management going overboard.

The reality in organizations seldom reaches the pitch suggested in the last paragraph. We find some personnel managers have changed their titles and nothing else, although most have modified their approach to some extent and many have introduced initiatives in some parts of their work – like management development – with an HRM flavour. After research in 1984–5 it was possible to report (Mackay and Torrington 1986) that most personnel managers did not like human resources management and regretted the need to be more 'hard-nosed' or 'tough'. Many of these respondents were hankering after the collective bargaining brinkmanship of the 1970s, and it would be unrealistic to suggest that this attitude is still widely held among personnel managers at the end of the 1980s. Human resource management has now been assimilated, as personnel management has adapted to the decline of collectivism and the increase of opportunity, the rise of the consultant and the enterprise philosophy. The world has not changed after all, but it has moved on a bit.

Current and developing challenges for the personnel function

Before evaluating the influence of human resource management on the personnel function, we can consider some of the current changes which are likely to affect the evaluation. Which of the two emphases described above are the most appropriate for management initiatives in the following areas?

The *reduced assertiveness of trade unions* raises questions about collective bargaining, employee involvement and communication. How does management avoid the temptation of short-term advantage in exploiting union weakness that could bring the long-term problem of an alienated and unresponsive workforce? Is there a growing division between responses to trade unions in the private sector and those in the public sector, where the employer is likely to put a higher priority on union recognition and negotiation? There has been a great increase of team briefing and similar communication exercises. How effective are these in conveying accurate messages? How effective are they in achieving the objectives which the managers have for them? How do they affect the attitudes and feelings of employees?

A feature of the 1980s has been a *reduced investment in training by employers* (MSC/NEDO 1986). This has been accompanied by heavy government investment in the Youth Training Scheme and various schemes, like TVEI, to provide more 'useful' skills for children before leaving school because of the clear evidence that those with the poorest prospects in the job market are those without skills or qualifications. What types of training and development are being offered at the moment? How useful are these? Is there a shortage of skills or an unsatisfactory distribution of skills? Where are the shortages, for what types of job, and why do they exist? How can shortages be overcome? Is there a need only for more training, or are there other features, like unattractive working conditions, or ineffective selection that create shortages?

The *human resources development* aspect of HRM is receiving particular attention at the moment with an increasing investment in certain aspects of training. This is mainly in management development and in social skills training. What is the connection between these initiatives and the questions in the last paragraph? Is the practice of human resource development centred on activities to enhance self-confidence, poise, assertiveness and public relations at the expense of other types of skill? Is the concept of management 'competences' viable? Defining management competences that are generally acceptable and useful involves reducing them to elementary basics; are such competences compatible with the objective of producing a chartered manager of professional standing holding a DBA?

This array of questions shows the importance and range of the issues now being raised in the personnel area. Personnel specialists need to be equipped by their training and professional expertise to deal with them.

Methods of payment are being elaborated, following the experience of the yuppie phenomenon with the vogue for 'designer' pay arrangements with ten or a dozen fringe benefits, ranging from membership of health clubs to use of the company box at Ascot, although this is again for the few rather than the many. The number of people being *paid* for going to work seems to be declining. Most are now remunerated, rewarded, or compensated (a valuable prize awaits the person who can define a meaningful difference). What is the effect of all this elaborate packaging? Are approved deferred share trusts and save-as-you-earn schemes run because they have some impact on the behaviour of the people paid, remunerated, rewarded, or compensated, or simply because they are available? Do schemes producing prizes for nearly everyone that have to be awarded at an expensive dinner in the West End have any impact on working performance, or are they simply new products being vigorously promoted on the premise that new means better? The use of job evaluation continues to grow, but is it still appropriate other than as a defence against equal pay claims?

The use of consultants has been increasing in all areas of employment, with one estimate that there were over 1,000 operating in the personnel field (Wood 1983), since when the number has undoubtedly increased. This has been mainly as a way of 'saving' internal management jobs in company reorganizations to become leaner and fitter, but also to cope with the increasing range of mini-skills required in human resource management. There has to be expertise available in law, computer applications, job evaluation, equal value, team briefing, SSP, psychological testing, training, and many more areas that require expertise but which may not justify full-time appointments. What is the effect of this tendency on the management of the organization? In some cases there are inadequate internal resources to make the most of the external advisors' expertise and this can lead to heavy expense for little return. There is also some tendency for employees to mistrust consultants, seeing them as parasitic and not truly involved in the success or failure of the business. How can consultants be best used? How can the company ensure value for money from the services it purchases, especially in those areas – like management development and organizational restructuring – where the pay-offs are so difficult to assess and will probably not be seen for some years?

HRM and some theoretical formulations of personnel identity

Personnel managers have long spent their time bewailing the fact that they are misunderstood and under-utilized, and a part of this activity has been to disavow a previous identity in search of a new. The most persistent of these has been to disclaim a concern with welfare, even though this remains the most popular component of personnel management in the eyes of everyone else. The cruellest description was that of Drucker (1961: 243), who described it as: 'a collection of incidental techniques without much internal cohesion . . . *a hodge podge*'. As personnel people pull together more and more duties – pensions expert, data-protection guru, open-learning specialist and so on – this description may seem to be confirmed.

Some people have been attracted by *the employment contract* idea, which this author based on the original concept of Enid Mumford (1972). This sees personnel work as setting up, between employee and employing organization, a series of contracts which describe their mutual expectations, and then ensuring the fulfilment of those expectations.

Very similar is the 'man in the middle' approach of George Thomason, who saw personnel management as increasingly assuming a third-party role between management and employee, especially with the development of legislation. This put personnel managers between the two diverse sources from which they had evolved: 'the one paternalistically oriented towards the welfare of employees and the other rationally derived from corporate needs to control' (Thomason 1976: 27).

These last two views partly express the essence of HRM as well as personnel thinking, which was also found in the most vivid analysis of the personnel function by Karen Legge (1978), who identified two alternative methods of personnel people seeking power in organizations. The *conformist innovator* is the personnel specialist who identifies with the objective of organizational success, emphasizing cost benefit and conforming to the criteria adopted by managerial colleagues, who usually have greater power. In contrast, the *deviant innovator* identifies with a set of norms that are distinct from, but not necessarily in conflict with, the norms of organizational success. Power derives from an independent, professional stance for working with managerial clients.

While Legge describes a contrast between alternative approaches for personnel people in general, Shaun Tyson (Tyson and Fell 1986) uses a classification which works hierarchically, according to the amount of planning involved in different jobs. The *clerk of works* model describes personnel management carried out as administrative support, reactive to the needs of other managers and carrying little authority. The *contracts manager* is also reactive, but seeks to react to need by deploying procedures and systems rather than being only spontaneous. The *architect* pursues a more creative line, seeking to build the organization as a whole and working within the dominant coalition of the organization.

However persuasive this argument is to status seekers, it emphasizes 'management' rather than 'personnel'. In the words of Edmund Burke, this may be specious in theory but ruinous in practice.

Human resources thinking – revolution or re-jigging?

Most of those in the personnel function who espouse HRM are doing so in search of enhanced status and power. With the obsession about innovation that currently pervades management thinking, a change of label is a useful indication of innovation, even if you are not too sure that there is anything different in the package. Others align HRM with the planning and organizational growth aspects of Tyson's architect in making a further attempt to shake off the maligned welfare image, about which the personnel profession continues to be paranoid. Tyson himself is quite explicit:

> increasingly those in personnel are referred to as 'human resource managers'.
> Although perhaps an Americanism, this change of title does represent a development of the 'architect' model, with a greater emphasis on internal consultancy and organisation.
>
> (Tyson 1987: 530)

If, however, one considers the history and substantive content of personnel work, this perception seems inadequate. Personnel managers have been grumbling about their ineffectiveness for longer than any reader of this chapter will be able to remember, but they have still succeeded in growing steadily stronger as a professional group and commanding greater influence within the organization as the years go by. The membership of the Institute of Personnel Management exceeds the combined membership of the Institutes of Marketing, Administrative Management, Industrial Managers, and Purchasing and Supply, despite having appreciably higher entry standards. Board-level representation of personnel is now taken for granted to an extent that would have been unimaginable twenty years ago.

The review of historical development at the beginning of this chapter demonstrated that personnel management has grown through assimilating a number of additional emphases to produce an ever-richer combination of expertise. This is the counter to Drucker's 'hodge podge' charge: the mixture of activities requires a common thread of expertise and understanding as well as an appreciation of many specialisms. Personnel posts would not be found so extensively in board rooms and similar management council chambers unless there was a strong expertise that the other senior members of the organization found necessary. Shaun Tyson used a metaphor from construction. Let us use one from medicine. The general practitioner carries professional standing and respect because of a wide-ranging expertise, while acknowledging the specialized expertise of consultants and kindred specialisms.

The personnel manager is a general practitioner in personnel, dealing with many issues, running many programmes and producing many plans. Sometimes there is a need for special skills the personnel manager does not possess or have available; then the consultants are called in or the 'patient' is referred to a training school, assessment centre, or some other source of special treatment. The personnel manager orchestrates the use of those skilled resources, and that requires a high degree of expertise.

It is averred by some current researchers that personnel managers lack organiza-tional power: they do not have any impact on selection decisions that continue to discriminate against women or blacks; they are powerless to prevent a demagogue company proprietor from abrogating collective agreements. This view convinces academic researchers but puzzles most practitioners, because their perspectives do not coincide. Management research in most disciplines concen-trates on decision-making, especially that carried out at the very pinnacle of the organizational hierarchy. Management is usually seen as a unity to which other people and groups respond.

The reasoning behind the argument of this chapter is that power may not be a strong feature of the personnel function – or indeed any management function – but authority is: the authority of expertise. Individual managers, at all levels, spend very little time actually making significant decisions and most of their time nudging things to happen, clearing obstructions, calming fears, generating enthusiasm, getting things done. The main vehicle is the personal network of contacts (Kotter 1982), through which the manager seeks favours, information, advice, suggestions, and practical help from a great number of people inside and outside the organization. In return the manager is asked for favours, information, advice, suggestions, and practical help. The currency of these exchanges is mainly expertise and secondly power.

Some advocates of HRM talk of 'the manager in charge of personnel' rather than 'the personnel manager', urging lateral movement across a variety of manage-ment specialisms or the abandonment of specialisms altogether, with the all-singing, all-dancing manager who concentrates on deploying resources in a neat equation so that the sums are right whatever the resources happen to be. The danger with that is of the baby disappearing with the bathwater. Alistair Mant reminds us of how asset-stripper Jim Slater was asked at his first Annual General Meeting of Crittall Hope, the window manufacturer, what the company would be making now that he was chairman. His alleged reply was that the company would be making money; and the subsequent lack of emphasis on the product led to decline of the business and the departure of Mr Slater.

There is no more trite remark than that the most valuable resources of a business are its human resources. What is more important is that the most difficult aspect of management is managing human resources, which are relatively inflexible and where mistakes are hard to rectify. The manager-in-charge-of-personnel-for-the-time-being is likely to lose the essence of success in the same way as Jim Slater.

HRM is no revolution but a further dimension to a multi-faceted role. It will probably embellish personnel expertise and authority in two ways, by finally making training important and by helping managers grant more dignity to working people by concentrating more on getting the contract right and less on supervision and motivation. Personnel management remains a distinctive management specialism whose practitioners derive their expertise from an understanding of one or more of the ways in which people, individually and collectively, engage with the need to be employed and the needs of organizations to employ them.

The recruitment, development and management of resourceful humans is a more complex, interesting and expert task than the management of human resources. This is needed at all levels in all organizations as a specialist activity, no matter how skilful line managers become with their 'competences', and no matter how exotic the offerings of consultants. If we stretch the general practitioner metaphor a little further, we can see the line manager as being like a patient successfully managing health and ill-health; diet, exercise, paracetamol, abstinence, sleeping off hangovers, sweating out fevers, and wrapping up warm in cold weather. Occasionally the GP personnel manager is called in to diagnose a puzzling set of symptoms, to carry out some specialized treatment or procedure, or to advise on a particular problem. Even more occasionally the personnel manager will call up the expertise of the consultant, but the personnel manager remains the selector of the consultants, their monitor, and the manager of their services. This is another version of Thomason's man in the middle, not in between management and employees, but between managers and the host of external resources now available.

Line managers need from their personnel colleagues a distinctive, yet generalized expertise. This is where Legge's categorization is invaluable. Conformist personnel management innovators do no more than reflect the competences and values of their colleagues. Deviant personnel innovators are able to make a distinctive contribution to the totality of management, which becomes richer and more resourceful as a result.

Chapter five

The impact of corporate strategy on human resource management

John Purcell

The particular concern of this chapter is the impact of corporate strategy on the management of human resources. The focus is large multi-divisional companies. It seems sensible to ask how the behaviour of these firms influences the management of people at work by the corporate strategies they adopt, and by the controls they exercise on the behaviour of business units and subsidiary companies. The corporate office in many enterprises has four major roles: the development and execution of corporate strategies, the monitoring of divisional and operating subsidiaries' performance, the allocation of internal capital, and the treasury function managing relations with the external capital and money markets. All four, to a greater or lesser extent, impact on the management of human resources as the chapter seeks to illustrate. In the first section consideration is given to the position of large enterprises in the British economy indicating a concentration of economic power in excess of that found in many other industrialized nations.

A model of corporate strategy is developed in the second section derived from the well-known distinction between strategy and structure developed by Chandler (1962). Here three levels of strategy are identified. Decisions on long-run goals and the scope of activities constitute first-order strategy. These, in the normative model, directly affect and lead to decisions on the way the enterprise is structured to achieve its goals, what is termed second-order strategy. Both first-order and second-order strategy provide the critical context in which functional strategies are developed. Our concern is with those to do with human resource management, what are termed third-order strategies. The term strategy is used throughout to indicate that the focus is on those decisions which have a major and long-term effect on the behaviour of the firm (Hickson *et al.* 1986) as opposed to day-to-day operating decisions. The rest of the chapter attempts to trace the effect that first and second order strategies have on human resource management especially in relation to subordinate, non-managerial employees.

The multi-divisional firm in Britain

Estimates of the size of diversified companies are surprisingly difficult to obtain, especially in the service sector. In 1985 half of the employed workforce in manufacturing worked for 560 enterprises each with 1,000 or more employees; a third worked for 104 enterprises with 5,000 or more people and a quarter in the 48 firms of 10,000 or more employees. These enterprises were even more important in the sector when their contribution to gross output was examined and especially when one looked at their proportion of the total wages and salaries bill in manufacturing (60 per cent). In the late 1970s, before the major recession of the early 1980s, there were more large firms in manufacturing and their share of employment was even greater. The substantial decline in manufacturing employment, of around 40 per cent between 1978 and 1986, was especially marked in large enterprises and large establishments. Table 5.1 shows, however, that the average number of establishments owned by large firms has continued to increase so that, while numbers employed have fallen, the accumulation of establishments owned by large enterprises has continued to rise. This is probably a reflection of the increasing pace of mergers and acquisitions and the investment in greenfield sites.

Table 5.1 Average number of establishments owned by large enterprises in UK manufacturing, 1958–85

	Enterprise size (no. of employees)			
	2,000 and over	5,000 and over	10,000 and over	20,000 and over
Year				
1958	12	21	30	44
1978	19	29	42	56
1985	20	37	40	60

Source:
1958 Historical Record of Census of Production 1907–1970
1978 Report of the 1978 Census of Production PA 1002 HMSO 1981. Table 12.
1985 Report of the 1985 Census of Production PA 1002 HMSO 1988. Table 12.

The concentration of employment in manufacturing is not the whole story. *The Times* list of the largest 100 industrial companies in Britain, according to company annual reports in 1986, showed that 79 of them employed over 20,000 people – only 24 of them were in manufacturing. Not all of these employees worked in the UK but we can assume that well over half, and probably over three-quarters did so. *The Times* 100 list excludes the banking, insurance, and finance sector where the dominance of a few large firms is evident in any high street.

Table 5.2 gives further details of the largest industrial companies in the UK. The 5.3 million employees working for the top 100 is equivalent to approximately 25 per cent of the working population in employment in the UK, while the top 20 companies have nearly two million employees (equivalent to just under 10 per cent of the employed population). Comparisons of industrial structure and concentration are difficult to make but it has often been noted that concentration of ownership is greater in the UK than in other major industrialized nations (George and Ward 1975).

Table 5.2 Top UK industrial companies: employment and turnover, 1986

	No. of employees (m)	Turnover (£ billion)
Top 20 enterprises	1.98	17.97
Top 50 enterprises	3.78	26.53
Top 100 enterprises	5.30	34.22

Source: Times top 1,000 1987.
Notes: UK registered companies: includes public-sector trading companies (post, steel, coal and gas) and excludes banking, insurance, finance, and management services. Employment includes overseas employees. Billion equals thousand million.

Not all of these large enterprises are diversified and not all of them have a multi-divisional structure but the evidence is clear that diversification and divisionalization has been growing rapidly and is likely to continue. Figure 5.1 shows the changing structure of the top 200 UK enterprises. The rise of 'related' business and conglomerate enterprises and the concomitant decline in single businesses is most noticeable.

Figure 5.1 Diversification strategy of top 200 UK corporations (% distribution by number of companies)

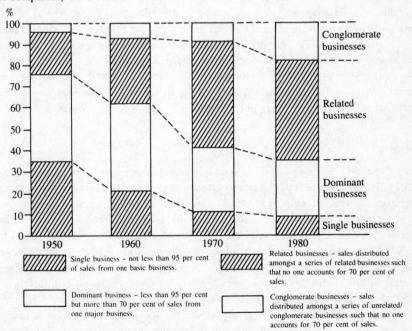

Source: Channon 1982. Reprinted with permission from *Long Range Planning*, vol. 15, no. 5, copyright Derek Channon 'Industrial Structure', 1982, Pergamon Press PLC.

Since the collection of these data the substantial merger and acquisition wave of the mid-1980s is likely to have altered the picture with a probable further growth in 'related' and especially 'conglomerate businesses' seen in the rapid emergence of firms like Hanson with the acquisition of the Imperial Group, London Brick, and the UDS Group. Such firms are often loosely described as multi-divisional. The multi-divisional firm emerged in the USA as the most effective way of managing diversified business combining tight control over the financial performance of subsidiaries, restructuring of the firm to meet product market needs through the creation of product market related divisions, and the centralization of resource allocation and strategic planning. The multi-divisional structure is commonly seen as 'a superior organizational form since it separates strategic from operating decisions. It makes visible the contribution of each division to profitability and hence increases the probability of optimizing resource allocation within the organization' (Hill and Pickering 1986). The authors cite a variety of studies, all finding that multi-divisionals are generally associated with superior profitability in the USA. While the picture is more mixed in the UK, studies by Steer and Cable (1978) and Thompson (1981) give evidence of better performance in profit terms.

Eighty-two per cent of the 144 large enterprises studied by Hill and Pickering in 1982 were organized along multi-division lines. They observed, however, that there were a variety of structures and practices within the generic descriptive term. Multi-divisional firms can have quite complex structures with each division organized into strategic business units (SBUs) and with a number of operating subsidiaries, wholly-owned companies and establishments. The extent to which head offices and divisional headquarters are involved in operational management varies considerably. This variety within the multi-divisional form will be discussed at the end of the chapter since variations in structures and styles are of substantial importance in assessing the impact of the multi-divisional company on the management of human relations, but first we must consider the meaning of the term strategy especially in relation to the role of the corporate office.

Strategy

The distinctive feature of multi-divisionals is that their internal operating procedures are more refined and differentiated than those found in functional or holding companies. The decision to move to a multi-divisional structure, from say, a centralized functional firm or to adapt the configuration to emphasize local profit centres, is a strategic decision of substantial importance in its consequences for employee relations, as discussed later. The decision to reorganize might have been triggered by strategic decisions taken earlier, for example, to diversify. One useful way of distinguishing between types of strategic decisions is in terms of upstream and downstream. 'Upstream', first-order decisions are concerned with the long-term direction of the enterprise or the scope of its activities. Clearly these decisions will have implications for the type of people employed, the size of the firm and the technology required. If an upstream decision is made to acquire a going concern a second set of considerations apply concerning the extent to which the new firm is to be kept apart from or integrated with existing operations, and about the nature of the acquired firm's relationship with its new owner. These can be classified as more downstream, or second-order, strategic decisions. This is similar to Chandler's (1962) distinction between strategy and structure and his oft-quoted dictum that structure follows (i.e. is downstream from) strategy. The difference here is that decisions on strategy (the type of business undertaken now and in the future) and on structures (how the firm is organized to meet its goals) are both of strategic importance in that they have long-run implications for organizational behaviour, are taken in conditions of uncertainty and commit resources of people, time and money to their attainment.

It is in the context of downstream strategic decisions on organizational structure that choices on human resource structures and approaches come to be made. These are themselves strategic since they establish the basic parameters of employee relations management in the firm, but are likely to be deeply influenced by first and second decisions as well as by environmental factors of law, trade unions and external labour markets. These are termed here third-order strategic decisions. At its simplest therefore three levels of strategy are evident as seen in Figure 5.2. The concern of this chapter is primarily with first- and second-order strategies, not with strategies *within* human resource management (see Ahlstrand and Purcell 1988) nor with the outcomes, nor the environmental forces which provide the context in which strategies are formulated and implanted. It will be appreciated, as the model implies, that the actual conduct of human resource management, let alone employee-relations behaviour, is influenced by an enormous variety of forces interacting in a complex and dynamic way. The purpose of the chapter is to draw attention to the impact of corporate strategies which, with a few exceptions (Thurley and Wood 1983; Batstone, Ferner, and Terry 1984) has been largely ignored.

In theory in this idealized, normative model, strategy in human resource management is determined in the context of first-order, long-run decisions on the direction and scope of the firms' activities and purpose (location, technology, skill requirements, etc.) and second-order decisions on the structure of the firm seen in its internal operating procedures (levels of authority, control systems, profit centres, etc.). What actually happens in employee relations will be determined by decisions at all three levels and by the willingness and ability of local management to do what is intended in the context of specific environment conditions and forces.

One principal objection needs to be raised on the nature of the model. Like many such models it implies rationality in the process of decision making: a carefully planned series of decisions where human resource management is designed to mesh with organizational structures which in turn derives from first-order strategies. But strategic decisions are characterized by the need to cope with uncertainty, to integrate management activity in various fields and are concerned with change. A political process model to strategic decisions is more appropriate.

71

Figure 5.2 Three levels of strategic decision making

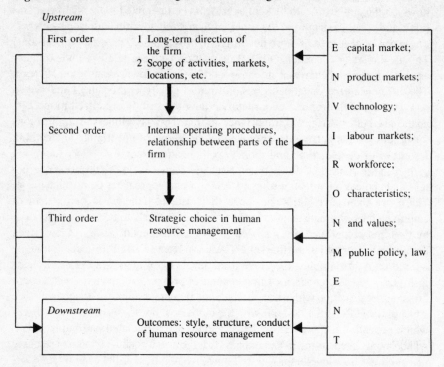

'Strategic decisions', writes Johnson, 'are characterized by the political hurly-burly of organizational life with a high incidence of bargaining, a trading off of costs and benefits of one interest group against another, all within a notable lack of clarity in terms of environmental influences and objectives' (1987: 21). The process is especially complicated in the area of human resource management. Since it is difficult to determine the ends (what is the purpose of human resource management?) and the means to achieve these uncertain ends, it is also difficult to measure whether the firm is successful in its personnel or human resources policies.

One of the problems with the rational, normative model of strategy formulation as described and prescribed by many books on corporate strategy is that it tends to de-personalize and reduce analysis to a common currency of figures and hard data of markets, shares, discounted cash flows and rates of return. Questions of values or purpose beyond the 'bottom line' are acutely uncomfortable to strategic decision makers. In the rational model, phenomena which cannot be reduced to figures such as 'motivation', 'good industrial relations' or 'good employment standards' are easily discounted or ignored. If it were possible to prove that 'enlightened or progressive' approaches to the management of people at work were invariably associated with higher productivity, lower unit costs and improved profit, and that exploitative, coercive systems failed, life for the social science researcher and human resource executive would be easier. As it is, little can be conclusively proved because of the complexity of variables and the impossibility of monitoring and measuring all the relevant dynamics and relations. If some 'proof' is obtained over a short period of time in specific circumstances, it is often found to be impossible to replicate. This ambiguity in human resource management, and the relative weakness of the function in the corporate corridors of power (Hegarty and Hoffman 1987), often leads to a situation where decisions on first and second order strategy are taken without consideration of their effects on the conduct of human resource management. Third-order strategy concerned with the management of people is increasingly required to fit the strategies and structures of the firm especially as counter-vailing requirements in the environment (trade-union power, industrial demo-cracy proposals, income policy and labour law) appear to have receded in the 1980s. It is more difficult to argue 'we can't do that because . . .' than it was a decade ago.

We need now to consider how trends in first order and second order strategy, especially toward diversification and decentralization, affect the management of human resources. Our concern is firstly to trace the logical consequences which flow from first order strategies on the scope of the enterprise activities for employee relations. This will entail an examination of portfolio planning techniques. Next, within the multi-divisional form the critical question is second-order strategy concerning the relationship between parts of the business and the management of interrelationships. This will take us into a discussion of different types of multi-divisional companies seen in terms of integration or separation of divisions and centralization or decentralization within divisions. We will also consider the evidence for profitability and effectiveness and the link with employee relations. Third, there is a need to consider the relationship between the corporate office and business units. How are different styles and approaches likely to impact on human resource management?

First-order strategy: portfolio planning

We noted earlier the growing tendency for large companies to be diversified. One of the critical issues facing the corporate office, especially the chief executive officer (CEO) is the allocation of capital to the various parts of the business and the identification of growth areas within the portfolio and outside for possible acquisition. This involves the use of portfolio planning developed as a means of identifying the attractiveness of various parts of the portfolio of businesses as an aid to capital allocation and determining the appropriate mix of businesses held by the enterprise. It is based on two prime premises. First, there is an experience curve: 'average costs will decline as the accumulated experience associated with selling, producing, engineering and financing [a] product increases (Hamermesh 1986: 10)'. Among the most common reasons for this proven relationship are:

economies of scale (or scope) in manufacturing, marketing, engineering, and financing; labour efficiencies; product standardisation and process improvements. The strategic implications . . . are that the company with the most accumulated experience can have the lower costs and therefore a company should invest rapidly and early to accumulate experience (ibid.)

The experience curve is associated with market share. In theory the company with the highest market share will have the greatest accumulated experience and the lowest cost and therefore generate the most profit. Second, market growth is not constant. Eventually – and the time scale can vary enormously – most markets for a given product reach a mature state of slow growth and may then decline. Firms with a dominant share of a mature market are likely to wish to diversify by switching cash from the mature business into new markets with growth potential, and gain early experience to build market share and invest heavily to keep it. Portfolio planning is defined by Hamermesh as 'those analytic techniques that aid in the classification of a firm's businesses for resource allocation purposes and for selecting a competitive strategy on the basis of the growth potential of each business and of the financial resources that will be either consumed or produced by the business' (ibid.). It was estimated in 1982 that half of the Fortune 500 companies in the USA use some form of portfolio planning (Haspeslagh 1982). Goold and Campbell (1987) in their study of sixteen major British diversified companies showed that while the formal statistical use of the techniques was not widespread, the thinking behind portfolio planning was often employed.

The most well known system is that developed by the Boston Consulting Group (1970; Hedley 1977) if only because of its mnemonic qualities: cash cow, star, dog, and wild cat (or question mark) as shown in Figure 5.3. The purpose of the model is to help the strategic planners classify the various business units in the portfolio in terms of their potential for cash generation or cash usage. High market-share businesses, assuming the experience curve, will have lower costs than their competitors with smaller shares and should be able to generate more

Figure 5.3 Portfolio planning growth-share matrix

		Market share *(Relative competition position)*	
		High	Low
Market growth *(Business* *growth rate)*	High	STAR	? WILD CAT
	Low	CASH COW	DOG

profit. Market growth indicates the likely demands for investment. When there is high growth there will be substantial demands for investment in terms of new plant, equipment and technical innovation. Low-growth markets require less investment. The model combines the two axes and leads to generalization about corporate and business strategy.

- *Stars (high-share, high-growth)* are in an advantageous position. While they require high levels of investment their dominant position in the market often allows them to produce sufficient profits to finance further growth.
- *Cash cows (high-share, low-growth)* produce large profits and positive cash flows. They require modest amounts of capital to maintain their market share, renew equipment and to keep in step with technological change. The cash surplus is used to finance the stars where necessary and particularly to help develop new business ventures in growth markets, the wild cat or question-mark businesses.
- *Wild cat, question-mark (low-share, high-growth)* businesses compete in rapidly growing markets with the aim of moving up the experience curve ahead of the competition. Market growth in new markets is difficult to predict and the gaining of experience and efficiency in situations of uncertainty can be difficult. These businesses are therefore uncertain and require substantial investment in excess of their own profitability.
- *Dogs (low-share, low-growth)* do not produce much profit and are not worth investing in. Two options exist: either divest the business or act to pare costs down to the minimum to squeeze out the surplus value.

A slightly more sophisticated version of the portfolio-planning model is the nine-box matrix original developed in the General Electric Company in the USA. Industry attractiveness includes market growth by covering other factors such as industry profitability and market potential and size. Market share is included as one of the factors in business-unit position but this will include an assessment of the unit's technological base, actual profitability, and size (for more detail see Hax and Majluf 1983). In both models 'the purpose of the strategic mandates is to create a pattern of capital spending whereby a business receives funding early in its life so that it achieves a strong (i.e. profitable) competitive position. Then, as its market matures the business will produce the cash flow that will find other, more rapidly growing businesses . . . (and) facilitate the creation of a port-folio of businesses in which the sources and uses of funds are nearly balanced (Hamermesh 1986: 16).

It is not our concern to debate the strengths and weaknesses of portfolio planning for strategic management (see Hamermesh 1986 for a useful analysis and more recently Porter 1987a). The question of concern here is the implications that flow from it in terms of second-order strategies and third-order human resource matters. At a general level the most important implication is that the enterprise is seen not as a unified business but a collection of businesses. Portfolio planning says nothing about long-term aims or purpose of the firm and by its analytical methods finds no place for history, tradition or cultures. Firms excessively committed to portfolio planning tend to ignore or find difficulty with that aspect of corporate strategy which determines 'the kind of economic and human organization it is or intends to be, and the nature of the economic and non-economic contribution it intends to make to its shareholders, employees, customers, and communities' (Andrews 1980: 18). Hamermesh refers to this as 'institutional strategy', others use terms such as goals, values, missions. In employee relations we refer to it as 'management style' being the preferred way of managing employees: see, for example, in corporate philosophy statements (Purcell 1987). Portfolio planning tends to drive out, or at least drive down, questions of style and non-economic issues *and* positively encourages different approaches to employee relations in different segments of the business (Schuller and Jackson 1987).

This comes about in two ways. First, the identification of business units as the prime unit of analysis (sometimes referred to as strategic business units or SBUs for short) is a critical feature in the creation of the multi-divisional company. Business unit managers are given responsibility for the determination of their success within the confines of the strategic mandate. Corporate office rules and regulations which limit unit managers' freedom of action come to be resented, are seen as an unnecessary overhead cost and are often too general to be applied in detail in each unit. Thus, what may be termed the *administrative control system* of head office rules and regulations, symbolized in human resource management by the personnel manual, tend to be out of place, resented or ignored by profit-responsible unit managers facing different circumstances. If centralized rules cannot be applied and if, in their place, there is no guiding logic or set of standards on appropriate employee-relations management, then the requirements of the financial targets set by corporate headquarters will dominate unit management behaviour. This *performance control system* (Mintzberg 1979) establishes, through annual budgeting and monthly reporting (often reinforced by incentive pay and stock options for unit managers), appropriate financial targets for the unit within an agreed mandate for capital expenditure. How the unit manager achieves this is up to him or her. We will look at the effect of different types of performance-control systems later. Here we note the implication of separating the enterprise into quasi-independent units and a tendency for central standards on non-economic conduct to be weakened or abandoned altogether.

There is nothing inherently wrong in separation and decentralization and there are many advantages to be gained from avoiding over-centralized, bureaucratic systems, allowing unit managers to design their own employee-relations strategies for their circumstances. There are two difficulties however. First, the implication is that inter-unit comparisons drawn by trade unions and employees themselves are to be avoided or minimized and employee involvement in strategic affairs through corporate consultative committees and collective bargaining, employee trustees in pension funds, and worker director schemes are out of place. If the logic of portfolio planning is a separation of business units (second-order strategy) then employee relations similarly needs to be separated and decentralized. Employees and the unions which represent them must, from a management point of view, adopt a unit perspective and be concerned with the parochial needs of the unit, not the strategic thrust of the enterprise.

The need for boundary maintenance becomes critical if the enterprise seeks to implement the logical consequences of portfolio planning for its human resource strategies. This is not simply because unit managers are given responsibility for profit generation and business strategies in their unit but because the type of employee relations needs are likely to differ substantially between different segments of the matrix. This is hardly ever discussed in the analysis of portfolio planning methods. One small exception came from Arthur D. Little, the major American consulting firm in their development of the concept of strategy centres. They suggest that the wild cat requires an 'entrepreneur' with a free-form or task-force structure and an informal or tailor-made communication system. Stars need a sophisticated manager, managing a semi-permanent task force or product divisional structure with more formal, tailor-made communication systems. Cash cows place emphasis on administration within a business divisional structure and with a formal or uniform communication system. The dog has a manager who is an 'opportunist milker' in a paired-down division. The communication system is 'little or none . . . [a] command system' (Brown and O'Connor 1974: 21). Brown and O'Connor in their review of corporate planning are even more explicit suggesting that 'Dog businesses should be run by tough, hard-bitten individuals who are prepared to liquidate people and facilities'[1] (ibid: 16).

Clearly the type of human resource management will vary considerably. This variety is likely to be greater if, as is probable, the size of the business units varies according to the product market life cycle and the unit's share of the market. Cash cows are likely to be large stable units; wild cats small and experimental; stars medium to large and growing; dogs medium-sized and declining.

It is likely that *wild cat business* units will wish to avoid most of the rigidities associated with larger, stable firms. What is required is a flexible operation with employees willing and able to work in a variety of areas and with broad skills. Overhead costs associated with personnel departments, formal job grading schemes and work study are expensive for small units in growing markets when change is likely to be both continuous and unpredictable (for a further exploration of these issues in high technology firms see Kochan and Chalykoff 1987).

Star businesses face the problem of managing larger and growing units. It is likely that there will be a growth in occupational differentiation with skilled, semi-skilled, clerical, technical, and professional staff, because of the adoption in some businesses of sophisticated, technically advanced dedicated technology. At the same time the high rates of investment and technical change require continued flexibility and cooperation in the management of change. As demand grows the need for continuous operations is likely to develop in order both to meet market need and to utilize capital equipment as effectively as possible. The free-form structure of the wild cat is likely to be replaced with more formal structured systems with the growth of sophisticated human resource management designed by professional staff but implemented and managed by the line managers. If there is strategic thinking in human resource management these units are likely to wish to develop employee-relations policies based on high individualism paying above market rates to recruit and retain the best labour, careful selection and recruitment systems to ensure high quality and skill potential, emphasis on internal training schemes to develop potential for further growth, payment system designed to reward individual performance and cooperation, performance and appraisal reviews, and strong emphasis on team work and communications. At the same time, as in many green-field sites, careful consideration will be given to questions of unionization and it is here in new plants (implying heavy capital investment typical of stars) that we might find single-union deals, pendulum arbitration, and new forms of employee representation. In short, technical and capital investment is matched by human resource investments, at times reaching near the ideals of human resource management. The assumption is that the future is good for star businesses provided the market continues to grow and their share of it continues to be high.

Market maturity and the management of *cash cows* brings a need for order, stability and predictability: in short, structured systems of collective bargaining, job evaluation, work study, and the adoption of the modern sophisticated method of managing a highly unionized workforce. The need is to ensure continuing high rates of return on investment sufficient to meet the corporate need for profit generation for use elsewhere in the enterprise. Depending on the tightness of the performance control system and the profit requirements of head office, cash cows can, however, sometimes slip into forms of indulgency patterns (Gouldner 1954) or management slack in discretionary behaviour (Williamson 1975). Here there is tolerance of over-manning, restrictive practices and general inefficiency since the unit is profitable; there is little pressure for change and the costs associated with removing these customs and practices might be deemed too high. Given the size of the unit and the fact that it has been in business for a number of years or decades it is also likely that various overhead costs linked to employee relations will exist such as sports and social clubs, subsidized canteens, employee discount shops, and various welfare services. We might expect to find elements of paternalism. Other costs might well be seen in office facilities and time-off arrangements for shop stewards, especially full-time shop stewards and conveners and a sizeable personnel department. These are affordable because of high profits, are likely to have grown up over a period, and are justified on the grounds of their contribution to labour peace and harmonious labour relations. The requirement is for management to maintain the cash cow, not to be innovative and entrepreneurial, or pare costs down to such an extent that there is a hostile reaction while earning high profits. At the same time, given market maturity, profit improvements are less likely to come from marketing and sales expenditure than from improved efficiency and resource usage, especially labour productivity (McMillan, Hambrick, and Day 1982).

Clearly such business units are vulnerable to market changes and they may slip into a *dog mode*. Either they lose market share because of better performance by competitors, perhaps triggered by entry into the market by overseas companies or technical or product innovations developed elsewhere – for example Japanese competition, or they are caught by a general decline and instability in the market as in the recession of the early 1980s. While:

> occasionally it is possible to restore a dog to viability by a creative business segmentation strategy, rationalizing and specializing into a small niche . . . (usually) the only prospect for obtaining a return from a dog is to manage it for cash, cutting off all investment in the business.
>
> (Hedley 1977: 11–12)[2]

In short, action is required to 'harvest' as it is euphemistically called in the nine-box matrix, through a management acting as an 'opportunist milker', the term used by Arthur D. Little. Since there is little prospect of increasing market share, attention is turned to the business unit itself to cut costs in order to improve margins. This might require the use of a 'command system' of communications (another Arthur D. Little term) where vigorous efforts are made to improve productivity, not through investment but by work intensification, reduction of 'surplus' labour, cutting overhead costs like welfare benefits and concession bargaining. 'Turnaround management' can emphasize employee involvement as a means of achieving productivity improvements without investment. The alternative is to sell or liquidate the business (and a hostile reaction by the workforce to cost-cutting measures is likely to accelerate the closure). This may in any case be the obvious course of action even if profitability and productivity improve since a better price can be gained for a going concern and rationalization costs such as redundancy payments can be offset against profit on corporation tax. The most important consideration is to ensure that there is no form of cross subsidy to the dog from the cash cow either in investment, corporate subsidy in loss making, or 'artificially' supported rates of pay. It may well be appropriate to allow earnings to rise in the star and cash cow but dogs need to be treated as an independent, stand-alone unit where pay movements are linked to ability to pay, and ability to pay is a function of cost reduction not price improvement. This separation of units is one way to reduce the size of the exit barrier (Harrigan 1980). It has also been noted that 'a sense of obligation to workers in plants which would be closed by liquidation of a dog business may also seem as a barrier to exit' (Christiansen *et al.* 1982).

In sum, different businesses in the portfolio require different types of employee relations and must thus be treated as separate units. This differentiation and the emphasis on market share tends to drive out corporate institutional strategies concerned with non-economic matters such as values, standards and social responsibility. The management of human resources thus becomes an operational responsibility and brings with it the need to weaken or inhibit cross-unit comparisons and trade-union interest in strategic management, while developing local, unit-based loyalties.

Second-order strategy: internal operating procedures

The implication of portfolio planning was seen firstly in the need to develop a variety of businesses in different segments of the product-market life-cycles and secondly to manage these differently according to market need and position. This has considerable influence on second-order strategies concerning the structuring of the enterprise, in the preference for performance-control systems and difficulty in imposing administrative controls and institutional strategy. One of the difficulties associated with product-portfolio systems is the definition of the business unit. What exactly is the market the unit is designed to serve? The term multi-divisional company portrays an image of relatively large organizational structures designed to trade in general markets. Hill and Pickering noted in their study of 144 British companies that while most had opted for the divisional form the tendency was for the number of divisions to be relatively small. Each division was likely to have a number of operating subsidiaries (on average 10.4 per division). It was therefore by 'no means valid to assume that there is a direct one-to-one relationship between a division, one distinct business and one end market' (1986: 31). They go on to note that 'as companies have become more diverse, rather than increasing the number of divisions they have increased the number of activities within each division' (ibid.: 33). It could be argued that the existence of large, complex divisional structures inhibits the full logic of portfolio planning since in each division there are likely to be a variety of businesses within the various segments of the portfolio grid.

A further difficulty is that these large divisions were liable, by their very size, to exert political and economic power at the corporate level. They 'had become so powerful that they restricted the power of head office, limiting its ability to impose strict financial discipline' (ibid.: 35–6). Thus, the critical advantages of portfolio planning specifically, and multi-divisional companies generally, were not being fully realized either in the structuring of business units or in the separation of strategic management (especially capital allocation and financial control) at head office from operational management at unit level. A growing response noted by Hill and Pickering to these difficulties has been a further twist in the internal operating procedures to decentralize and reduce the power of the divisional tier:

> Several companies had moved away from a structure where the divisional tier mattered as a management unit . . . towards one where [it] only had a minor role. This downgrading of the divisional tier was accompanied by a further decentralisation of short-run decision making power to subsidiaries within divisions . . . while long-term strategic functions and financial control functions were centralised at head office (ibid.).

Hill and Pickering asked their corporate office respondents to indicate across a range of decisions, which level in the enterprise had responsibility for decision making. At head-office level a reasonably clear picture emerged with responsibilities for legal functions, relations with financial institutions, long-term planning, investment decisions and acquisitions largely placed in the corporate office. Head offices often were involved in, but shared the responsibility with lower levels, decisions on financial control, public relations, management development, and personnel. They were rarely involved in marketing, production, buying, or industrial-relations matters.

The responsibilities of operating subsidiaries was the reverse of head offices with prime responsibility for marketing, production, buying, and industrial relations, and a shared responsibility for personnel and management development, financial control, public relations, and investment. Divisional offices were in a curious position:

> No decision taking area was identified where, overall, it could be said the divisional head office had the main responsibility . . . . This does perhaps raise questions about the appropriate role of divisional head offices . . . and whether the issue in organisational design is not so much about divisionalisation as about decentralisation' (ibid.: 39).

The authors go on to note that there is a tendency for divisional head offices to be over-involved in the operating affairs of subsidiary companies and that this is associated with slow decision making, intra-organizational conflict and a lack of accountability and control.

The implication of Hill and Pickering's study is first that decentralization not divisionalization is the key attribute of diversified firms with a clear separation of strategic from operational responsibilities. Second, strong divisional offices appear to increase complexity and rigidity both upward through interference with strategy and downwards through involvement in operating subsidiary affairs. Thirdly, and of particular interest here, industrial relations and to a lesser extent personnel is defined in most multi-divisional companies as an operational responsibility. This takes on particular significance in looking at the effect of these factors on profits measured by rate of return on sales:

> Companies which allowed a stronger head office involvement in operating decisions tended to be less profitable. Similarly companies that involved their divisional head office in operating decisions also tended to be less profitable. These findings suggest that for optimum performance, operating functions should be decentralised down to the level of the operating subsidiaries. This view received support from the evidence of a positive relation between the responsibility of operating subsidiaries and profit in the case of buying, industrial relations and personnel decisions but, surprisingly, not in the case of production and marketing where no statistically significant

relation was found but the sign of the coefficient in each case was positive as expected.

(Hill and Pickering 1986: 47)

The data reported here related to the years 1978–80. Since then a number of enterprises have reorganized to remove or significantly weaken the divisional tier, for example, Tube Investments and GKN (Marginson *et al.* 1988) and restructured into smaller business units and operating subsidiaries. Some centralized firms have moved to create divisional structures and business units like BAA and British Telecom. At the same time there is evidence of further decentralization in collective bargaining to the local level, the break up of corporate wide job evaluation systems and a reduction in the size and role of corporate personnel departments. If further testing shows Hill and Pickering's findings to be largely correct (some caveats must be noted such as a response rate of only 28.8 per cent from the sample of *The Times* 500 companies) then it is likely not only that large firms will seek to create a multi-divisional structure but that further reorganization and restructuring will proceed to push for decentralization. This change in second-order strategies and the link between decentralized employee relations and profitability has profound implications for third-order human resource strategies in large firms.

Diversities in second-order strategies

Thus far we have assumed that multi-divisional firms will be generally similar in their behaviour and approach. Two further issues need to be addressed indicating variety and choice. The first of these relates to the approach taken by the corporate office in managing business units, what is termed by Goold and Campbell (1987) as strategy and style. The second looks more closely at the relationship between business units. The assumption of portfolio planning is that units can be managed as though they are unrelated to each other except in an ownership sense. We saw earlier that the growth of the multi-divisional firm has been particularly marked in related areas of business and this has been argued by Porter (1987a) as a more appropriate growth strategy than a collection of unrelated businesses managed in the portfolio method. Once units are related and are to a greater or lesser extent dependent on each other for the provision of goods and services (i.e. vertically integrated) then the pure logic of portfolio planning is harder to implement and may well be inappropriate. This in turn will have implications for third order employee relations strategies.

Corporate office control

The question asked by Goold and Campbell in their study of sixteen British-owned diversified companies was how does the corporate office manage its relationship with business units to ensure that value is added to the unit's performance. In their research model they identified two critical features of the process. The first is the extent to which the corporate office had *planning influence*. This 'concerns the centre's efforts to shape strategies as they emerge and before decisions are taken . . . . It is through planning influence that the centre seeks to improve the quality of thinking that surrounds major decisions' (1987: 36). The second was the *control influence* which 'concerns the way in which the centre reacts to results achieved . . . . Control influence arises from the targets that the centre agrees with its business units, the way the centre reacts to poor performance, and the frequency with which the centre monitors results' (ibid.). Three types of control influence were identified: flexible strategic control; tight strategic control and tight financial control. The critical differences are the amount of attention given to annual budget targets and monthly monitoring of results – i.e. the strength of the performance control system and the extent to which there are penalties for failure and rewards for success in target attainment.

These two dimensions are combined to produce three main categories which the authors summarize (ibid.: 10) as follows:

Strategic planning companies push for maximum competitive advantage in the businesses in their portfolio. They seek to build their portfolios around a small number of 'core' businesses, often with coordinated global strategies. The style leads to a wide search for the best strategy options, and tenacious pursuit of ambitious long-term goals. But decisions tend to be slower, reaction to poor performance is less decisive and there is less ownership of strategy at the business unit level. Financial performance is typically strong with fast organic growth, but, from time to time, setbacks are encountered. Companies with this style were BOC, BP, Cadbury Schweppes, Lex, STC and UB.

Financial control companies focus more on financial performance than competitive position. They expand their portfolios more through acquisitions than through growing market share. The style provides clear success criteria, timely reaction to events, and strong motivation at the business level resulting in strong profit performance. But it can cause risk aversion, reduce concern for underlying competitive advantage, and limit investment where the payoff is long term. Although financial performance in these companies has been excellent, with rapid share price growth, there has been less long-term organic business building. Companies with this style were BTR, Ferranti, Hanson Trust and Tarmac.

Strategic control companies balance competitive and financial ambitions. They support growth in strategically sound and profitable businesses, but rationalize their portfolios by closing down or divesting other businesses. The style focuses on the quality of thinking about strategy, permits businesses to adopt long-term strategies, and fuels the motivation of business unit managers. But there is a danger that planning processes can become superficial and bureaucratic, and that ambiguous objectives can cause confusion, risk aversion and 'political' manoeuvring. Strategic control companies have achieved profitability improvement and share price recovery, but have seen less growth and fewer major initiatives. Companies with this style were Courtaulds, ICI, Imperial, Plessey and Vickers.

The importance of strategy and style was vividly illustrated in the winter of 1986–7 in the hostile bid by BTR (a financial control company) for Pilkington (a strategic planning company). Pilkington is the world's leading glass maker which invented float glass in the 1950s and continues to invest heavily in R&D, developing global strategies, and making investments for strategic reasons even if the rate of return might be uncertain: a strategic planning approach. Interestingly the trade unions, and the St Helens community, the home town of Pilkington in north-west England, were active in defence of Pilkington and eventually, after the share price rose substantially, BTR withdrew their bid. What the unions and community feared was that if BTR were successful it would impose its particular management philosophy on Pilkington which would involve reducing costs[3] and pushing up margins for the benefit of the shareholder (BTR out-performed all but two of the quoted UK companies in terms of return to shareholders in the period 1974–86) but at the expense of jobs, community involvement and long-term development.[4]

The critical question is not whether the firm is profit maximizing but over what time period are profits expected or required to be achieved, and more contentiously who gains from the profits. Much of the literature on corporate strategy assumes that the only purpose is to service the needs of the shareholder. Other stakeholders; employees, communities, dependent suppliers, and customers are irrelevant. Not all companies take this view. In particular the strategic planners with long-term aims and objectives are the firms most likely to have a defined sense of purpose. In Hamermesh's terms these are the firms most likely to have an institutional strategy which includes non-economic values and beliefs. This is not to imply that they are soft companies or poorly managed, unable to take firm action when necessary but their approach to unit management is likely to be more benign and their capacity to design and inculcate a management style or corporate culture greater than other companies. Guest has suggested that only strategic planning companies have the capacity and commitment to develop human resource management (1987: 518).

Goold and Campbell, like so many authors in corporate strategy, say virtually nothing about human resource management assuming it to be an operational responsibility of unit managers. But the way these managers are themselves managed and motivated, and the freedom they have within financial targets is likely to influence their approach to employees and the extent to which they can invest in human resource programmes. The authors provide some fascinating insights here aided by quotes from their respondents. The two extremes, strategic planning and financial control, are contrasted.

Strategic planning companies
The centre acts as a sort of buffer to the capital market, protecting the business units from the need to satisfy the short-term performance criteria applied by the

outside investor. This allows business managers to concentrate on building their business rather than trimming their sales with a view to making half year earnings targets . . . . But lacking both market disciplines and clear internal targets . . . can mean that flexibility becomes tolerance and tolerance becomes looseness (pp. 198–9).

Although there are ultimate sanctions for non-performers, we did not get the impression . . . that managers who failed to hit their targets were in any imminent danger of serious reprisals (p. 68).

One of the features of these companies is their willingness to support subsidiaries that produce poor performance over long periods (p. 160).

Quoting Sir Hector Laing, CEO of United Biscuits, 'if things are going wrong you identify with management and help them out. At these times control should get more friendly not more fierce' (p. 68).

UB does not reward its managers with performance bonuses. Bonuses of that sort would jar with UB's culture which values family feeling and working for UB above individual effort (p. 68).

Financial control companies
There is no attempt to buffer the businesses from the requirements for short-term profits . . . by exposing all individual investments to this test, it goes much further than the capital market in applying tough standards (p. 207).

These companies have no formal planning systems, are concerned mainly with the financial results, control only against annual targets and apply strict short-term [2–4 year] pay back criteria to investment decisions (p. 111).

They are willing to act speedily to exit from the businesses that are not performing or do not fit (p. 126) . . . [and] are quicker to replace managers, fiercer in applying pressure through the monitoring process and more effective in recognising and acclaiming good performance (p. 132) . . . . Taken to extremes the style can encourage managers to milk their businesses by cutting back too far on investments (p. 202) . . . . [and the centre] has no wholly satisfactory means of ensuring this does not happen (p. 138) . . . . The style can cause risk aversion, reduce concern for underlying competitive advantage and limit investment where the payoff is long-term (p. 10).

In GEC 'we peer at the business through numbers' (p. 118) . . . . In any one year there are 20 managers who leave the budget review shaking in their shoes (p. 132) . . . . We asked Malcolm Bates of GEC how many years a manager could fail to meet his budget before expecting to lose his job. His response was telling and only partly tongue in cheek: 'How many years? You mean how many months. He might last for six months or he might not' (p. 129).

A quote from Tarmac: 'A division chief executive can only revise his budget downwards if he goes through some personal trauma. We can't stand the confessional . . . if they don't deliver they should feel very bad. They should feel that they have failed themselves and that life is awful. On the other hand if they succeed they will feel like winners. They will be basking. And they are rewarded (p. 131).

The authors go on to claim that financial-control companies 'generate high levels of motivation and satisfaction in their management' (p. 136) but offer no evidence for this. At the heart of this is a fundamental clash of values between long-term integrated 'family feeling' management teams and aggressive, short-run financially motivated managers (as in 'If you succeed, you are rewarded. If you don't you are out' p. 132). Presumably 'those who are out' or 'leave a review meeting shaking in their shoes' do not feel highly motivated – or rather they feel the motivation of fear. In many ways financial control companies adopt the logic of portfolio planning in that interdependencies between businesses are ignored and each business unit is given substantial independence within the confines of tight financial control. But the management style adopted within the unit is likely to be analogous to that found in the dog companies where cost cutting is emphasized, margins are pushed up and investment avoided unless there are clear pay-backs over short periods.

It is understandable that in periods of financial stringency and market instability pressure is placed on firms to improve performance by decentralizing to business units, applying demanding performance standards and closing down loss-making units. In effect, emphasis is placed more on control and less on planning (Hill and Hoskisson 1987). This, in turn, encourages further decentralization especially in terms of the administrative control system. Strategic shifts towards performance control are associated with structural shifts in internal operating procedures towards further decentralization leading to similar trends in human resource management strategies. But tight financial control systems and short-term investment pay-back requirements also tend to drive out long-term employee-relations investment at the unit level and destroy the basis of human resource management as part of corporate strategy.

Financial control companies, even when they gain abundant cash, do not appear to move back to the strategic planning style (ibid.: 235) and once a financial-control style is in place it is applied to all units irrespective of their market position and is unlikely to change until forced to by the shareholders. However, the capital markets approve strongly of financial control companies, for good reason. They:

'produced the best all round financial performance. They substantially outperform the industrial average. They have high profitability ratios and growth rates (achieved by acquisitions). Their main weakness is in organic growth, where fixed asset growth (4 per cent per year) has been less than inflation and less than half that of strategic planning companies (10 per cent per year) (ibid.: 161).

In short, financial-control companies produce excellent results for the shareholder, but few jobs are created and many disposed of through rationalization and restructuring. In contrast, strategic-planning companies with strong sales growth have created more jobs and, by their willingness to support subsidiaries with poor results over long periods, have disposed of less jobs in the recession than might have otherwise been the case. The returns to the shareholder, however, have been less good since 'strategic planning companies have the lowest stock growth . . . and earnings per share growth have been less satisfactory' (ibid.: 160). It is this that makes such firms more liable than others to hostile bids and acquisition battles like Pilkington with BTR.

Financial-control companies and increasingly pure finance companies and merchant banks like Merril Lynch and Morgan Stanley find it easy to raise the equity to engage in leverage buy-outs even after the stock market crash in the autumn of 1987. According to *Fortune* magazine (February 1988) these financial buyers:

> have moved into control of corporations because they see opportunities for restructuring, cost cutting, divesting – and for squeezing out record cash flows. Growth isn't on their minds and neither are capital expenditures . . . . Because the financiers are obsessed with reducing debt and getting their money out, they are expert in thinking about *today* . . . but . . . the financiers seldom care much about the company as an institution (and are poor) at encouraging innovation and preserving 'core skills'. . . . Most financiers insist that the efficiency they're injecting into these companies is a social good. They are generally frank to admit, however, that social utility is not why they got into this business. Money is.
>
> (*Fortune* 1988: 16–32)

Before we leave strategic styles it is worth noting that international comparisons provided by Goold and Campbell indicate that institutional strategy is not inevitably driven out. They argue that the Japanese giant enterprise, Matsushita, is in most respects a financial-control company but:

> finance, personnel and training are all fully centralised . . . . Personnel and training exist to create 'harmony' . . . . In other words the central role of these two functions is to help build and maintain the Matsushita culture . . . . [In this enterprise] people are seen as *the* critical resource [emphasis in the original] (ibid.: 283).

Looking at all the overseas companies they cite (IBM, Hewlett Packard, GE, and Matsushita) they conclude, in analysing their success, that

> perhaps most importantly, there are a series of things concerned with corporate objectives and culture that seem to matter. Agreement on basic directions for

the long-term development of the business, and on how to treat people within the firm, are perhaps the most essential common features of these companies (ibid.: 281).

This is a critical part of first-order strategy but for reasons they do not analyse is not widespread in Britain or the USA. Here, stock-market emphasis on short-term financial results makes the adoption of non-economic values as part of corporate strategy less likely. In such circumstances professional human resource management comes under increasing pressure.

It is important to note that the well-known examples of sophisticated human resource management embedded in corporate strategy (IBM, Hewlett Packard, Marks and Spencer) are exceptions which prove the rule. In these companies the values and approach of the founders of the company are much in evidence (as is the case in Matsushita) and they tend not to have deviated much from their core businesses. By 'sticking to the knitting' (Peters and Waterman 1982) and growing organically they have been able to maintain and articulate core values as part of their strategy. This raises the critical question of the distinction between diversified and undiversified, or critical function firms.

Related businesses, vertical integration, and diversification

One factor which makes it more likely that a strategic planning style exists and for corporate value statements to have meaning is the relatedness and extent of vertical integration and interdependence of business units. Hill and Hoskisson (1987) distinguish between financial, synergistic, and vertical economies in the way multi-divisional firms are structured. Financial economies are found when the superior allocative properties of the internal capital market are maximized by choice of style and strategy. These enterprises are likely to diversify into unrelated or loosely related activities and take on the attributes of financial control, and to a degree strategic control, companies. They are likely, out of choice, to ignore the interdependencies which happen to exist between parts of the enterprise (Goold and Campbell 1987: 118). For example subsidiaries are not required to trade with other parts of the enterprise, nor to offer preferential terms.

Synergistic economies exist where common techniques, skills, or market knowledge are utilized across a range of products. These companies are capable of organising around a core activity or critical business and are usually concerned that acquisitions match and enhance their business mission and core philosophies. Vertical integration is where a closely coordinated and integrated chain of activities from raw material sourcing to final distribution allow for vertical economies to be realized. Banking and multiple retailing companies exhibit some of these properties. Computer companies like IBM and Hewlett Packard are also organized around base skills and integration mechanisms. Such companies can emphasize administrative coordination. They can be decentralized in the sense of giving substantial responsibility to unit managers for the implementation of strategies and policy and for profits but in the context of coordinated integrating structures. Internal labour markets can be organized across the firm, not just within the unit. They are more likely to have well organized personnel departments in the corporate office (Sisson and Scullion: 1985) than others and they are capable of emphasizing core values in the way in which employees, customers and suppliers are to be treated. They are much more capable than others of being 'value driven', of 'respecting the individual', of 'viewing themselves as an extended family' and of following the dictum that 'customer relations simply mirrors employee relations' (Peters and Waterman 1982). The important point here is that the *potential* for strategic human resource management is greater in such companies. This is not to imply that the potential is realized.

This type of firm is, however, becoming rarer, at least among large enterprises. Channon has observed that the pattern of diversification has grown substantially and:

> today large companies tend in the main to be highly diversified both by range of business and by geography . . . Diversification was continuing amongst many of the organizations engaged in related businesses which seemed likely to make them unrelated concerns in the future.
>
> (1982: 79)

There is counter evidence to this as some firms like BET, Cadbury Schweppes and Dalgety have sought to divest businesses which do not fit a slimmed-down version of the portfolio organized around a broad core business. However, there is little evidence to suggest that these firms have at the same time changed the nature of their internal control structures. The dominance of performance control systems appears to remain intact.

Conclusion

Hill and Hoskisson have hypothesized that:

> as firms grow by vertical integration or related diversification, they will become increasingly constrained by information processing requirements to focus on attaining financial economies. [And that] under conditions of either high or increasing uncertainty, vertically integrated firms will focus on realizing financial economies.
>
> (1987: 338, 340)

The 1980s have been marked by uncertainty in product markets and, as we have seen, short-run pressures in the capital market have generated unprecedented uncertainty even for the largest firms. In these conditions corporate strategy increasingly is focused on ways of realizing financial economies. Firms which emphasize the achievement of financial economies are 'characterized by relatively high degrees of decentralization of decisions to divisions, decomposition between divisions, and consequently, high accountability for divisional profits' (ibid.: 334). It is these firms which emphasize the performance-control system; which often examine their businesses along the lines suggested by portfolio planning principles and which tend towards financial control, reducing the emphasis on long-run strategic planning. These types of first order strategies and second order strategic decisions on the structuring of internal operating procedures come to exert a strong influence on third order human resource management policies. It becomes harder to develop integrated and meaningful institutional strategies or management style at the corporate level, and – to the degree that short-run rates of return on investment, emphasis on margin improvement, and tight financial controls are imposed on unit managers – harder at the unit level to develop and maintain long-run human resource policies.

This pessimistic conclusion is difficult to avoid. It is the contention of this chapter that current trends in corporate strategy in many large diversified companies render the ideals of human resource management, as specified by Guest (1987), unobtainable. There is nothing new in this. Herman, in his study of corporate power concluded that 'The present state of evolution in economic freedom has produced an environment dominated by vast impersonal organisations that pride themselves on their ruthlessness and respond only to material incentives' (Herman 1981: 32). Mintzberg noted that 'the control system of the divisionalised (company) drives it to act, at best, socially unresponsively, at worst socially irresponsibly. Forced to concentrate on the economic consequences of his decisions, the divisional manager comes to ignore their social consequences' (Mintzberg 1979: 424).

The criticism of diversified companies is not restricted to their economic power and damaging social consequencies. Porter (1985, 1987a) has attacked portfolio planning and argued forcibly for a renewed emphasis on interrelationships between units and horizontal strategy. Piore and Sabel (1984) have argued that the economic consequencies of conglomerates and their search for multi-national diversification has had damaging consequences for the US economy. The criticism of the effects of diversified, multi-divisional companies on employee relations presented here is another twist of a familiar story. It is odd, then, that the current wave of interest in human resource management is so optimistic and implies that a major reconsideration of personnel practice is underway. The belief is that corporate executives and line managers have discovered the need to encourage employee involvement, team work, and integrated reward systems (ideas which have been around for a long time) as a crucial element of their corporate and business-unit strategies. Changes are, of course, taking place and there is much experimentation, some very exciting, as the old order crumbles. But in many diversified firms, in Britain at least, the material conditions for these to be translated into long-run strategic decisions placing human resource management as the, or even a, critical function in corporate strategy, do not exist. What ought to happen, as prescribed by the burgeoning literature, is a long way from being realized.

Notes

1. This might seem the ultimate self-sacrifice for the manager if his or her job is to go also. However, 'as a practical matter, it takes some time, perhaps two or three years to liquidate a dog business. At the end of this period there will undoubtedly be other opportunities in the organization for its manager and his staff' (ibid.).
2. Brown and O'Connor are, again, rather more explicit 'for dog businesses an early demise is the appropriate policy. Needless to say, they should receive no investment, not even to repair a leaking roof in the factory. If possible such a business should be sold to an organisation that does not realise it is a dog; if not, it should be abandoned' (1974: 16).
3. Hanson Trust, a very similar company to BTR, has cut, on average, 25 per cent of labour costs out of acquired companies (Porter 1987b).
4. BTR, through a subsidiary company, acquired the major Australian firm ACI in 1988. Within three months the whole of the human resource planning department at head office was closed down. No opportunity was given to the director of human resource planning to present a human resource strategy.

Chapter six

Selection and appraisal: reconstituting 'social relations'?

Barbara Townley

Introduction

There appears to be a growing trend on the part of management to the use of more systematic selection and appraisal procedures. In itself this might be taken as evidence of a greater professionalization of the personnel function and worthy of no additional comment. However, this would be to neglect the fact that an increasing application of these procedures is to sections of the workforce *for whom this has not previously been the case*. No longer confined to managerial levels, careful selection screening and regular formal monitoring of performance are increasingly becoming the experience of those at lower levels in the organizational hierarchy, especially blue-collar employees. Evidence in the UK shows a small but perceptible trend in this direction, whilst the practice of Japanese and USA companies and their UK subsidiaries illustrates well-developed policies in these areas.

On one level this may be seen as an organizational response to a changing economic context where high numbers of job applicants prompt management to be more rigorous in selection, and concern for costs oblige the more systematic checking of work output. This chapter will argue, however, that rather than their being seen as 'technical' readjustments prompted by immediate concerns with competition and efficiency, selection and appraisal are integral to what has been identified as HRM. The latter is understood as being characterized by an increasing emphasis placed on the *attitudinal and behavioural characteristics of employees*, factors which readily lend themselves to monitoring through selection and performance review. Selection and appraisal, in other words, are identified as contributing to an *overall approach to the handling of labour relations*. Management is also aided in this by modern 'technology' – personality and psychometric tests, biodata, and performance appraisal reviews – which give both the semblance of being objective and scientific and, concomitantly, efficient.

This is not to argue, however, that concern with behavioural and attitudinal characteristics is a recent employer interest. It was characteristic of the labour-management philosophies, for example, of the early Quaker employers (Child 1964) and American welfare capitalism (Brandes 1976; Ozanne 1967). Its emergence in the present context, however, is associated less with managerial philosophy than with the changing nature of production requirements. More systematic selection and appraisal procedures, it will be argued, are being introduced *in response to the problems of monitoring* raised in the move away from the direct and technical supervision of work, to the greater degree of 'discretion', or 'flexibility', being devolved to the individual and/or work group. This chapter will examine the evidence from surveys and case studies for the increased use of more systematic selection and appraisal procedures, and illustrate the extent to which behavioural and attitudinal factors are highlighted, before going on to account for these developments in greater detail.

Employee selection

Behavioural and attitudinal characteristics are most readily identified by personal interest and personality tests. Lewis (1985: 157) says of the latter 'this method provides recruitment and selection with an overlay of scientific respectability. It isolates the psychological dimensions of a candidate and attempts to accurately measure them'. Supported by research into motivation theories which indicates that employees respond differentially to various work environments and personnel policies designed to elicit effort, testing attempts to identify personality profiles or 'types' – 'bright achieving leaders' or 'approval-seeking humanitarians' – whose needs are seen as corresponding to the organizational ethos (Owens and Schoenfeldt 1979). Its significance as Guest (1987: 511) points out is that 'human resource management, based on these assumptions about employee motivation will therefore be viable in organizations employing workers with these orientations or *able to recruit and select such workers*' (emphasis added).

The recent economic climate has emphasized the laying off rather than the recruitment of labour. It is difficult therefore to say to what extent practices in UK companies are changing, if at all. Some research indicates a low orientation towards testing or the systematizing of procedures, but highlights the difficulties of generalizing about company behaviour in recruitment (Wood 1985; Windolf and Wood 1988). However, the limited survey data which is available indicates an increasing interest in the use of testing generally, and personality testing in particular. An early survey undertaken by the BIM (1963: n=350, sample drawn from BIM members) revealed 2.4 per cent of companies using personality tests, increasing to 7 per cent in a 1969 survey of the use of psychological tests in personnel work (Miller and Hydes 1971: n=828, sample drawn from IPM members). A later survey by Sneath *et al.* (1976: n=495, sample drawn from Dun and Bradstreet Guide to Key British Enterprises) reveals a relatively low level of use of personality and interest tests – 10 per cent for managers, 7 per cent technicians and supervisors, 3 per cent clerical and secretarial, 2 per cent skilled operatives – and these usually for purposes other than selection where the majority of tests examined aptitude and attainment. Evidence from a more recent survey by MacKay and Torrington (1986) however, although confirming that work sampling and trade knowledge tests still predominate, indicates a growing interest in personality and personal interest tests. Sixteen per cent of companies used the former and 17 per cent the latter in the recruitment of blue-collar employees. The figures for white-collar employees were 40 per cent and 16 per cent, and for management 67 per cent and 9 per cent, respectively, again confirming that use varies according to the position being recruited for, but illustrating a growth in the use of personality testing. Lewis (1984) also affirms personality testing is on the increase.

Biodata or 'personal history inventory' – essentially an extended application form or questionnaire – is also being increasingly introduced into selection decisions. It seeks information on the kind of experiences a person has had and involves the candidate answering a range of questions concerning personal life history and background. This is then used to build up a profile of the candidate to be measured against 'suitable' profiles of successful incumbents. Informed by a social learning approach to behaviour and motivation, it assumes or predicts 'relatively stable value orientations and associated work goals and preferences' (Guest 1987: 511), learnt from outside the workplace. Evidence of 'stability' in areas, for example, of financial responsibility or family commitments, are thought to predict continuing stability (Lewis 1985). Biodata, therefore, attempts to identify those employees with 'appropriate orientation' – appropriate that is to the motivation and reward structures of the organization. Designed as a filtering system in the initial or pre-selection stages of recruitment, its emergence is partly in response to the vastly increased volume of applications for jobs in the present economic climate. As such it is essentially recommended as a method of identifying those candidates who may be rejected rather than as a process for selection.

Its use, however, is not restricted to selecting those for entrance into the organization. It is being used in several organizations, for example in the finance sector, as the first stage in determining who shall have access to management development programmes. Several companies in this sector have introduced 'tiering', the gradation of the workforce according to the prediction of individual potential for advancement, with access to different training and development programmes according to the level of attainment or the 'tier' achieved. Initial access to assessment programmes, which determine the tiering level, is dependent on a minimum 'score' being achieved on the biodata questionnaire. The use of biodata to determine the 'core' workforce involves an analysis of the biographical details on background, experiences and interests of the present workforce in order to obtain a profile or an indication of those items associated with successful candidates. Questionnaires are then subsequently given to future entrants with those having similar 'profiles' being recruited onto development programmes.

The biodata questionnaire reflects a range of theories from psychology and sociology which have attempted to account for success and social mobility, thus questions refer to educational qualifications of applicant and parents; father's occupation; the number of different house and school moves during childhood; familiarity with an urban or rural environment; position in the family in relation to siblings; the nature of the family background (closeknit etc.), and the degree of importance placed on doing well at school etc.; the time spent on school work and the approaches to deadlines; educational achievements and whether this was ascribable to luck, interest, hard work, etc.; school discipline; leisure activities; contact with adults and the stability of the friendship network; employment experience; career expectations and goals; requirements from a job; individual goal setting and planning; responses to new activities and tasks, etc.

This 'personal history inventory' is a relatively new method of screening applications. Robertson and Makin (1986) in a survey of selection methods for managerial posts found that only 6 per cent of organizations made use of it, however there were indications that it was under serious consideration in other organizations. To an extent, the use of biodata is dependent on the computerization of personnel, which recent surveys indicate is still relatively low but estimate will increase rapidly (Hall and Torrington 1986). Growing interest in computerized or automated selection testing (Bartram and Bayliss 1984; Grant 1987) may also indicate that biodata will be an addition to the repertoire of future selection techniques. It is also an area in which specialist management consultants are also beginning to build up an interest.

Although some research indicates a degree of validity in such techniques (Reilly and Chao 1982; Hough et al. 1988) the reliability of these methods in predicting actual on-the-job performance has been questioned with recent estimates of biodata estimating only a 40 per cent level of predictability (Smith and Robertson 1986). Biographical data has validity when these items share elements of the work behaviour being predicted. To be accurate, large numbers of job incumbents are needed to identify the relevant items which are associated with the particular job in hand. There is also an indication that there is some decay in the procedure over time (Lewis 1985). It is often stressed in the literature that the value of such techniques can only be assured where there is validation of the methods against future performance and only when methods devised are organization-specific rather than off-the-peg measures. Studies of recruitment and selection procedures, however, indicate generally a limited validation of selection methods (Mackay and Torrington 1986; Wood 1985).

Although evidence from UK practice is rather unsystematic, both Japanese and American practice indicate that a great deal of importance is attached to recruitment and selection methods with these often incorporating several selection or screening devices, in particular, psychological testing and biodata. This practice also informs local management approaches, as is evidenced by case studies of their UK subsidiaries. White and Trevor (1983: 124) argue that 'one of the most significant aspects of Japanese thinking about personnel is in its approach to the issue of recruitment and selection'. Their study of Japanese subsidiaries in the UK emphasizes the investment of time and resources by senior management in such procedures, with each firm establishing and following a definite recruitment policy. In manufacturing establishments this policy was to structure the workforce into two distinct groups: young employees, usually school leavers with no previous work experience, and skilled employees. In terms of individual prerequisites there was an emphasis on 'potential' but more particularly on employee attitudes and character. A great deal of importance was placed on 'loyalty', 'seriousness' and 'commitment' and selecting people 'with a deep sense of responsibility', good workers having a desire 'to get on' (White and Trevor 1983: 103). Attitude was more important than technical competence – 'brilliant but awkward people would not fit in' – the inference being that whilst training could provide those with ability with the requisite skills, little could be done by the company in the important area of engineering the right attitudes.

For White and Trevor (1983: 124) 'care and selectivity in building up the workforce is a normal feature of the Japanese approach in Britain', a conclusion which is supported by the examples provided by the establishment of the Nissan plant at Washington and Komatsu at Newcastle. Both followed a conscious recruitment policy with rigorous selection procedures being applied to production workers (Wickens 1988; Crowther 1988). Recruitment of staff involved a carefully structured exercise lasting 18 months. Initially twenty-two supervisors were selected first by a senior management team during a week-long selection procedure. Primary interviews produced a shortlist of candidates who then underwent aptitude tests, occupational personality tests, and group exercises. The investment of managerial time was also replicated in the selection procedure for production workers, where the initial pre-screening device was an inhouse matrix questionnaire asking for biographical details. Subsequent testing of those who successfully completed this stage was designed to assess individual attitudes as well as there being a number of exercises to assess aptitude and ability (IRRR 1986).

The location of a new plant in a green-field site has obvious advantages for management. However, there is some indication that some UK-based companies, with established workforces, for example Austin Rover and Ford, are also modelling themselves on their Japanese competitors and paying increased attention to recruitment and selection methods. At Austin Rover recruitment now involves two-day assessments to which families are encouraged to attend to determine whether the 'individual and company aspirations converge' (IRRR 1986) – a far cry from the casual employment practices of former times.

Examples from the USA also show the importance attached to selection techniques as practised by large companies associated with HRM (Foulkes 1980). In some cases, however, selection testing based on personality criteria merely confirm the view of its being 'a frequently misunderstood and abused selection method because of the failure to understand what testing involves' (Lewis 1985: 157). As practised and recommended by some management consultants in the USA this facet of HRM owes more to 'union busting', where procedures advocated are designed to secure a compliant – non-unionized – workforce. The following comes from evidence given to a US Congressional Hearing on the role of management consultants specialising in helping employers 'select employees who are least susceptible to unionisation'. The 'type' to avoid is therefore:

someone who is too bright or skilled for a job . . . avoid hiring leader types . . . avoid prestige seekers . . . if the employee holds office in several outside clubs, look at this as a potential red flag . . . be sceptical of hiring the young swinger [sic.] – the youngest member of a family of more than one child should be carefully questioned in this regard . . . [avoid] that person loving a challenge and always ready for competition . . . [who] is adventurous, has a wide range of interests and is willing to try his hand at anything.

(Oversight Hearings 1979: 196)

As one union organizer remarked 'to stay non union, hire dull, dumb, introverted, antisocial, unimaginative types'. The use of selection techniques to 'weed out' employees on attitudinal or political grounds has led some States to introduce legislation prohibiting some of the more obvious aspects of this discrimination, on the grounds of protecting civil liberties (Munchus 1985; EOR 1985). The possibility of litigation under equal opportunities legislation also resulted in American corporations reviewing their use of selection testing in the 1960s and 1970s (Dulewicz 1984).

Again careful selection in the USA is especially apparent in the context of establishing new plants, where, for example, recruitment of production workers to a new GM plant saw senior executives explaining over a three-day period the new working philosophy under which they would be operating (Wood 1986a). The establishment of a new plant gives the added advantage of being able to take into consideration labour issues in the prior decision of plant location and there is some indication that the nature of the labour force is a factor influencing the location decisions of multi-nationals in the UK (Maguire 1986; Morgan and Sayers 1984). These strategic location decisions are usually complemented by careful selection procedures as, for example, in Livingston and Silicon Glen (*Financial Times* 18 January 1988).

Selection, by definition, involves a process of discrimination, and the opportunity for management to emphasize employee 'acceptability', or the 'good bloke syndrome', rather than 'suitability' residing in task-based criteria, has been well documented in the discussion of recruitment and selection decisions (Silverman and Jones 1973; Blackburn and Mann 1979; Oliver and Turton 1982; Jenkins 1986; Jewson and Mason 1986). However, the extent to which these factors are in fact elevated over task-related abilities has been questioned (Wood 1986b; Windolf and Wood 1988). The argument being made here is that there seems to be a move on the part of some management to more systematic selection procedures for sections of the workforce for whom this has not previously been the case; and that selection is overtly based on the grounds of attitudes, motivation and behavioural criteria. Management is aided in this by the possibility of institutionalizing or regularizing this procedure through mechanisms such as testing and biodata. Recruitment and selection decisions are, in this context, being identified as part of a conscious and integral approach to labour-relations issues, and characterize the policy of those companies which have been identified with HRM. It is an area, it is predicted, to which increasing attention will be paid in the future.

Appraisal

Survey data indicates that increasing attention is also being paid to employee appraisal. Fortunately, in comparison to recruitment and selection, there have been more systematic, longitudinal surveys on its use (Gill *et al.* 1973; Gill 1977). A feature identified by the most recent survey (Long 1986), and one of most concern here, is the extension of appraisal systems to groups of employees not previously included, in particular, an extension of appraisals from managerial levels to include a greater number of blue-collar and secretarial staff. For first-line supervisors this has increased from 60 per cent in 1977 to 78 per cent in 1985; for clerical and secretarial staff the increase is from 45 per cent to 66 per cent but for skilled and semi-skilled employees the increase is from 2 per cent to 24 per cent. In addition, almost a third of the organizations indicated an intention to extend their appraisal procedures to cover more job levels in the organization. Data from Mackay and Torrington (1986) indicate that 30 per cent of manual employees, 62 per cent clerical and secretarial, and 70 per cent of supervisory staff are appraised. A comparison may be made with the US, however, where a recent survey indicates that figures on coverage are: 91 per cent first-line employees, 88 per cent office and clerical and 63 per cent skilled manual workers (Bureau of National Affairs 1983).

Several commentators have identified changes in payment systems as being the main contributing factor to the increase in performance appraisal. Developments in harmonization, and in particular the establishment of integrated payment systems have been associated with appraisal for manual employees (IRRR 1984, 1987; IDS 1987). Equally the move away from 'bureaucratic' age/wage or seniority based payment systems to merit- or performance-related remuneration, is seen as an important factor especially in white-collar employment. Long (1986: 15), however, does not see this interest in appraisal as being directly attributable to the more recent discussions concerning performance related pay. The number of companies citing the assessment of salary increases as one of the main purposes of performance review has remained at the 1977 level of about 40 per cent, with only 15 per cent carrying out a salary review at the same time as the performance review. (This is unlike the USA where there is a more direct link between pay and performance). The exception to this is at more senior managerial levels with a direct relationship between pay and performance.

Another aspect of appraisals which Long's (1986) survey uncovered was their emphasis on assessing current performance rather than future development, the latter having been the reported focus in previous surveys. This may reflect, as Long suggests, declining opportunities for advancement, or alternatively that separate procedures are in operation to assess potential. The emphasis on current performance and in particular on the 'marginal' performer, attention to whom has sharpened over the last few years, has been attributed by Long (1986: 49) to the immediate economic context:

> In situations of low growth, stiff market competition, and scaled-down manpower levels, organisations can no longer carry under-performers, the new culture demanding satisfactory performance against job requirements. In addition higher standards of performance are required to meet the challenge of changing markets.

Whilst there may be some validity in stressing 'efficiency' criteria, this fails to account for another finding of the survey – that of increasing emphasis being placed on 'social' rather than task-based criteria in the appraisal of non-managerial staff. Whilst managerial jobs are overwhelmingly assessed in a results-orientated approach to performance, trait-rating is used almost exclusively in non-managerial performance review. Eighty-nine per cent of the non-managerial appraisal schemes used trait-rating compared to 11 per cent of those for management and professional employees. Long (1986: 29) concludes that 'primarily personality oriented schemes were without exception for non-management grades'. Even where 'job related' behavioural criteria were used these were 'no more than personality trait criteria presented as behavioural statements' (Long ibid.: iii). In the few cases where specifically job-related criteria were used to assess non-managerial employees this was accompanied by an overall performance rating which, in some cases, was subject to forced distributions. There was also a difference in the amount of time spent in performance-review discussions, with those for managerial staff lasting on average twice as long.

Although the survey offers an overview of appraisal systems, a more detailed analysis of their operation has to rely on case studies and reports into their usage. The finance industry provides an interesting example of the extension of appraisal systems to clerical and secretarial employees. Increased competition in the sector has led to the move towards performance-related pay with, for example, the three largest building societies introducing some measure of performance-related pay (PABB 1988). The following example of appraisals, taken from one of the clearing banks, is used to determine the transfer, promotion, and financial reward of clerical staff. As with the survey findings, these examples indicate that the criteria used in evaluation are rarely defined exclusively by categories of performance-related knowledge.

In order to analyse the criteria identified reference is made to Offe's (1976) three-fold typology of 'norms', which he identifies as being attached to job roles and which become the focus of assessment. He distinguishes between 'technical rules' which are functional for the operation of the work task; 'regulatory norms' which function in allowing or facilitating the operation of cooperative work processes, for example, references to 'carefulness' or 'economy'; and 'extra functional norms' which are functionally irrelevant for the work task but which 'prop up the authority structure of the organisation, for example, those which check loyalty to the aims and interests of those in authority' (ibid.: 30). Although having a degree of intuitive appeal, an attempt at classifying the criteria according to the typology identified indicates that it is easier to operate within a continuum, not least because of the difficulties of distinguishing between task and 'social' components of work.

Although varying in the degree to which the organizations define their terms it is possible to identify the importance of Offe's regulatory and extra-functional norms. Criteria identified by the bank for appraisal of clerical staff include: technical knowledge and ability; output and accuracy; judgement and reliability (whether the individual may be relied upon to take the correct initiative in the face of uncertainty); initiative (which is variously defined as resourcefulness, enterprise, and energy, but also includes the approach to and the need for supervision); cooperation (involvement, adaptability, and contribution to a team effort – but also willingness to undertake more tasks); promoting the corporation's image (appearance, conduct, customer/colleague relations); reaction to change (a negative reaction includes unadaptability, inflexibility, and not understanding, accepting, or coping with change – the extent to which management's willingness to explain and plan for change is taken into consideration is not known); and attitude to authority. The assessment of future potential which accompanies this is almost wholly concerned with 'social' criteria and includes the supervisor's assessment of the need for success (responses to encouragement, criticism and challenges); personal qualities (assertiveness, degree of self-discipline, and determination); career attitudes (goal setting and commitment to tasks); (the demonstration of) professional standards and qualifications; relationship with management (including degree of diffidence and respect); relationship with others; creativity ('innovative' approaches to challenges); outside knowledge and involvement (knowledge of 'broader issues', community, social or professional involvement).

Advice accompanying the appraisal document states that it is important to assess what people have done rather than personality characteristics, and appraisers are warned against leniency/severity, the halo effect, contrast, and similarity with the appraiser, reliance on critical incidents, etc. However, as with recruitment and selection, there is a search for 'types' as the advice states: 'It is not necessary that individuals fulfil every aspect of a dimension although research indicates that these traits are normally seen together'. There is even the allowance for self-assessment scores on the performance-appraisal review, though the parameters of the assessment are well defined.

Case studies reporting appraisal systems as they have been applied to manual employees (IDS 1987; IRRR 1984, 1987), although including some UK companies, have largely cited examples from plants having American or Japanese parents. The latter have either no-union or single-union agreements, and again reflect the identification of HRM with American, Japanese, and non-union practices. There are variations in the appraisal systems cited: the extent to which they required an overall assessment of the employee (associated with the American and Japanese systems); the extent to which the amount of pay to be determined by the appraisal system was fixed or discretionary (the latter being associated with both the Japanese and American companies); the procedure used and the degree of 'self-assessment' allowed and the number of factors assessed (ranging from those which addressed the acquisition of specific skill modules to those which identified between 10 and 18 different aspects of performance – the greater number being associated with the American and Japanese companies); whether there was a 'safe' middle option, or a forced choice between above- or below-satisfactory performance (the latter was associated with procedures operating in a Japanese company). As with the survey evidence the case studies reaffirm the position of line management in the operation of these schemes: 'supervisors are the linchpins of performance appraisal' (IDS 1987: 4).

As with the earlier examples cited, however, criteria identified for appraisal show a large emphasis on regulatory or extra-functional norms. Criteria which may be identified as being primarily 'task-based' include: attendance, timekeeping, productivity, quality and job knowledge. Other criteria towards the opposite end of the continuum, however, include references to 'dependability' – the extent to which the individual is inclined to follow standard procedures and the amount of supervision required; 'flexibility' – variously defined as a willingness to 'help out', take on or learn other jobs; 'initiative' – the ability to cope with the unexpected; personal contact skills – the ability to get on with others; leadership and determination; and a criterion in the appraisal system from a Japanese subsidiary was an explicit reference to work undertaken 'beyond the contract' which included an interest in self-development and participation in *voluntary* training courses!

The changing locus of control

Developments indicate the introduction of more systematic procedures in selection and appraisal and, in particular, a growing importance being placed on behavioural or attitudinal criteria. What factors may account for this? For Offe (1976), although arguing the inherent impossibility of an 'objective' assessment, the principal factor giving 'peripheral' elements, as he terms them, prominence, is the nature of work organizations. He identifies features such as the size and complexity of organizations and increased hierarchical and functional differentiation, as leading to more complex systems of internal control, the latter usually involving an increased emphasis on normative orientations. This is required especially where there is a 'discontinuity of task' between subordinate and superior which renders the latter unable to judge whether the technical requirements of the task have been fulfilled. Control therefore has to rely on 'peripheral' elements, those 'normative and ideological requirements defined as necessary to the task but not related to its technical fulfilment' (Offe 1976: 28). The emphasis on extra-functional norms is also identified as becoming more important as the move is made from work with things, through work with symbols to work with people – roughly from industrial-production workers, to clerical employees and management.

Offe's explanation, as with his typology, raises the immediate problem of how the 'technical' components of work as opposed to its social construction may be identified (Cockburn 1983; Manwaring and Wood 1985) as well as the validity and utility of the distinction (Wood 1986b). Whilst the assertion that extrafunctional norms increase in relevance according to the nature of work may account for the emphasis on attitudinal criteria, and its emergence in parts of the service sector for example, where competitive advantage is perceived as relying on those having direct customer contact, it does not allow for developments among production workers in manufacturing. Equally the identification of an overall trend in the size and functional differentiation of organizations does not allow for a more disaggregate analysis, nor does it account for the emergence of these factors in a specific industrial or historical context.

The actual nature of the changes in work organization which may be identified, for example, amongst blue-collar production workers for whom the introduction of selection and appraisal systems has been identified includes: the introduction of broad-banded pay scales, harmonization and integrated payment structures, the move away from specific job descriptions, an emphasis on mobility and 'functional flexibility', pay scales linked to skill acquisition – in other words the introduction of the prospects of upward internal mobility through the development of an infrastructure of an internal labour market. Does what is being outlined therefore depict the emergence or development of internal labour market employment conditions for categories of employees for whom this has not previously been established? In this context selection and performance appraisal may appear as 'natural accompaniments' – the assumption of a high degree of job security and the building up of a 'core' workforce placing a premium on selection techniques; and the requirements of monitoring performance as a basis for upward progression necessitating appraisal.

Rather than concentrating on the employment conditions characterizing an internal labour market, however, it is of value to consider the changes in the nature of work organization which have been identified, in particular the importance attached to increased individual discretion, and the implications this has for the administration of work. Changes in work organization which require the exercise of discretion – the use of judgement, filling in 'the gaps' and taking initiative – produce specific control problems for management. It requires that those in authority are satisfied that the task is being done in accordance with broader organizational objectives. The question then becomes how to control discretion. How may senior levels in an organization ensure that the potential areas of error in the exercise of discretion are avoided, how may the possibility of 'deviant' behaviour be minimized?

One method which has been identified is through the elaboration of the employment contract – the specification of the details of the effort reward relationship through work rules and personnel policies. Characterized as 'bureaucratic control' (Edwards 1979) or the growth of the 'internal state' (Burawoy 1979), this 'objectification' (wage rates attaching to jobs rather than workers, the development of job categories, work rules, promotion procedures, wage scales, disciplinary procedures, etc.) is seen as a mechanism where, although predictability may not be fully ensured, uncertainty may at least be confined within narrow limits. Such an approach places great faith in the 'rationality' of rules whilst ignoring the inherent drawbacks of such an approach – the impossibility of specifying rules for every contingency; the inherent discretion in, and therefore the possibility of conflict over, the interpretation of rules; the double-edged nature of codification as definitions of what 'is' also prescribe what 'is not'. These are all factors which lead to the inevitable juridification of the employment relationship, and by enforcing rule-following ultimately undermine any move to the exercise of discretion.

Discretion, by definition, obviates the exercise of bureaucratized procedures. However, where work cannot be effectively secured or fully guaranteed through a system of formal rules then other systems which attempt to minimize the potential areas of error in the exercise of discretion have to come into play. The emphasis shifts from *formal rules* as to how the work *is* to be done, to *implicit expectations* as to how it *should be* done. This relies on informal regulation or rather shared norms of understanding, a common grammar of interpretation. Discretion requires the internalization of the organization's 'goals' or 'norms' to ensure that the individual interprets the area of discretion correctly from the organization's point of view (Fox 1974). Hence the emphasis on the creation of these shared norms, through 'commitment', or the importance of a 'strong organisational culture', which is evident in the literature on HRM (Walton 1985a; Guest 1987).

One of the functions of appraisals, rather than its being seen as the 'objective' measurement of individual performance, is to communicate organizational norms or 'culture' and reinforce this process. Edwards (1979), in an examination of one of the facets of 'bureaucratic control', Polaroid's job assessment or appraisal procedure, illustrates the operation of such a system. As Edwards notes, and as was illustrated by the examples given earlier, a lot of assessment is concerned with work behaviour – such as dependability and thoroughness, work habits, and personal characteristics – rather than actual production achieved. What is learnt through the appraisal procedure are work habits, attendance, attitude, and other personal characteristics. 'Exceptional' workers become defined in terms of those who set examples to others in methods and use of time, suggest ways of improving the job, increase the effectiveness of the group, display cooperation and enthusiasm etc. These criteria also become the basis for promotion (Edwards 1979).

Edwards (1979) identifies three criteria which are rewarded in the Polaroid scheme: 'rules orientation', dependability and identification with the company. He asserts, however, that these criteria are emphasized differentially according to status in the organization with those higher in the organization being assessed on their internalization of norms whilst lower-level employees are assessed on their rules orientation. The examples of appraisals cited from the finance sector and the case studies, however, show that the criteria of dependability and identification with the company are equally important at all levels in the organization.

The criteria identified by the appraisals emphasize regulatory and extra-functional norms – readiness to adapt, avoidance of conflict, loyalty to the dominant interests in the organization, and the acceptance of the cultural pattern of the dominant groups. 'Commitment' becomes the equivalent of both the knowledge of, and conformity to, the attitudes and values of superiors, co-workers and subordinates. Whilst appraisal is in terms of compliance, it is compliance with a much more nebulous construct of norms, and not with bureaucratic rules as Edwards (ibid.) argues.

This communication or reinforcement role for appraisals finds some support in the survey evidence. An identified trend in appraisal schemes is the opportunity for the individual being reviewed to read the completed form (operating in 92 per cent of the organizations), and in some cases (83 per cent) being able to record dissenting opinions. Long (1986) welcomes this as a move to more 'openness'. There is a question, however, as to what this 'openness' represents. Where appraisals function as a system of communicating managerial and organizational expectations and ethos to subordinates, 'openness' is a prerequisite in indicating those aspects of behaviour and attitudes which are primarily valued. The extent to which 'openness' represents the move towards a more participative, less judgemental, system is questionable. There has been no move to improve or widen appeals procedures. Only half of the organizations had a formal appeals procedure, with moreover, access to appeals remaining at the same level as that reported in the 1970s. Equally only 0.02 per cent of organizations gave non-managerial employees performance-review training notwithstanding the view in the literature (Randell et al. 1984) that successful appraisal requires the positive involvement of both parties to the review. Perhaps the fact which weighs against the view of appraisals representing anything other than a control function was the fact that self-assessment or self-rating was rarely used as a review tool. The reported lack of follow-up on action, training, and development plans, reflecting the findings of earlier research (Rowe 1964), also questions the sense of priority attached to appraisal as a 'two-way' communications system in most organizations. As with selection only a small number of organizations attempted to validate their review methods, 11 per cent in the case of potential review methods (Long 1986).

Appraisals in this context represent a return to much more personalized or 'simple' forms of control. Indeed the extent to which this was precluded under 'bureaucratic control' is doubtful. For Edwards (1979: 132) bureaucratic control – 'the most important change wrought by the modern corporation in the labour process' – is built into the formal structure of the firm, rather than personal relationships between workers and bosses. Its superiority lay in its establishing an 'impersonal force of company rules/company policy as the basis for control' (ibid.: 131), replacing the rule of supervisory command or personal power with the rule of law. It also has the added advantage of obscuring the source of regulation. This presumes a high degree of standardization and objectivity which, even if attainable in an appraisal system, cannot preclude the inevitable inequality which results from different employees being assessed by different people. One of the findings of the Long (1986) survey and a major criticism of the performance-review procedure is that most appraisal systems are viewed as suffering from the unequal standards applied by different appraisers. Appraisal is likely to be felt, and, indeed, is designed to be felt, as the exercise of personal power. As Long (1986: 11) remarks 'whatever else it might be, performance appraisal is a personal event between two people who have an ongoing [*hierarchical*] relationship' (emphasis added). Appraisals more accurately reflect the rating of the relationship between manager and subordinate than anything else (Child 1980).

Rather than obscuring the source of power, appraisal represents the very personalized applications of power especially, although not exclusively, when related to monetary reward, and in doing so deliberately reinforces the role of the supervisor or immediate superior. The role of the line manager is a factor which is reinforced throughout the appraisal survey and case studies, and is another feature which has been identified as characterizing HRM (Storey 1987b). In 98 per cent of the organizations the immediate superior was responsible for carrying out the performance review, with the second level reviewer being the superior's superior. There was also the indication that line managers would be involved more in the preparatory stages of the design and implementation of a new or revised appraisal system (Long 1986).

Any obscuring of power which might arise comes from the reference to 'scientific' procedures, the application of 'impersonal' (in the sense of not having been personally designed) procedures of 'empirically verified' measuring devices, and the bureaucratized mechanics of the process (standardized forms, annual assessments, etc.). Although the procedure might be bureaucratized and systematically carried out this does not render the evaluation systematic, predictable, or objective. As has been noted 'ratings do not employ measuring rods which can be validated to any meaningful degree apart from group judgement' (Livernash quoted in Offe 1976: 115). The essence is personal or individualized control through the semblance of a uniformity of procedures and given the emphasis on subjective, extra-functional, norms this is bound to be the case. As Fletcher (1984: 22), writing on appraisals concludes 'the goal of objectivity in appraisal schemes seems further away than ever . . . our perceptions of what is real and valid in the world *rest on a consensus of shared beliefs*; appraisals of performance are no exception to that rule/those rules' (emphasis added). Indeed the function of appraisals, it is argued here, is the reinforcement of those shared beliefs.

The importance of appraisal as outlined, however, lies not only in its emphasis on the attitudinal and behavioural characteristics of employees, but also in its emphasis on the individual. The underlying ethos of appraisal is what Offe (1976) has termed the 'achievement principle', i.e., the reward of individual work, achievement or performance. However the focus on the 'productivity' of the individual has the result of defining the individual as the *unit* of work. The social or collective element of work is obscured or hidden. This is despite the fact, as Offe (1976: 81) notes, 'that the social organization of work, the extent to which the parameters of work organization are already defined, the reliance on at least a degree of "team cooperation" effectively render impossible the attempt to locate the success of any one individual'. This contradiction between cooperative production and the simultaneous retention of individual success is seen as further reinforcing the elevation of peripheral work behaviour. In addition it contributes, as was identified by Edwards (1979), to the finely graded division and stratification of workers, and may provoke narrow self-interest and individualism – reflecting the individualistic ethos which some have identified as the defining characteristic of HRM.

Conclusions

The argument in this chapter is that changes in the nature of work organization will result in a greater emphasis being placed on behaviour control:

> if control in work organisations is through 'technical rules' it is hardly a problem should the worker possess a distinct cultural identity. Once control is through the worker's 'normative orientations', the necessary control in work will depend on the removal of any basic cultural differences between him and his superiors.
> (Wickham 1976: 9–10)

The changes in work organization being referred to are the increased emphasis on 'flexibility' or the requirement for the greater exercise of discretion, whether this is in response to working with a greatly reduced workforce, the introduction of just-in-time production, or a competitive strategy which places an emphasis on high-quality products. The changes which have been associated with the introduction of selection and appraisal, and HRM generally, have been primarily associated with moves toward 'japanization' or 'flexibility' and the concomitant move away from 'bureaucratized' procedures. The latter being primarily identified as complementing a well-defined and bureaucratized production system – mass production and mass markets – by providing predictability but failing to provide 'flexibility' in a changed economic context.

With a diminution in the extent to which rules may prescribe the way tasks are performed, the nature of regulation over labour must also change – changes in 'hard technology' are seen as bringing forth changes in the 'software' of control. The emphasis becomes the total behaviour of the individual rather than specifically 'productive' behaviour, and it is that facet that selection and appraisal mechanisms are designed to identify and mould. However, this is not to offer a simplistic 'control for control's sake' argument. The norms which have been identified, especially in appraisal, reinforce production and work requirements by emphasizing criteria which indicate a willingness and ability to work without supervision, undertake a number of tasks and instil these aspects in others.

The development outlined was recognized by Nichols (1980: 289), amongst others, who wrote of the 'socialisation' of capitalism,

Naked coercion being ruled out, given unionised workforces and other considerations – and bureaucratic control in the end being insufficient anyway, for
rules can cut two ways, not only specifying what must workers do but what
they need not – it becomes yet more important to call forth a new flexibility
in workforces. In short the more far-sighted employers come to more fully
appreciate the need to 'involve' workers in their work and to elicit from them,
individually and collectively, their productiveness as social labour.

The tension for employers is between treating labour as engaged under a market
relationship of a freely negotiated contract and treating it as engaged in a continuing
social relation between employers and workers. The tension has been identified
by Streeck (1987) as being one between contract and status. There are advantages for employers in sustaining the view of employment as a market relationship
– management's power takes the form of authority, i.e., it is based on voluntarily-
given consent; the contract may be terminated at the will of either party. There
are, however, disadvantages, in particular, with a view to gaining the degree of
commitment required from employees to both the enterprise and the work
involved. Many facets which have been identified with HRM reflect an attempted temporary resolution of this tension by attempting to obscure the 'market'
component and highlight the 'social' (in Streeck's terms there is an emphasis on
status rather than contract). As a result, greater attention is being paid to the aspects
of personnel policy which can regulate this, in particular, in the areas of employee
selection and appraisal, but also communication and financial participation
programmes. The former have the added advantage for management that they
are usually firmly established under the umbrella of managerial prerogative.

Management is also aided in this by the development and application of
'technical', 'methodical', 'rational', 'scientific', and 'calculated' measures, giving
both the impression of the attainment of objectivity and reinforcing a technicist
concept of work. Both selection and appraisal appear under a veneer of scientificity
– the rational application of measuring systems or techniques to a socially organized
work environment (Hollway 1984). Whilst these techniques may achieve a reduction of subjectivity there is a danger of their acquiring the status of objective or
technical legitimacy. This claim to technical proficiency is also likely to be
supported and reinforced by the 'professional' personnel manager in the claim
to a new source of legitimacy as organizational diagnostician, or increasingly,
by specialist management consultants (MacKay 1987; Torrington and MacKay
1986).

Moves in the directions outlined, however, will vary according to the particular circumstances at the disaggregate level. Nor can it be assumed that these moves
will necessarily meet with success. Resistance to the introduction of such schemes
may be anticipated, for example, in strongly unionized areas. It is of note that
companies which abandoned the introduction of performance appraisals for its
manual employees did so because unions jammed the grievance procedure (IDS
1987). Equally, assumptions about a move to HRM cannot be 'read off' from the

existence or implementation of, for example, performance-appraisal schemes per se. Whilst the argument here has been that the reinforcement of behavioural norms is the primary function of appraisal systems and this is required in cases where the move from direct control requires the greater exercise of discretion, this is not to deny that appraisals also have a direct function of monitoring performance. For example, the introduction of performance appraisal into the public sector with bonus pay for civil servants, performance related pay in the NHS, appraisal for teachers and university lecturers, 'good practice' allowances for GPs etc., has to be understood within the context of public-sector restructuring, and serves as a reminder of this monitoring function in a cost-cutting environment. In this context, concerns with reinforcing behavioural norms are secondary to 'accounting' and disciplinary concerns.

It has been said that managerial strategies are routes to partial failure (Hyman 1987). There are perhaps two caveats which may be identified as undermining the strategy of increased reliance on personal control through selection and appraisal procedures – one contextual and the other inherent. The contextual variable relates to a potential area of conflict which may emerge between the State and corporation, as the latter requires greater 'flexibility' and the former has regulations in place which presume, and require, a fairly high degree of bureaucratization, e.g. equal opportunities and unfair dismissal legislation. The inadequacies of enforcement in these areas and moves to deregulation indicate that this may not be an unsurmountable obstacle for management. The second caveat relates to the attempt to encourage greater discretion and individual judgement in a context where the parameters for their use are heavily constrained or circumscribed. The result is unlikely to be the exercise of discretion and judgement, i.e., creativity, to be harnessed by the organization, but rather the inevitable ritualization of those particular norms which become identified as valid in the work context.

Chapter seven

Corporate training strategies: the vital component?

Ewart Keep

The purpose of this chapter is to examine the importance of training and development to human resource management policies. Subsumed under the general
heading of training will be the issues of selection and recruitment. The inter-
relationship between training and recruitment strategies is usually a very close
one, not least because if an organization wishes to improve the skills of its
workforce, it has the choice of either training its existing employees or recruiting
pre-skilled labour that has been trained elsewhere. As training and recruitment
are to some extent substitutable, it is difficult to study either activity in isolation.

The chapter opens with an attempt to offer a working definition of HRM, and
goes on from this to outline the importance of investment in training and development as a test of whether an organization is treating its employees as a resource,
or as a cost or commodity. The implications of training activity for employee
motivation and wider aspects of HRM are discussed. The chapter then examines
the evidence that training has an effect on economic performance at both aggregate
and company levels, and instances the ways in which international comparisons
have acted as a spur to the adoption of HRM in the UK. The types of change
in training that have recently taken place are surveyed, and it is argued that the
evidence indicates the centrality of these changes to evolving HRM practices.
Following on from this, some potential problem areas in terms of current
managerial attitudes towards training are discussed, and a number of underlying
structural factors adduced to explain these barriers to the widespread adoption
of HRM policies. The chapter concludes with some brief remarks about the
prospects for the widespread adoption of HRM, and the need for further research
on the factors that impede its spread among UK companies.

Evaluating HRM: some potential problems

It seems prudent to begin by highlighting some of the problems that confront
attempts to evaluate any aspect of what might be termed the human resource
management movement. Earlier chapters have indicated that human resource
management can cover a broad spectrum of approaches and practices, and that
there appear to be at least two basic definitions of HRM – one which might be

termed 'tight', the other 'loose'. The latter category appears to cover the adoption by companies of almost any relatively systematic approach to the deployment and utilization of labour, and can embrace casualization, numerical flexibility, even de-skilling. The former emphasizes the centrality to competitive advantage of investment in the training and development of all levels of the workforce, of improved communication with the workforce, and of the motivational benefits that are attendant upon these developments. This tighter definition could perhaps be said to describe a specific school of thought within a broader HRM movement – one which might be termed human resource development (HRD). The main British proponent of this style of approach has been the Manpower Services Commission, or, as it is now to be known, the Training Agency.

The fact that, at its most basic, the term human resource management can be held to cover so wide a range of philosophies and practical developments, causes obvious problems for those seeking to evaluate the centrality of any individual aspect of the deployment of human resources to this web of activity. Also, it needs to be borne in mind that the debate about the nature and importance of HRM is taking place against a still rapidly changing and much more competitive economic environment, within the context of which many very different strategies and forms of re-structuring have been adopted by British enterprises. Some of these responses to more demanding and uncertain market conditions, such as the growth of large conglomerates, the development of new management structures and cost controls, and increased pressure to contain and reduce labour costs, have often had very direct and profound effects upon the way in which workforces have been managed. However, the degree to which the resultant changes can be ascribed to the adoption of anything that can usefully be termed human resource management, is open to question. In many senses the types of developments mentioned above have tended to reduce the importance of the workforce to that of simply another element within a matrix of managerially-led cost-reduction activities. Thus, in some organizations at least, recent developments have led labour to be treated to an even greater degree as a commodity, rather than as a genuine resource.

Moreover, in attempting to assess how widespread has been the actual adoption of the various component concepts that make up HRM, it is difficult to separate fact from the bandwagon effect that has occurred. The general terminology of the HRM movement has gained widespread currency, and, in the area of training and development, efforts on the part of the government and bodies such as NEDO, the MSC and the CBI, have certainly raised the profile of these HRD activities. However, the degree to which the adoption of the appropriate phraseology on the part of managers actually reflects new and different attitudes and practices among its users is less certain.

Another problem that confronts any inquiry in the field of HRM is the lack of reliable quantitative information. For example, one can identify two obvious lacuni in the areas of manpower planning, and recruitment and selection. Furthermore, information on the training and development practices of British companies is also very crude, and such data as is currently available is of relatively limited value. If the term HRM has any meaning, it ought to indicate the adoption of a comprehensive and coherent approach towards employment practices, yet it is precisely the degree to which such an approach is being adopted by individual companies that is so difficult to gauge from the fairly patchy aggregate data in our possession.

A final problem that faces those who seek to evaluate or analyse the HRM movement, is the fact that the time scale of enquiry is too limited to easily enable any definitive judgements to be made. HRM as a subject for study in Britain has simply not been in existence sufficiently long to allow a final conclusion to be made concerning its long-term impact and significance. What follows can therefore at best offer an interim judgement on a still-evolving situation.

The importance of training strategies within HRM

Notwithstanding the difficulties outlined above, the purpose of this chapter is to argue that training and development should be regarded as central to anything that can sensibly be termed HRM. In so doing it is suggested that the loose definition of HRM is not one that helps reliably apportion the motivation for and importance of changes that are taking place in the management of the workforce, in that it tends to act as a 'catch-all' banner under which a huge variety of very different developments can be lumped. As has been mentioned above, the underlying impetus for many of these changes, such as casualization and numerical flexibility, has little to do with a desire to develop the workforce, or to treat employees as a resource.

By contrast, the case that the adoption by companies of a strategic approach towards the training and development of their workforces represents a vital component of any worthwhile or meaningful form of HRM (or HRD) is easily made. If the term human resource management is to be taken as something more than an empty 'buzz phrase', then the word human, in this context, can only relate to the employees, present and future, of the enterprise. The use of the word 'resource', as opposed to commodity or cost, implies investment therein. The word management, for its part, implies that strategies aimed at the motivation, development and deployment of this resource and its associated investment will be directed in such a way as to maximize its potential. Training is a prime investment in human resources that plays a vital role in securing these goals. Companies that, for whatever reasons, are inclined to treat their employees simply as a cost or commodity, and who hence fail to invest in training and development activity cannot meaningfully be said to be practising human resource management.

It can also be argued that there is a solid economic rationale that is likely to bind the incidence of training to the development of wider human resource management policies. If a company has invested in training its workforce, it then makes sense to develop policies that will help to retain these employees and to motivate and develop them in such a way as to put to best use their skills, thereby maximizing the return on investment. With a lowly-skilled workforce, whose training has mainly been in the form of an unstructured, on-the-job acquisition of experience, there is far less incentive to retain them and their loyalty, as the cost of loss and replacement is likely to be lower.

Furthermore, training and development activities have implications for attempts to motivate and involve the workforce. One of the primary objectives of HRM is the creation of conditions whereby the latent potential of employees will be realized and their commitment to the success of the organization secured. This latent potential is taken to include, not merely the capacity to acquire and utilize new skills and knowledge, but also a hitherto untapped wealth of ideas about how the organization's operations might be better ordered. These motivational aspects of HRM are bound up with investment in training and development insofar as such investment is a powerful signalling device, which enables employers to confirm to their employees that they are being regarded as important to the company's future success. Obversely, there is little use in firms claiming to their workforces that they have become people-centred organizations that regard their employees as important and valuable, if they subsequently refuse to invest in people. Actions speak louder than words and employees have normally not been slow to notice inconsistencies in the messages emanating from management. Thus a failure to treat expenditure on training as a necessary investment can rapidly undermine the credibility of an organization's attempt to adopt HRM practices.

The role of international comparisons

Above and beyond the abstract logic of this proposition, there is evidence that suggests that training and development activities have an effect upon relative competitiveness and economic performance, at both the aggregate level of the national economy or industrial sector, and at the level of the individual enterprise. In terms of a national policy debate about the need to secure improvement in Britain's training performance, the most important comparative study was 'Competence and Competition', which was undertaken by the Institute of Manpower Studies for the MSC and NEDO (1984). Other, more detailed studies, undertaken by the National Institute of Economic and Social Research (NIESR), have tended to underline the weakness of specific aspects of the British training effort when compared with that of other European countries (see, for example, Prais and Wagner 1981; Prais 1985; Steedman 1987; Prais and Wagner 1988).

Other research undertaken by NIESR, using studies of matched plants in two industries, metal-working and kitchen furniture manufacture, in Britain and West Germany, has pointed to the results that spring from the relatively low levels of training and technical competence that were found in the British plants (Daly, Hitchens, and Wagner 1985; Steedman and Wagner 1987). These deleterious consequences included a slower adoption of new technology, a less adventurous use of it where it was adopted, more frequent breakdowns of machinery and longer periods of down-time as a result. The overall effect was that West German

112

productivity was found to be markedly higher – over 60 per cent greater in both industries. In the case of the kitchen-furniture industry it was further suggested that the low skill levels among the British workforce reinforced, as well as reflected, the decision of British manufacturers to abandon the high-quality end of the market to German producers and to concentrate their efforts at the lower, mass-produced end of the market (Steedman and Wagner 1987: 85–7).

Such international comparisons have formed the major spur to the government and MSC's attempts to improve the quality and quantity of the British training effort, there being in the government's view – to quote a Cabinet minister – 'a clear and well-proven link between training and industrial performance' (*THES* 9 January 1987). International comparisons have also been one of the main forces motivating change on the part of individual companies, particularly those operating in increasingly competitive international markets. The direct relationship between overseas exemplars of good HRM and training practice and change in British enterprises can be seen in the cases of Lucas Industries, Jaguar Cars, and the British Steel Corporation. These organizations, faced with severe overseas competition, in terms of both price and quality, mounted major study exercises to see what lessons about the motivation, development and deployment of workforces could be drawn from best practice abroad. As an executive at Jaguar put it, 'we were up against the wall in the early 1980s and we had people going overseas, particularly to Germany, to see how and why competitors like BMW and Mercedes managed to be successful' (*Self Development* November 1986: 1). One of the chief messages that emerged from the visits to Germany was that German companies appeared to 'have a much greater commitment to training and development' than their British counterparts (*Self Development*, November 1986: 2).

In the case of BSC, senior managers looked in detail at HRD methods in Japanese steel-making companies, as well as drawing comparisons with some of its European competitors, most notably the Belgian firm SIDMAR. Another example of a British company's reflections on Japanese personnel and training policies, based on research undertaken in Japan, is given in Brown and Read (1984).

Changing company training strategies

The result of such comparisons, and of the forces for change generated by increased competitive pressures, has been to convince some senior British managers of the need to lay far greater stress upon the importance of HRD activities within their companies. This step change in the importance attached to training and development activity has been accompanied by the equally vital acknowledge-ment that training needs to be regarded as an investment, rather than as a cost. Thus, according to Peter Nicholson, chairman and chief executive of the Forward Trust, 'Our key investment is in people' (*Self Development* November 1987: 3), or, as Sir Dennis Rooke, the chairman of British Gas put it: 'We must transform the perception of training expenditure so that it is no longer seen simply as a cost, but is regarded as an investment to be evaluated alongside investments in capital equipment' (*Self Development* November 1987: 3).

As well as supportive statements from company chairmen, there are now a number of companies operating in the UK, usually large employers, that appear to have progressed some way towards successfully developing training and HRD systems that are integrated into wider business planning and strategy. It is these companies that tend to be cited as the leaders of the HRM movement in Britain. Among them can be numbered firms such as Jaguar Cars, Lucas Industries, and ICL. They join a select band of companies, such as IBM, Hewlett Packard, and Marks and Spencer, who have a long-standing commitment to the type of employment practices and strategic consideration of personnel issues that are now styled as constituting HRM.

There is not space to undertake here a detailed analysis of the changes that have been introduced within many of these companies, but even a brief description of developments indicates the basic thrust of HRM in practice, and, in so doing, underlines the centrality of the role afforded to training and development within such changes. The companies cited below have by no means followed a single, uniform pattern of development, but in most cases there are common strands running through the initiatives that they have instituted.

To begin with, the integration of training and development into wider business planning has been seen as crucial. Instead of being activities peripheral to the achievement of corporate objectives, the human resources of the organization are seen as a vital factor in corporate planning, and training and development as able to make an important contribution to the achievement of business objectives. Allied to this has been the clear requirement that such integration, and the heightened profile for HRD activities that goes with it, should command the participation and support of the most senior levels of management (Beattie 1987; Bowen 1987: 10; Brady 1987: 5–6; Hendry and Pettigrew 1987: 30). Certainly in companies such as Jaguar Cars, British Airways, and British Steel, the message that training and development were to be treated as important has been passed down very firmly from board level.

Apart from a top-down approach, the aim has been to create an integrated and coherent package of complementary measures aimed at altering many aspects of the employment relationship. These include greatly enhanced efforts in the area of corporate manpower planning and forecasting (Beattie 1987), an area in which British companies have in the past generally tended to be particularly weak. Within this area, the issue of succession planning has assumed considerable importance, particularly in those organizations which, because of large-scale redundancies and recruitment freezes in the past, now find themselves faced with significant age bulges in key sections of their workforces.

Hand in hand with improved manpower planning have come various attempts to upgrade the quality of those being recruited. As one chief executive put it, 'a company is only as good as its personnel – so it's vital to choose and train the best' (Upton 1987: 29). This outlook has found expression in moves towards the creation of more systematized, sophisticated and objective systems of selection and recruitment (Ballin 1986: 25–6). These have, for example, included greater interest in the use of psychometric testing, more concerted efforts to specify the skills, competences, qualifications and qualities being sought from applicants, and the increasing use of assessment centres.

Companies' efforts to improve the quality and suitability of those they recruit, has in turn given an added impetus to the need to forge closer links with educational institutions at all levels within the education system (Ballin 1986: 26). Improved contact on a continuing basis with local schools, sixth-form colleges, and further education colleges is being seen as an important first stage in the process of shaping and channelling the job choices of prospective young entrants into the local labour markets in which the companies operate. At the level of graduate recruitment, the renewed emphasis upon the crucial importance of managerial expertise as a corporate resource has led to considerable efforts being directed into targeted links with selected higher-education institutions. Demographic trends, in the shape of a major decline in the number of young people coming onto the job market in the first half of the 1990s, means that the priority afforded to industry/education liaison activity is likely to increase still further.

Another common factor among many of the firms that have been identified as having adopted HRM policies, has been moves to increase the use of formal performance and/or training-needs appraisal procedures (Upton 1987: 28; Hendry and Pettigrew 1987: 31–2). In one or two cases, the use of a training-needs appraisal system has been extended downwards to cover the entire shop-floor workforce.

Efforts to upgrade the skills base of the managerial workforce have also usually been high on the agenda of the leading HRM practitioners. That this should be the case is hardly surprising, given the relatively low qualification levels of many British managers and the traditionally poor record of most UK companies in the area of management training and development (an issue to which we will be returning below). Such efforts have often been made in conjunction with measures to enhance career planning and introduce greater use of job rotation and lateral transfers.

On the shop floor there have been a large number of changes, not least in terms of the introduction of training in support of greater functional flexibility. This has frequently meant multi-skilling for craft workers, as well as equipping production operatives with the skills necessary to undertake routine maintenance on the plant that is in their charge. Other developments have included moves to systematize and upgrade the provision and recording of hitherto informal on-the-job training. Another measure, and one that has attracted considerable interest, has been the efforts that have gone into the provision of enhanced opportunities for self-development, most notably through investment in computer-based open-learning systems. Probably the best-known example of this has been Jaguar Cars

(Simpson 1986; Richards 1986), but similar developments can be found in Lucas Industries, the Rover Group, BSC, and a number of other companies.

Increased competition has led some organizations to adopt a strategy of attempting to compete in terms of quality rather than price, and in such cases training has been closely associated with attempts to improve product quality. In manufacturing this has meant not just the introduction of quality circles and statistical process control (SPC) methods, but also various initiatives to build a quality approach into the production process through major improvements in the motivation and competence of the workforce at all levels. One example of this has been within British Steel, which is introducing a package of measures, originally promoted under the title of total quality performance (TQP), aimed at securing competitive advantage through a higher-quality product. The most important training element within TQP has been the decision to identify required standards of competence for every level of activity, and to undertake training and development needs assessments of the corporation's entire workforce against these criteria.

In the services sector the drive for quality has most often been seen in attempts to improve the levels of customer care or customer service being offered. British Airways and British Rail are the two perhaps best-known examples, but there are many others, not least in retailing (Upton 1987: 26).

This extensive range of activities has normally been accompanied by major financial investment in the area of training and development. This has meant both increased injections of capital, to finance items such as new open-learning centres, and also rises in the general level of recurrent spending on training.

In nearly all the published case studies of companies that have embarked upon such changes, training and development have been seen as an integral part of wider strategies aimed at the creation of new working practices and a better motivated, more self-reliant workforce (Ballin 1986: 24). Thus, for example, it is often hard to draw firm lines between new methods of training and new forms of communication. Team briefings are an example of management attempting to improve communications with their employees, but they can also be used as a training opportunity and as a means of reinforcing the message of team-training exercises. Frequently, many of the wider changes in areas like communications and management structures have carried with them major requirements for training and re-training. Finally, there has been a general acknowledgement that training has acted as an important lever in promoting cultural change within those companies that have been attempting to upgrade the importance attached to the workforce's contribution to organizational success.

The place of training in the HRM literature

However, despite the centrality of training to the practice of HRM, its place within the HRM debate has not always been paramount. A significant proportion of the literature, whether prescriptive or analytical, has been concerned, either explicitly or implicitly, with addressing the issue of whether HRM is different from traditional personnel, and, if it is different, in what ways this difference is made manifest. This has been an important debate, though one which might have been less diffuse had all participants drawn tighter definitions of what they meant by the term HRM from the outset.

Perhaps more seriously, in some of the prescriptive, how-to-do-it literature, training and development is hardly placed centre-stage. To take two examples, Armstrong (1988), and Pigors, Myers, and Malm (1973), each devote more space to the issues of management leadership and organizational redesign. Whether this balance of emphasis is correct is open to question. It may not accurately reflect the strategy and priorities of leading HRM practitioners, and it can be argued that focusing on the decisive role of management leadership is not easily reconciled with HRM's implicit concept of tapping the knowledge, expertise, and ideas of the workforce at large. This is particularly the case when one considers the somewhat more formally structured approach adopted overseas towards employee involvement, not least in the area of decision making about training. It should be remembered that it is often training systems containing an element of co-determination, such as that in Germany, that have been identified as examples of good practice that should inform British employers and policy makers. On a somewhat different tack, the prescriptive value of the notion of management leadership may well prove to be something of a blind alley, in that the exercise of leadership is such a subjective activity and one that is extremely ill-defined, not least by managers themselves (Hirsh and Bevan 1988).

Problem areas in the field of training and development

There are, however, more important problems with the centrality of training to HRM than a simple mis-focusing on the part of some of the prescriptive literature. Despite the high-profile examples of good practice on the part of a number of large companies, a great deal of evidence suggests that at aggregate level the broad mass of British employers may not yet have accepted the vital importance of training and development activities and acted accordingly. Given the centrality of training to the success of meaningful forms of HRM, it seems likely that if this evidence is correct it has serious implications for the widespread adoption of HRM in this country.

To begin with, such statistics as are available indicate generally low average per capita spending on training and development by British companies. An MSC-sponsored survey found that, on average, employers were spending only £200 per employee per annum on training, which represented 0.15 per cent of company turnover (MSC 1985). No less than 24 per cent of the establishments surveyed had provided no training of any kind in the previous 12 months, and 69 per cent of employees had received no training during this period (MSC 1985: 23). By contrast, it has been alleged that leading employers in West Germany, Japan, and the USA spend up to 3 per cent of their turnover on training and development, and that employees in these countries tend to be trained to far higher levels than their counterparts in the UK (NEDO/MSC 1984). A report prepared in 1985 by Coopers and Lybrand Associates for the MSC and NEDO on British companies' attitudes towards training concluded that:

> few employers think training sufficiently central to their business for it to be a main component in their corporate strategy; the great majority did not see it as an issue of major importance . . . training [was] rarely seen as an investment but either as an overhead which would be cut when profits are under pressure or as something forced on the company as a reaction to other developments.
>
> (Coopers and Lybrand 1985: 4)

Beyond the apparently comparatively low priority afforded to training activity, there are a number of specific areas within the field of British training and development that it can be suggested are likely to prove particularly problematic with regard to the spread of HRM policies and practices. A number of the most important of these problem areas are discussed below.

The very clear example of a potential barrier to the take-up of HRM are current levels of management education and training in the UK. Recent research (Mangham and Silvers 1986; Handy 1987; Constable and McCormick 1987) has served to underline the extreme poverty of British practice in this area, with levels of education and training that are very poor by international standards. Mangham and Silvers point out that 'over half of all UK companies appear to make no formal provision for the training of their managers', and that in companies employing more than 1,000 people fewer than one in ten senior managers received any training (1986: 1). Handy cites another survey which indicated that 36 per cent of middle managers had received no management training since starting work (1987: 10), and goes on to suggest that 'management training in Britain is too little, too late, for too few' (1987: 11). If HRM means something, one might at the least expect a significant investment in the managerial segment of workforce, but on current evidence this would appear not to be generally the case in much of British industry and commerce.

In the wake of the Handy Report there is currently a flurry of activity in this area, mainly centred on the creation of the Charter Group of two hundred leading companies who are to take the lead in promoting and implementing good practice in management education, training, and development. New qualifications are proposed and a code of practice has been launched. As yet it is too early to judge to what degree these efforts will have any significant impact upon the problem of an under-educated and under-trained managerial workforce, but it must be said that the difficulties experienced by the Charter Group in attempting to agree a firm commitment to an entitlement to a specific number of days off-the-job management training, are not particularly encouraging. Indeed, the fact that the fairly rudimentary provisions that make up the code of practice have been hailed as a landmark in British management education and training is a reflection on the paucity of what has gone before.

Moreover, given the scale of the backlog of training needs among the existing managerial workforce, even the most dramatic improvement in provision will take a considerable length of time to achieve widespread effects. Or, to put the problem another way, John Banham, the director-general of the CBI, admits that current training levels among British management represent 'a relatively blank sheet with which to start to prepare the managers we will need for the 1990s and beyond' (*Personnel Management* December, 1987: 8). The danger is that large areas of the sheet will continue to remain unmarked by progress.

Low levels of management training and development have other, less direct, implications for the widespread adoption of HRM. For, in the light of the limited training opportunities available to management, it is perhaps not altogether surprising that managers have in their turn often tended to regard a lack of training on the part of their workforce as something that does not constitute a serious problem. For example, Steedman and Wagner's comparative study of matched manufacturing plants in the British and West German kitchen furniture industry (1987), revealed worrying assumptions about training on the part of the British employers that contrasted markedly with those of their West German counterparts. Despite the fact that only about 10 per cent of the British workforce held any kind of vocational qualification, as against the 90 per cent of the West German workforce who had passed through a three-year period of craft training (1987: 91–2), British managers appeared unconcerned at the disparity. They were, moreover, apparently willing to accept the limitations that were being imposed by low skill levels upon productivity, product innovation and the ability to adopt and utilize new technology.

The reaction of many companies, particularly in the retail sector, to the introduction of the more advanced, two-year Youth Training Scheme, appeared symptomatic of broadly similar attitudes to the need for and value of extended periods of training for young-people employees (Pointing 1986). The MSC's announcement of the decision to extend the duration of YTS from one year to two was greeted with widespread concern on the part of companies that they would be unable to 'fill out' the training to occupy two years (Pointing 1986). These views existed despite the fact that under the widely respected West German dual system of apprenticeships, the vast majority of young entrants to the labour market undergo a 3-year period of training, not only in manufacturing companies, but also in the retail and commercial sectors.

On a wider front, firms' reactions to YTS give even greater cause for concern. The scheme has been hailed as the most important development in British vocational education and training since the 1944 Education Act, and the foundation upon which subsequent improvements in upgrading the quality of the adult workforce can be built (Manpower Services Commission, 1988: 15). Despite these expectations on the part of government and policy makers, the majority of employers are still not participating in YTS (Leadbeater 1987), and many of those who do still choose to see it as a measure aimed at the young unemployed, rather than as a period of foundation training for all their young employees. The result is that large numbers of YTS trainees leave the scheme to take up a job that carries with it no opportunities for training. The fact that such attitudes towards YTS are held by a significant proportion of British management, it can be argued, reflects a series of limiting assumptions on their part about the levels of knowledge and skill that are required and used by their employees. These assumptions stand in the way of a recognition of the importance of investing in people.

Underlying factors that impede the widespread adoption of HRM

The examples cited above of barriers to the spread of improved training and development, and thereby the spread of successful HRM policies, raise questions about the extent to which HRM is likely to extend beyond what is at present a fairly select group of companies. At another level, these barriers are themselves merely symptomatic of a number of underlying structural factors that inhibit British employers from placing greater emphasis upon the importance of the people they employ, particularly in the area of training. A large number of deep-seated structural explanations have been advanced to explain Britain's poor performance in training and development, and this chapter is not the place to undertake a thoroughgoing exploration of such complex issues. Nevertheless, there is some value in outlining a number that are particularly germane to the adoption or otherwise of HRM policies.

One that has already been touched upon is the variety of other strategies for survival and growth that are available to British employers. It seems reasonable to expect that companies will, at least partly, tailor their approaches to the management of the people they employ on the basis of the product markets in which they compete. For some companies operating in the UK this has meant efforts to compete through mass-volume production and the sale of standardized product lines. The result in terms of skill requirements and people management techniques tends to be a mass of relatively lowly skilled operatives, who are managed along more or less Taylorite lines. Examples of those following this type of route would include sectors as diverse as the fast-food chains and parts of the clothing and footwear industry. Companies operating in this way are unlikely to find the full-blown HRM model relevant to their perceived needs.

The growth of the British multi-national, particularly in the wake of the end to exchange-control regulations, has meant the opening up of new avenues for growth. The figures on overseas acquisitions and investment contained in many British company annual reports indicates that there has been a significant move to shift productive capacity and investment overseas. One indicator of the scale of this activity is the fact that in 1987 British companies spent $31.7 billion on acquisitions in the USA (Rodgers and Tran 1988). The result has in some cases been to effectively marginalize the importance of the British component of the companies' manufacturing operations. In such circumstances it is open to question whether these companies are going to bother to invest heavily in re-skilling their UK workforces, when, through overseas acquisition, they can buy new workforces pre-trained.

Another strategy, and one that has commonly been adopted by some large British companies, has been growth and profitability through a cycle of takeovers, followed by divestment of those parts of the new company that no longer fit the approved product mix, or which are failing to turn in adequate levels of profit in the short term. The food industry is a sector in which such practices have been rife in recent years. It can be argued that companies that follow this path are likely to lack the long-term commitment to their subsidiaries that is a prerequisite to securing a reasonable return from any heavy investment in training and re-training. In this connection it is noticeable that most of the firms cited as leading examples of HRM in Britain tend to be single or closely related product companies, rather than large conglomerates or holding companies.

The counter-pressures against investing in people referred to above are compounded by other factors. For, despite the CBI's recent report on relations between industry and the City, the overwhelming balance of evidence suggests that the relative absence in Britain of the type of long-term relationship that exists between banks, stockholders, and company managements in West Germany and Japan,does create damaging pressure that forces companies to adopt a short-term view of the trade-off between investment and profit. These difficulties are compounded by stockmarket and takeover pressures, which materially affect industry's ability to invest in long-term projects, such as training and research and development, at the expense of short-term profit margins (Dore 1985; Walker 1985; Parker 1986; Fifield 1987).

These short-term financial pressures assume a still greater significance in the UK because of the dominance of financial management and accounting systems that militate against people-centred investment (Hayes and Garvin 1988; Allen 1985; Kaplan 1985; Benjamin and Benson 1986). As Jonathan Fox, the director for personnel and corporate affairs at Norsk Hydro, pointed out in a recent article, such systems hinder attempts to change employment practices:

we have not helped this drive towards innovation by the way we assess our business performance; for if we examine the core of our decision-making process it is based on an accounting system which counts the cost of what we do and ignores the consequences of what we fail to do. We need to know more about the cost of not doing things. The absence of initiative, poor teamwork, under-utilisation of people's talents, quality, safety, are not part of the financial model.

(1988: 38)

Added to these difficulties is Britain's persistent failure to evolve and maintain a coherent national system of vocational education and training. In a situation where there is no statutory requirement to train, a policy of recruiting skilled labour rather than developing it internally is an economically rational strategy for individual companies. The threat of seeing skilled labour 'poached' is one that makes it all the harder for those companies that do train to treat training expenditure as an investment.

A final major underlying impediment to the spread of HRM remains to be discussed; that relating to the ability and willingness of many British managers to banish informality in personnel practices. As has been pointed out, the whole tenor of HRM suggests rigour, and a systematic and coherent approach towards managing and developing the productive capacity of the workforce. Unfortunately it can be argued that many of the basic processes and procedures that ought to underpin HRM simply do not have widespread currency among British employers, and often operate very patchily even within organizations that are attempting to formalize their employment management systems.

In this context, the example of recruitment and selection is an instructive one. If HRM indicates the widespread adoption of a more people-centred approach to organizational management, then it might reasonably be expected that significant effort would be made towards obtaining the right basic material, in the form of a workforce endowed with the appropriate qualities, skills, knowledge, and potential for future training. The selection and recruitment of workers best suited to meeting the needs of the organization ought to form a core activity upon which most other HRM policies geared towards development and motivation could be built.

In fact much of the evidence that is available tends to indicate that there are real problems in this crucial area of personnel management activity. In many organizations, recruitment and selection are apparently conducted in a haphazard and informal fashion, a circumstance which appears to reflect the enormous strength of resistance that exists towards any attempt to institute more thorough, formalized and objective systems. In the past, studies of the recruitment process have pointed to the entrenched traditions of informality (Blackburn and Mann 1979; Courtney and Hedges 1977). Wood, in a further study of recruitment practices (1986b: 11) has suggested that,

> the new human resource management is concerned to develop the conditions in which new ideas and tacit and diagnostic skills can flourish. This implies far more intensive selection, aimed at gauging both an ability and commitment to harness and develop working knowledge in order constantly to improve performance than appeared to be the norm from the study reported in this article.

Collinson's study (1988) of equal opportunities practices in the recruitment systems in a number of sectors illustrates how deep-seated are the difficulties that face such developments. This research covered a wide variety of jobs, ranging from semi-skilled manual and clerical posts to managerial vacancies in some sixty-four workplaces. The companies in which his investigations were conducted were usually large, including national clearing banks, insurance companies, hi-tech companies, food manufacturing, and the mail-order business. It seems not unreasonable to suggest that some of these organizations, particularly among the banks and insurance companies, would have identified themselves as practitioners of HRM policies.

The picture painted by the case studies however, is one of informal arrangements, often blatant sexual discrimination, and the use of vague and subjective selection criteria, with the result that employees were taken into employment or promoted on grounds that had little or nothing to do with ability or suitability. In two cases (Collinson 1988: 63–69) informal selection processes allowed candidates who were the least well-qualified, or who had scored lowest on the selection tests, to be selected over the heads of better qualified and apparently more able candidates. The earlier study by Wood (1986b) found extensive evidence of similar informal practices.

Collinson attributes the prevalence of these informal arrangements to the desire on the part of line managers for autonomy, and the weakness of many personnel departments (1988: 3–4). This weakness was reflected in an inability to implement policies, either due to remoteness from operational levels in the organization, or through subordination to line managers (1988: 4). More depressingly still, the study revealed that 'even many personnel managers had not been trained in selection and interviewing methods' (1988: 3).

If the organizations under study had been small businesses, in unprofitable or declining sectors of the economy, the results might have raised fewer problems for anyone suggesting a widespread adoption of HRM policies and practices by British employers. As it is, of the forty-five companies involved, only three employed fewer than 1,000 people in the UK, and all but two maintained corporate personnel or HRM departments, and had formalized recruitment and selection policies (Collinson 1987: 32). In the event these policies were not being implemented, or were being subverted.

This evidence begs a number of questions about the likely willingness of some managers to adapt their working practices to meet the demands HRM poses. One of the central weaknesses in much of the literature on HRM is that it takes little account of the possibility that rational self-interest on the part of some managers might impede the adoption of the measures it prescribes. In reality, there are few forms of change that do not constitute a threat to someone, and in this respect HRM is no exception.

This threat takes a number of forms. The first is the problem of managing a more self-reliant workforce of the sort that HRM aims to create. Traditional styles of management, based on authoritarian, non-participatory tenets are unlikely to sit easily alongside demands to communicate with and to involve employees, particularly in circumstances where the management workforce is itself ill-equipped to meet the challenge. Bearing in mind the education and training of British managers, it is open to question how genuine would be their welcome for a better-educated, better-trained, more self-reliant and questioning workforce.

British industrial-relations history adds to this problem with a system whose heritage of management/workforce relationships has normally centred on the achievement of more or less passive compliance on the part of the workforce to management's instructions, rather than on securing their active commitment to shared goals. It seems not unreasonable to suggest that many managers who have grown up within the context of such a system are unlikely to be entirely happy at the thought of abandoning familiar tried and trusted methods.

At another level, HRM threatens to circumscribe the degree of freedom of action afforded to line managers by demanding a more uniform, systematized and implicitly meritocratic approach to the implementation of company personnel policies. In this respect it is possible to draw some parallels between the prescriptions offered by the proponents of HRM, and the recommendations of the 1968 Royal Commission on Industrial Relations. At first sight these two might appear quite dissimilar, but their juxtaposition is not entirely fanciful. A common link is provided by their calls for greater formalization and regularization of both personnel procedures and the conduct of collective bargaining. The Donovan Commission wanted to see an end to informal bargaining arrangements, and suggested a reform of collective bargaining structures, greater use of formalized written agreements, and the development of corporate industrial relations strategies. HRM, in a similar way, lays stress upon the need for a strategic formulation of HRM strategies at corporate level, and on the value of a thorough systematization, at all levels of management, of previously informal, loosely-linked personnel policies and practices. Paradoxically, HRM is calling for this at a time when British Industry is witnessing a greater devolution of decision-making power to line managers, autonomy of smaller units within larger businesses through the creation of profit centres, and new systems of financial control.

Industrial relations research after Donovan identified a number of underlying forces that tend to sustain informality in bargaining relationships and in the exercise of managerial control of industrial relations (see for example Terry 1977; and Armstrong and Goodman 1979). In much the same way, it is possible to identify similar forces that are likely to militate against the adoption of more formalized personnel practices in many British companies.

As Lee and Piper (1987: 7) point out, the prescriptive literature on HRM and personnel tends to assume the actions of 'rational people operating within efficient technical systems'. As we have seen from Collinson's (1988) study of recruitment practices discussed above, this is often not the case. Systems may exist, but they are open to manipulation and distortion by those who operate them. Managers as individuals have a number of goals, only some of which are shared with those of the organization that employs them. These unofficial goals, such as maintaining standing with one's subordinates and avoiding unnecessary conflict, are often realized through the discretion which informality imparts to the manager in the exercise of his or her decision making. Thus the ability to recruit and promote those who do not pose a threat and who conform to one's own stereotypes, and the possession of the organizational leeway to do favours for selected employees, social peers, friends, and relatives, are arguably important to many managers.

None of this sits very well with the sorts of restraints imposed by HRM's demands for meritocratic objectivity in management decision making as it affects employees.

Conclusion

This last point brings us back to the crucial issue of how genuine much of the interest in HRM really is, and the degree to which this apparent enthusiasm is likely to be translated into action. At present, genuine HRM policies, as defined in this chapter, appear to be confined to a relatively limited group of large companies (Coopers and Lybrand 1985: 9). They are often ones chiefly competing in international markets, in which it is harder to ignore the deficiencies caused by Britain's traditionally low levels of education and training.

This chapter has argued that training and development are activities central to the reality of anything that can meaningfully be termed human resource management. Indeed, it can be suggested that training effort is one useful litmus test of the reality of the adoption of HRM/HRD policies within British firms. If the training and development of its employees is not afforded high priority, if training is not seen as a vital component in the realization of business plans, then it is hard to accept that such a company has committed itself to HRM.

Unfortunately, as has been outlined above, there are a number of deep-seated factors that appear to militate against significant improvements in the area of training and investment in people. These in turn have implications for the widespread adoption of HRM policies. In view of the importance of many of these barriers to change, it is perhaps surprising that, at least to date, they have not been addressed in detail by much of the literature on HRM. Certainly many of them require further investigation, and it would seem important that they constitute part of any future research agenda.

On the wide issue of the long-term significance of HRM in Britain, it is still too early to reach any final judgement. To date, the number of companies in which it is practised is limited. A number of important potential obstacles to its progress have been identified. There is a danger that progress will, to echo the words of the Handy Report, be a case of too little, too late, for too few. If this proves to be the case, the result will not only be to further widen the qualitative disparity between best and worst personnel practice among British employers, but also to heighten the contrast discussed earlier in this chapter between the employment strategies of most British companies and those of their overseas competitors. In a world where international competitive advantage is increasingly likely to turn upon the skills, knowledge and commitment of an enterprise's employees (Cassels 1985: 439), the economic consequences of such an eventuality are painful to contemplate.

Chapter eight

Financial participation

Tom Schuller

Introduction

Two interrelated aspects of the debate on the nature and character of HRM form the focus of this chapter, which deals with the one dimension of employee participation. First is the notion of a shift to a managerial approach which seeks to elicit commitment rather than to ensure compliance. One of the more commonly stated arguments in favour of employee participation – of whatever kind – is that it will enhance commitment; if the employees are directly or indirectly involved in company affairs, at whatever level, they will be more committed to the effective implementation of decisions than if such decisions are unilaterally imposed. More generally, and leaving aside the arguments of principle, their effort and enthusiasm will be greater, with consequent benefits for efficiency. The second aspect is the attention paid to changing the nature of the relationship between management and employees by focusing on employees as individuals rather than dealing with them collectively. In some instances the promotion of this individual focus may be deliberately intended to undermine more collective forms of employee identity, notably trade unions; in others it is a matter of setting up parallel machinery which may or may not complement existing machinery and procedures for collective bargaining. This too has been a long-running theme in the debate on participation.

The chapter picks up these two themes in the following way. Its focus is on the issue of 'financial participation'. This term has a variety of meanings. The most common association is with profit-sharing, but to identify financial participation with profit-sharing alone is already to foreclose discussion of alternative conceptions. I shall argue that in a review of HRM it is worthwhile taking one step back and considering a broader range of forms of financial participation. Alongside profit-sharing I shall use as an example employee representation in the management of pension funds. This kind of participation is indirect, and it is concerned with a form of ownership that is at least partially collective. It therefore differs in two respects from profit-sharing schemes, which are designed to give individual employees direct shareholdings in the companies in which they are employed. By contrasting the two approaches we can begin to get some purchase on how to analyse critically this aspect of HRM, and to set it in relation to other aspects.

Participation over the decade

It was only just over ten years ago that the Bullock report on industrial democracy was published (Bullock 1977). Participation was firmly identified in the public – and to a lesser extent in the managerial – eye with representation at board level. I shall not review the report's proposals, except to note three features relevant to the changed employment context. Firstly, the report dealt only with large companies, those with over 2,000 employees. Secondly, the proposals were for worker directors to be elected through trade-union channels – the so-called single-channel system. Other forms and levels of participation did not fall within the remit of the committee. Thirdly, the proposals prompted a massive and hostile response from most employers, with members of the committee facing audiences of up to 1,000 managers as they sought to disseminate the report up and down the country; nevertheless, it is to be remembered that although the three employer members of the committee signed a minority report, they did not dissent from the principle that there should be employee representation at board level. Such was the nature of the economic circumstances of the time that major industrialists were willing to concede a principle that had been fiercely resisted up to then. But the extent of that commitment was revealed by the burying of the proposals following the change of government in 1979 (Schuller 1985).

Over the decade since the report's publication the ground has shifted dramatically. The nature of this shift is very familiar: a change of political administration, with a radical Conservative government committed to economic restructuring and reducing the influence of trade unions; a massive growth in unemployment; a major shift in the pattern of employment, including a decline in manufacturing, a growth in services and a rise in part-time and peripheral employment; an emphasis on breaking down productive units into smaller cost centres; and a shift in the pattern of ownership, including a wave of mergers and takeovers and a large-scale programme of privatization. Outside the area of paid employment there has been a determined thrust to attack collective forms of welfare and to promote the ideology of individualism. 'Industrial democracy' is hardly heard of as a term in the debate on how organizations should be managed; instead the talk is of employee communication and a range of other approaches such as briefing groups, quality circles and the like. It is in this context that financial participation has assumed a new prominence.

Individual and collective participation

One way of bringing the diverse developments that can be grouped under the heading of 'financial participation' into relationship with each other is to map them out on a spectrum running from the individual to the collective. Table 8.1

sets out a simple spectrum. At one end, and with only a very tenuous connection with participation, we have personal equity plans and the privatization programme. I have included these primarily as an index of the government's efforts to promote a shareholding democracy, epitomized by the Chancellor of the Exchequer's stated wish to see the aggregate number of shareholders overtake the number of trade unionists in the country, a symbolic cross-over point where individualism takes over from collective organization.

Table 8.1 Forms of financial participation

Financial participation	Ownership
Privatization	Individual
Personal equity plans	
Profit-related pay	
Profit-sharing:	
APS	
SAYE	
Share option schemes	
ESOPs	
Workers' cooperatives	
Management buy-outs	
Pension fund participation	Collective
Wage-earner funds	

Secondly, there is profit-related pay, an attempt to use fiscal incentives to link pay levels more closely to economic performance. So far, this initiative has signally failed to take off. In October 1987 there were 146 profit-related pay schemes registered with the Inland Revenue, with a further 97 applications awaiting approval. This is a minimal outcome from a total of some 26,000 requests for guidelines following the launch of the scheme. An Incomes Data Services survey of 50 companies that had expressed a strong interest in 1987 showed that only 2 had actually proceeded to register. The problems identified as discouraging further progress were the difficulty of using profit as an indicator of company performance, the complexity of the scheme and – particularly relevant to our consideration of HRM – the lack of any evidence that such schemes create any long-term commitment to the company (IDS 1988a).

We come now to initiatives which affect the pattern of ownership. At the individual end are the various types of profit-sharing scheme: approved profit-sharing (APS), SAYE schemes, and discretionary share-option schemes. I shall return to these shortly. ESOPs, or Employee Stock Ownership schemes, are a largely American phenomenon. The underlying idea has been around for many years, but impetus has been given recently by a number of legislative initiatives promoted by Senator Russell Long. The basic format of an ESOP is that a company places stock into a trust on behalf of its employees, allocating the stock to individuals according to salary or some other formula. The stock is held on the employee's behalf until he or she leaves the company or retires. Russell (1985) reviews the evidence on the effect of ESOPs and concludes that they:

> do appear to promote more harmonious relations between labor and capital . . . . In most cases, however, they appear to bring about only a cosmetic change . . . rather than a structural one. One sign of the largely symbolic nature of these programs is the heavy stress that is often placed on the way these plans are communicated to workers. Apparently, if workers are not frequently reminded by management of the existence of these plans, the danger is that they might easily forget about them, and the plans will have no effect (p. 26).

Other researchers attribute a rather more substantial effect to the schemes, but cautiously so (Klein and Rosen 1986).

Two other instances of ownership patterns which depart from the traditional forms are management buy-outs and worker cooperatives. Since 1980 there have been some 1,720 buyouts, of which 100 had had a value of more than £10 million, with a value of £4.7 billion (McRae 1988). The cooperative movement has continued to grow, despite an adverse overall economic climate, and has diversified out of its stereotypical business areas of wholefoods and printing works. Any overall review of financial participation should take such trends into account; here however we are concentrating on the way financial participation fits into a supposed general strategy of HRM, which makes these instances somewhat peripheral.

A final example of financial participation, and one that is closer to our theme, is that of the Swedish wage-earners funds, which finally came into existence in 1984, after a prolonged and painful gestation period (Gill 1984). The funds are financed by a tax on profits above a certain level for large firms and a payroll contribution from small employers. There is majority employee representation on the management boards of the funds. Where the local trade union so requests a fund is obliged to transfer 50 per cent of its voting rights to it, thus, in principle, establishing a link between ownership and control at the two different levels. The Swedish initiative is clearly of great potential interest, but evidence on its impact is so far very slim, both as regards investment patterns and the use of influence within companies.

I turn now to the two principal instances of financial participation: profit-sharing and participation in the management of pension schemes. I have not selected these merely because they constitute different forms of financial participation. Both have a degree of history; more significantly, they derive from attempts to secure greater employee commitment to the organization, albeit in rather different ways.

Profit-sharing

Profit-sharing has a long history in the UK, reaching well back into the last century (see, for example, Church 1971). Over the last decade there has been a renewed upsurge in the incidence of non-cash-based profit-sharing schemes, fuelled mainly by the fiscal incentives provided by successive pieces of legislation: the 1978 Finance Act (introduced by the Labour administration as part of its electoral pact with the Liberal party) which encouraged approved profit-sharing or APS; the 1980 Finance Act, promoting save-as-you-earn share-option schemes; and the 1984 Finance Act which introduced discretionary share-option schemes. The first two are required to be made available to all full-time employees with at least five years' service; discretionary schemes are designed to benefit managers, and are sometimes known as executive share option schemes. (Details of the three schemes are listed below.)

- *Approved profit-sharing (APS) schemes (1978 Finance Act)*
  Profit-sharing schemes set up under the 1978 Finance Act involve the distribution to employees of shares, free of charge. Under a 1978 scheme approved for tax purposes by the Inland Revenue the company sets up a trust and periodically pays money to the trustees, who use it to buy shares in the company; these are allocated to individual employees and held by the trustees on the employees' behalf.
  An employee is not liable to income tax on the value of the shares allocated to him or her providing they are not sold for at least five years (reduced from seven years in 1985). Shares must be held in trust for the first two years; shares sold between two and five years from allocation attract income tax on a percentage of their value. A 1978 APS scheme must be open to all full-time employees who have been with the company for at least five years. The limit on the value of shares that may be allocated to any one employee in a given tax year has been increased a number of times; it currently stands at £1,250 or, if greater, 10 per cent of the employee's salary, up to a maximum of £5,000.

- *SAYE schemes (1980 Finance Act)*
  Savings-related share option schemes set up under the 1980 Finance Act involve the granting to employees of options over shares. Under an approved 1980 scheme companies give their employees options to buy shares at a set date in the future at a special price fixed at the outset – which must not be less than 90 per cent of the value of the shares at the time the option is granted.
  Like the 1978 schemes, an approved SAYE scheme must be open to all full-time employees of five years' standing. The shares under the option are bought with money saved under a special SAYE contract over a period of five or seven years, the maximum contribution being £100 a month. Employees are not liable to income tax on any gain they make through

exercising their option and acquiring shares at less than market value. Employees do not have to exercise their options; if for example the market value of the shares has fallen below the option price at the end of the fixed period, they may simply take the proceeds of their SAYE contract plus bonus tax free, in the usual way.

- *Discretionary share option schemes (1984 Finance Act)*
  As with SAYE schemes, share option schemes set up under the 1984 Finance Act involve the granting of options over shares, any gain realized when the option is exercised being normally free of income tax. But unlike the 1980 schemes, they are not linked to SAYE contracts and there is no obligation on the company to include all employees; options may be granted to all or any of its employees at the company's discretion. The limit on the value of shares over which an individual may hold options at any one time is set at four times his annual salary or, if greater, £100,000.

There is a massive literature on profit-sharing, some of it essentially proselytizing (e.g. Bell and Hanson 1984), others more analytical (e.g. Bradley and Gelb 1986). I shall not attempt to review the evidence generally, but use two recent studies to illustrate points relevant to the discussion in hand, that is the relationship between initiatives in the field of financial participation and broader human resource and corporate strategies.

The most substantial recent research has been carried out jointly by the Department of Employment and UWIST (Smith 1986; Poole 1988). Short telephone interviews were carried out with over 1,000 companies, of whom 303 were further researched by means of an interview with the company secretary or finance director. Twenty-one per cent of those contacted had some kind of all-employee scheme (including cash-based); a further 9 per cent had a discretionary scheme only. What evidence did the DE/UWIST survey produce that is of relevance to our discussion of HRM? First, the most commonly cited reason for the introduction of a scheme was 'to make employees feel they are part of the company', followed closely by 'to increase employees' sense of commitment to the company' and 'making employees more profit conscious'. Lowest of the declared aims came 'to help hold down wage claims'. When it came to an evaluation, companies generally rated the schemes successful in achieving these objectives. However it is notable that the highest rating for success was given to the tax efficiency of profit-sharing as a way of rewarding employees.

The survey investigated the styles of industrial relations pursued in the companies with profit-sharing schemes, and the existence of other forms of participation. It reports a stronger association with consultative than with paternalist styles of industrial relations management, and a clear relationship between profit-sharing and other forms of employee involvement, notably joint consultation. Profit-sharing is more likely to occur in firms where decisions on the introduction of new technology, the reduction or increase of the workforce and manning levels are made jointly. However this association does not extend into decision-making on other financial issues such as capital investment.

On the relationship between profit-sharing and collective representation, the survey reveals an association between the presence of trade unions in a company and the likelihood of a profit-sharing scheme being adopted. However, the presence of a staff association was a better predictor, and once the results had been standardized for size the relationship between union presence and profit-sharing becomes insignificant. It is predominantly larger companies, and especially those in the growth sectors of the economy, where profit-sharing has been introduced. These are the companies more likely to be involved in new technologies, and consequently to be paying attention to training and other aspects of HRM. All this was broadly to be expected. To an extent, therefore, it is possible that the introduction of profit-sharing forms part of a wider managerial approach. On the other hand it is clear that fiscal incentives have played a major part in the growth of such schemes, so that their innate attractiveness to management and their standing as an integral part of a coordinated strategy are difficult to gauge.

The DE/UWIST is unambiguous in its evidence on a further aspect of profit-sharing which has a bearing on their character as a managerial device. In only a very small proportion – around 10 per cent – of the companies where a scheme had been introduced was this done in any other way than by a unilateral management decision. In other words, the notion of profit-sharing as part of a sharing in *decisions* rather than cash looks rather thin. This is confirmed by another piece of recent research, carried out from Glasgow University (CRIDP 1987). This study was a postal survey, with some 360 firms replying out of 1,000 circulated. In hardly any case had there been consultation over the introduction of the scheme. The Glasgow team found, in addition, no clear relationship between the presence of a profit-sharing scheme and a particular style of industrial relations, nor any evidence for profit-sharing as an anti-union device. They did find a correlation between profit-sharing and other forms of participation, but one without statistical significance.

In short it is clear that profit-sharing tends to accompany other initiatives which could be classed as broadly fostering employee involvement. Yet much closer investigation would be needed to establish that profit-sharing was integrated in a planned way into these other initiatives; and far more detailed evidence to show whether or not it formed part of an integrated business strategy. Profit-sharing is clearly oriented to the individual employee, and its introduction has generally been effected without discussion with employee representatives; to that extent it can be described as potentially conforming to part of the HRM model, but in a weak sense only.

One further point deserves emphasis. Both APS and SAYE schemes are open to all employees, but with a service of qualification of 5 years, and only for full-timers. Of all three schemes it is the discretionary type that has been most popular. By June 1986, 562 APS and 541 SAYE schemes had been approved, compared with 1,676 discretionary schemes – even though the latter had been available for only a short time. Profit-sharing is in practice fairly clearly geared to core employees; it does not represent an instrument used to secure the commitment of the workforce as a whole.

Pension scheme participation

Pension funds are major capital holders, with assets of well over £200 billion. They have overtaken individual shareholders in the amount of assets they collectively hold. They represent a curious form of semi-collective ownership, in that members of pension schemes have individual entitlements to pension payments, but do not have ownership rights as individuals. Research also undertaken at Glasgow University, in the first part of the decade, showed that representation on the trustee boards of pension funds increased substantially in the latter part of the previous decade, following the publication in 1976 of a White Paper threatening the legal imposition of fifty–fifty representation. Over half of the companies surveyed had some form of representation at board level. Participation of this kind is not completely new – several companies had introduced it in the early part of the century – but in 60 per cent of the cases it had been introduced since 1976. In over half of the cases at least 40 per cent of the board were composed of member representatives, though many of these were drawn from the ranks of middle or junior management. Pension fund participation is therefore quite widespread, with at least the formal possibility of representatives taking part in the administration of significant amounts of capital (Hyman and Schuller 1983; Schuller 1986).

Evidence from the research relates to the review of HRM in a number of ways. In the first place it is clear that the introduction of participation did not form part of any overall strategy for increased employee involvement, although the companies taking part did often have other active initiatives in play. The major motive was, implicitly or not, the threat posed by the White Paper. Allied to this was the perception that pension funds in some sense belonged to the members; since it is 'their money', they are entitled to a say in its management – a matter of rights rather than managerial strategy.

It is worth remembering that the original rationale behind the establishment of pension schemes as legally independent of the companies was to preserve the pension rights of individuals even should the company go out of business. However, the watertightness of this separation has come increasingly into question. As the funds grew, with almost frightening rapidity, so companies became aware that the management of the funds had major implications for their own economic position, given that the investment performance of the funds could make a difference of millions of pounds to their asset/liability ratio and hence to the requirement of the company to make contributions. Second, pensions began to move into the mainstream of collective bargaining (Hyman and Schuller 1984) – a move accelerated by the dismissal or early retirement of many older employees. Third, this trend to early 'retirement' (voluntary or compulsory) helped to create massive surpluses within the funds. Their liabilities were reduced because early leavers generally receive smaller pensions, and their assets were swollen by the stock-market boom of the early and mid-1980s. Even rough figures on the amount of the surpluses are astonishingly difficult to secure, but they certainly ran into tens of billions of pounds. All of this meant that the management of the funds became very much an issue of corporate concern. Old-style pensions managers were increasingly supplanted by financial managers whose prime function was to manage the assets of the funds rather than to manage the welfare aspects of the scheme.

What, then, is the outcome of this conjunction of a growth in employee participation in the management of the schemes and the movement to integrate pensions management into corporate policy? Table 8.2 outlines the role played by member representatives, as reported by themselves and by pensions managers, both in responses to questionnaires and in the case-study research. The functions of trustees are broken down into a number of areas. The results show that member trustees were regarded as having a significant part to play in the personnel-oriented aspects of fund management. The respondents were unanimous in identifying the dissemination of information (on such matters as benefit entitlements) as the area in which member representatives make the most contribution, followed by the making of discretionary decisions (for example on the entitlement of an 'unmarried widow' to the pension of her deceased common law husband). Over half of all categories of respondent judged the contribution to be high in the dissemination of information, and only insignificant numbers reported that member representatives made no contribution at all.

Table 8.2 Contribution of member trustees to trustee board activities: as reported by pensions managers (PM), member trustees (MT), and case-study interviewees (CS)

| | Reported level of contribution (%) | | | | | | | | | | | |
| | High | | | Medium | | | Low | | | None | | |
	PM	MT	CS	PM	MT	CS	PM	MT	CS	PM	MT	CS
Dissemination of information	55	57	58	31	33	19	10	7	16	3	3	6
Exercise of discretionary powers	43	45	50	40	39	18	13	12	20	3	4	11
Monitoring of fund performance	11	33	29	40	41	32	36	21	35	12	5	4
Application and changes of rules	27	31	35	45	41	27	22	18	26	6	10	12
Investment policy	18	17	18	37	34	27	33	35	30	12	14	15
Appointment of managers/advisers	16	11	19	21	24	21	36	37	27	26	28	32

Source: Schuller (1986)

By contrast, the involvement of member representatives in decisions affecting the deployment of capital was very much smaller. Less than one fifth of all categories of respondent reported a high level of contribution by them on investment policy. Once policy has been decided it is essential that it should be monitored if trustees are to discharge their legal responsibilities, and it is noticeable that the pensions managers in particular rarely saw much of an impact by member trustees on the monitoring of fund performance. Equally significant is the low level of perceived contribution to the appointment of professional managers or advisers. In other words, member representatives were often seen as having minimal influence over the selection of the professionals to whom the management of the fund was entrusted. Over one quarter of all categories of respondent saw them as playing no part at all in this process.

Several reasons for this pattern were identified (Hyman and Schuller 1983; Schuller 1986). Some related to personal factors, such as lack of experience or training on the part of member trustees, or to perceived constraints imposed by trust law. Others related to structural factors, notably the removal of decision-making on investment issues to bodies such as sub-committees outside the trustee board, from which member trustees were excluded. There are, therefore, clear elements of inconsistency; employees are admitted into the management of a scheme, often on the basis that the assets in some sense belong to them; but while the investment of the fund comes to be seen as more integrally related to the corporate strategy of the parent company, the involvement of employees remains often marginal. Nevertheless, any assessment of this involvement must take into account the fact that in most instances participation is relatively recent. As member representatives gather experience, their influence may increase; at any rate, one cannot ignore the potential dynamics of involvement.

Recent moves by the government are designed to promote the idea of personal pension schemes, breaking up the collective identity of occupational schemes by encouraging individuals to make their own arrangements – essentially a return to the old money purchase system. Whether or not this will succeed remains to be seen. What this example of pension fund participation shows is that it is difficult to disentangle the issue of personal entitlements, and an individual's direct involvement with the company, from broader issues of corporate strategy. Pension schemes were originally introduced precisely in order to foster loyalty to the company – commitment, as the modern terminology would have it (Hannah 1986). That motive has largely disappeared, as companies wish more to promote flexibility and mobility. The perceived value of long service with a single employer has diminished, though many companies still have problems in working out their approach to investing in human resources and the time scale over which they can expect returns to such investment (Keep, this volume). Nevertheless, the commitment of employees remains a common stated objective, and the pension system has developed into one where there is a substantial measure of employee involvement in the management of massive sums of corporate capital, potentially at least, and in the administration of personal benefits. Identification with the company is still fostered by the existence of the scheme, and the legitimacy of the scheme is buttressed by the presence of member trustees. In other words, employees participate as individuals in the membership of the scheme and collectively through representation in its management; this representation, in turn, has both an individual aspect, relating to personal benefits and the provision of information on them, and a collective one in the shape of investment strategies which affect the management of the fund as a whole.

Conclusion

By drawing this contrast between two types of financial participation I have illustrated the difficulties involved in suggesting that there can be a straightforward shift of managerial strategy to focus on individuals through the introduction of participation, and at the same time to integrate this area with other areas of corporate planning. The recent growth in profit-sharing is largely the result of the fiscal incentives offered, the bulk of it going to executives. Although it often occurs alongside other forms of participation, and therefore in one sense can be seen as part of forward-thinking management, links with actual human resource development in the sense of a strategy to make better use of the labour force's skills and potential are far from clear. It is, if anything, a part of management for control rather then development.

Pension scheme participation appears at first sight peripheral to the HRM debate. Yet on the one hand it illustrates how implausible it is to attempt a clear-cut distinction between individual and collective forms of participation, with an often uneasy mingling of individual entitlements and capital management. As a form of indirect participation in collective ownership it seems far removed from the dominant HRM model. But it does engender its own form of commitment, cutting across many established barriers. Pension scheme management, moreover, entails planning on a long-term basis. In this sense it therefore offers itself for integration with other components of an HRM strategy. Yet the trends described above illustrate the ambiguities which persist in relation to the securing of employee commitment and the rationale for employee involvement.

Chapter nine

Human resource management and changes in management control systems

Nicholas Kinnie

Introduction

Conditions of increasing competition have focused attention on the role of company human resources policies within the wider business strategy. Changes in policies towards employees are frequently claimed to be integral to company success in the face of intensified market pressures. However, despite the importance of these issues, relatively little attention, to date, has been paid to the possible links between innovations in the management control systems (MCS) responsible for implementing the desired strategic changes and the management of human resources.

This chapter examines these possible links and has two aims. First, to consider the potential which exists for developments in human resource management (HRM) to contribute to the aims of the new MCS. Second, to examine the reasons which explain the degree to which these opportunities are, or are not, taken up.

In particular, this chapter examines the opportunities for HRM to contribute to the successful implementation of new financial and production-control systems. One of the principal aims of these new MCS is to widen the responsibilities of managers and supervisors and to increase their accountability to senior managers. A distinctive feature claimed for HRM is that line managers and supervisors become more involved in implementing an overall policy on human resources. Clearly, there exists an opportunity for these two sets of changes to support one another. The intended widening of line managers' duties might potentially include additional human resources responsibilities. The desired increase in managerial accountability creates the opportunity for them to become more involved in promoting a distinct HRM philosophy and approach.

However, the extent to which this potential is fulfilled is influenced by a number of factors. One key factor is the existence of human resource techniques which reinforce the MCS objectives by training, encouraging, and motivating managers and supervisors to take on these new responsibilities and accountabilities. In the absence of these supporting techniques it is unlikely that the benefits of these new control systems will be realized fully. The evidence, from the cases discussed here, shows that commonly these supporting techniques are absent because of the failure of human resource specialists to become involved during the implementation of new control systems.

This analysis is based upon research carried out in four manufacturing plants in 1985 and 1986. Data was collected by means of interviews with representatives of management and trade unions and by the study of written material. Brief details are given in Table 9.1 and further details can be found in Kinnie (1986).

Table 9.1 The four manufacturing cases studied

Name	Employees	Activity
Luxury goods	1,650	Manufacture of components
Hightech	8,000	Manufacture and assembly of components
Components	1,500	Manufacture of components
Consumer products	750	Mass production

These cases are drawn upon in order to explore the ways in which new management control systems have been developed. They are also used to illustrate the manner in which, and the extent to which a human resource management approach can be used to underpin the impact and effectiveness of innovations in MCS.

The chapter is divided into three main sections. The first describes the key innovations in management control systems focusing, in particular, upon production control and financial control. In the second section the range of opportunities for HRM to support the aims of MCS are then discussed in some detail and a catalogue of possibilities is spelled out. The third section turns to an analysis of the particular constituent techniques of HRM which would seem to be most relevant in this regard. The chapter finishes with a brief discussion of the reasons why these opportunities have not, so far, been more widely seized.

Innovations in management control systems

Changes are taking place in the systems used by managers to exercise control over their organizations, often in response to increased competitive pressures. This section examines some of the changes being introduced and considers their implications for managers and supervisors. In particular it examines the changes in financial management control systems (FMCS) and production control systems (PCS) using illustrations drawn from the four case studies. Before this, however, it is important to examine briefly the assumptions of the MCS model which embrace both FMCS and PCS.

Many studies have examined changes in MCS, stressing for example the production control aspects (Vollman *et al.* 1984) or the financial control aspects (Anthony and Dearden 1980). These studies employ a theoretical model which has the systems concept as its essential element. Here the components of the system are seen as integrated parts of the whole. Indeed, comparisons are frequently made with machines as representing simplified versions of organizations. Four key elements in the MCS process are commonly recognized: planning; goal setting; monitoring; evaluation. These elements are portrayed as stages in a continuous cycle (Lockyer 1983: 26; Anthony and Dearden 1980: 19).

Changes in these MCS affect the allocation and control of decision making throughout the organization. Their effect is to change the rules and procedures governing the exercise of autonomy by managers and supervisors. Two distinct trends were recognized in the organizations studied as a result of changes in the MCS. First, there was a widening of the responsibilities of lower-level managers, either through an increase in their autonomy or because new tasks were added to their job. Second, there was a move towards increasing the accountability of line managers as their performance became more clearly identified or easier to measure. Lower-level managers found that they were given greater responsibility for running their departments, but their actions were more closely scrutinized in one way or another by top managers. They soon recognized that they were 'free to succeed, but not free to fail'.

These trends are illustrated in the two following sections which look first at changes in FMCS and then at innovations in PCS.

Financial management control systems

A number of FMCS can be recognized, although this section is concerned in particular with cost centres and profit centres (Anthony and Dearden 1980). In the first, inputs or costs are measured in monetary terms but no attempt is made to measure output in the same way. Control is typically established by means of setting budgets, perhaps with the involvement of lower-level managers against which actual expenditure is compared – allowing budgets to be reset in the future if necessary. In the second, financial performance is measured in terms of the difference between costs and income. The aim here is to measure performance in terms of profits, which are seen as broader than looking simply at costs or incomes.

Perhaps the most common change to cost centres is the move towards delegated budgets whereby a global budget is broken down and a specific budget is allocated to managers lower down the line. In this case managers will enjoy greater discretion than previously since they have the ability to authorize expenditure. At the same time, however, they are now held personally responsible for the expenditure incurred against the budget allocated. For example in 'Components' supervisors were for the first time made responsible for allocating their manpower against a number of different budgets as part of a new internal accounting procedure. At monthly intervals their labour costs were compared with the budgets by senior managers. The aim of this system, and many others like it used elsewhere, is to improve the control over costs. Managers now have the ability as a result of employing information technology, to monitor detailed data on labour, materials, and machine costs and hence attempt to exercise control over these costs.

The introduction of profit centres puts even greater emphasis on the autonomy and accountability of lower-level managers. This change is commonly part of wider organizational changes involving a move from a functional to divisional structure. The essence of the change is that managers are now responsible for maximizing profit rather than minimizing costs. It is possible, for example, under the cost-centre system to reduce costs and achieve budget, but in doing so sacrifice quality or customer service. The broader responsibilities of profit centres are more attractive in an environment in which quality and customer service are being increasingly recognized as important (Donaldson 1986). The new system aims to free managers from head office restraints and encourage them to use their initiative to develop new ways of improving efficiency. At the same time, however, they realize that senior managers now have a more sensitive set of instruments for both monitoring and evaluating their performance.

Production control systems

Production control systems are used 'to ensure that a factory produces the quantity and mix of products necessary to satisfy the customer demand created by design sales and marketing efforts' (Senker and Beesley 1985: 52). They are used together with inventory and material control systems with the aim of achieving the efficient use of materials, plant, and working capital. Two quite distinct developments in PCS can be recognized. First, the emergence of 'just-in-time' (JIT) or Kanban purchasing using Japanese manufacturing techniques (Schonberger 1982). This approach which makes sparing use of high technology is aimed at reducing work-in-progress to a minimum. Second, the use of computer-based techniques such as materials-requirements planning (MRP) systems and manufacturing resources planning (MRP II) (Senker and Beesley 1985). MRP systems are based on company material requirements while MRP II covers all the companies' activities including financial management (MacBeth 1988).

JIT has been described as a 'pull' system whereby the assembler pulls the part or sub-assembly from the supplier departments. 'Kanban's core objective is to obtain low-cost, high-quality, on-time production. To achieve this, the system attempts to eliminate stock between successive processes and to minimize any idle equipment, facilities, or workers' (Aggarwal 1985: 9). The most common application of JIT is where group technology or cellular manufacturing has been established.

Here the focus is on the product rather than the manufacturing process. Cells, or mini-production lines manufacture a family of parts repetitively to replace the long lines of machines performing the same operation (Schonberger 1986: 10). This concept may be combined with two others: total quality control (TQC) and total preventative maintenance (TPM) (Schonberger 1986: 7).

An example of this change was seen in 'Consumer Products' where the production process was designed around a team of employees led by a team leader who was responsible for the output of a product from raw material to packaging.

The team leaders had wider responsibilities than their equivalent foreman would have had since they were responsible not only for output and costs but also for quality, maintenance, and overall levels of efficiency. However, these team leaders' performance also became much more immediately visible: the JIT concept quickly shows up any failure to achieve production targets.

Changes such as these are designed not only to improve efficiency but also to make direct and indirect cost savings. Apart from the direct savings coming from reduction in stocks of materials and semi-finished goods there were also more indirect savings. The new system was also designed to reduce numbers in staff such as progress chasers and inspectors who were regarded as non-productive overheads whose costs should be minimized. The overall aim was to achieve a 'leaner' less-bureaucratic management and administrative structure. A longer-term aim was to improve the quality of decision making and hence improve productivity. It is argued that better decisions will be made by team leaders who are 'on-the-spot' compared with more senior line and functional managers who are more distant from the decisions.

MRP and MRP II systems tend to be used where a very large number of components are assembled for the final product, particularly in mass production. The second of these techniques involves computer applications, often leading to the development of very sophisticated packages. Some systems extend beyond the materials requirement area to include production planning, shop loading, scheduling, and inventory control. These have been described as 'push' systems whereby once targets have been set the detailed targets and data are then 'pushed' through the organization. An example of such a change was seen in 'Hightech' where a highly sophisticated PCS integrated a number of previously separate data bases covering inventory, work-in-progress, and machine performance. The project, costing several thousand pounds, was a central element in the reorganization of the business.

Systems such as these will have a profound effect on the jobs of managers and supervisors. For example in 'Hightech' the new system reduced managerial discretion in some areas and expanded it in others. The new PCS included the provision for the automatic prioritizing and scheduling of work, thus potentially removing some areas of autonomy. However, at the same time managerial and supervisory responsibilities were expanded to deal with quality control and motivation of employees. These systems also increase the visibility of supervisory performance because they are on-line and real-time rather than paper-based. For example, the new PCS in 'Luxury Goods' provided comprehensive and up-to-date figures on all aspects of each department's performance to management. Data covering output, manning levels, and machine usage was now available in a matter of minutes rather than days.

These systems were also designed to make their contributions to cutting costs and improving efficiency. PCS data in 'Luxury Goods' was used to reduce the amount of absentee cover required and ensure the correct mix of skills for particular jobs. Information such as this was particularly useful in dispersed or split departments where manning levels are reduced since supervisors are able to make the best use of the resources they have available to them.

This section has discussed some of the implications of introducing new MCS in the finance and production functions. In particular it has identified the changes taking place in the jobs of managers and supervisors as a result of the new control systems. The overriding theme is the increase in both the responsibility and accountability of managers and supervisors. Frequently they have more duties, but this is not within a vacuum. Alongside these new responsibilities financial or production constraints are drawn more tightly and more precisely by higher managers. The clear implication from this is the rising skill demands placed on these managers and supervisors. The following section looks in some detail at the human resources aspects of these new demands made on managers and supervisors, and the opportunities these present for HRM to contribute to the achievement of the goals of the new control systems.

Opportunities for developments in human resource management to support the aims of new management control systems

This section draws on the preceding discussion of innovations in MCS and considers two issues in detail: the potential contribution that changes in HRM might make to the achievement of the aims of new control systems; and the extent to which these opportunities are taken up in practice.

Innovations in MCS lead to often quite dramatic changes in the jobs of managers and supervisors. In particular, they alter managerial relations with both subordinates and superiors, and provide the opportunity to achieve both MCS and HRM goals at the same time. However, evidence from the cases studied here shows that there are a number of obstacles which must be overcome before this potential can be fulfilled.

The discussion of these opportunities and obstacles which follows focuses on the MCS objectives of firstly, widening managerial and supervisory responsibility, and secondly increasing accountability to senior managers.

Wider responsibilities

The widening of managerial and supervisory responsibilities prompted by new FMCS and PCS provides the opportunity to put into practice some of the concepts associated with HRM. Two possible changes are identified: the chance to practise more individualistic human resource techniques; and the opportunity to achieve greater flexibility.

Team leaders and individualism

The new MCS can involve either simply adding to managerial and supervisory duties, or redefining the role to one of 'team' or 'group' leader. Typically, the team leader, in addition to his production responsibilities, becomes responsible for quality and inspection of the goods or services involved. Indeed, he is often required to work alongside his team members rather than simply supervise.

In the human resources field team leaders have the opportunity to become more involved with the motivation and training of those whom they lead. Rather than leaving such responsibilities to specialist departments or dealing with the group via the shop stewards they now become directly responsible for dealing with members of the team. Indeed, 'Kanban has its roots in employee motivation and assumes that workers will perform at their best when entrusted with increased responsibility and authority' (Aggarwal 1985: 9).

This extension of responsibility provides the opportunity to practise more individualistic human resources techniques. The aim of these is to increase individual employee commitment and attachment to the organization. For example, in 'Consumer Products' the team leaders found themselves responsible for the first time for communication and appraisal. Once a month all production in the firm was stopped for half an hour to allow the team leader to pass on and collect information about the company and team performance. At 6-month intervals team leaders were to conduct appraisal interviews with the team members, where they would review the past 6 months and set budgets for the next 6 months. These changes in 'Consumer Products' were largely successful because the team leader role was part of wider managerial changes and was consistent with the changes in technology.

A similar emphasis on individualism was experienced with the MRP II system in 'Hightech'. One effect of the change was to take away from supervisors some aspects of discretion such as shop loading which they had previously enjoyed. New responsibilities were added to their role, however, including more direct control over the discipline of their subordinates. Particular attention was to be paid now to issues such as timekeeping of employees. Supervisors were able to input directly into the new system and could create clockings, if, for example, someone had genuinely forgotten to clock in. In addition, supervisors were to keep log books to record any persistent pattern of lateness and absenteeism, and then be prepared to find out why employees were not at work, and if necessary to take action against them. In this case, however, the supervisors were ill-equipped to carry out this new role and had little prior warning of the change.

Flexibility and delegation

New PCS are also designed to allow managers and supervisors to improve the flexibility of their sections. On the technical side efforts are concentrated on reducing set-up time to allow smaller production runs, reducing work-in-progress, and improving the integration between different departments. The aim is to allow the production facility to be able to respond much more quickly to the demands of the market. Similar objectives are set for the flexible use of employees. For example in 'Luxury Goods' the improvement in information created the potential for supervisors to make the best use of their available resources by moving employees more frequently between jobs. A similar example is given by Child

(1984: 216) in the retail sector when referring to the precise knowledge provided by electronic point-of-sale technology which 'has enabled retail managers to redeploy staff between departments and to schedule the hours of part-timers accordingly, with attendant economies'.

Supervisors in 'Luxury Goods' were, however, reluctant to use the new system and tended to rely on their established practice of making decisions on the basis of a 'rule of thumb'. Typically this involved moving men around and borrowing from other departments to achieve current needs and seeking a permanent solution once production was underway. Many supervisors prided themselves on this ability to 'juggle' with men using their experience, and through 'swop' arrangements with other supervisors. As others have noted, resistance of a subtle kind is possible where 'the supervisors' skills of fixing and by-passing the formal systems through a mixture of experience, cunning, personal contacts, and trading of favours or indulgencies, could appear to count for nought overnight' (Rothwell 1984: 23). Commonly supervisors knew what was required of them but were disinclined to use the new systems blaming technical and access problems to explain their behaviour. They claimed that the system was slow to collect data, had a long response time and there was a shortage of computer screens which made it difficult to gain access to the information which was available. One consequence of this attitude is to undermine the credibility of the PCS since MRP systems depend upon the accurate and comprehensive input of information. If managers and foremen begin to resent the system because of its intolerance of informality the result can be that 'inaccuracies tend to find their way into important MRP files' (Aggarwal 1985: 9).

Increased accountability

The new control systems are designed not only to widen managerial and supervisory responsibilities, but also to make them more accountable to senior managers. This might be achieved in two ways: by more regularly monitoring the performance of key indicators and by evaluating individual managerial and supervisory behaviour on the basis of these indicators.

Monitoring and quality

An essential element of the new MCS is an enhanced provision for monitoring performance. On the technical side this often takes the form of much closer attention to quality control than previously. On the financial side delegated cost centres, for example, are designed to provide regular detailed feedback on expenditure measured against budgets. Managers and supervisors are often held directly accountable for the expenditure in their section whereas previously accountability was at a much higher level. The information potentially available is now more up-to-date and accurate than that produced by earlier systems.

For example, the new FMCS installed in 'Components' required supervisors to resolve any 'mismatches' between the number of employees budgeted for on their section and the number actually in attendance. They were required to allocate the manpower for which they were responsible under a number of headings and account for any surplus or shortfall. These inputs were fed directly into the internal accounting system and replaced the manual method of 'crewsheets' which supervisors filled in every day to account for the number of employees on their section. A monitoring device built into the system meant these mismatches could no longer be ignored, whereas previously as one manager put it 'all the information was on "bits of paper" and the supervisors could hide behind the inefficiency of the system'.

The intention of this system was to increase the degree to which supervisory actions were visible to senior management. In doing so the objective was, in the words of one senior manager, 'to get our supervisors to supervise'. The actual outcome was somewhat different since there was some opposition to the new system from the supervisors. They resented what they saw as a tightening up on their own activities and demanded changes in their payment system to compensate for this.

Evaluation and goal setting

Perhaps the most direct way of evaluating the role of managers and supervisors is to introduce profit centres. Here managers and supervisors are held directly responsible for the overall performance of their section which can be measured against goals which have been set for them or they have participated in setting. However, this kind of MCS will not be suitable in all circumstances, particularly where it is difficult to measure output or inappropriate to measure profit. In these cases managers' and supervisors' performance can be evaluated through the PCS. For example, one consequence of the PCS in 'Luxury Goods' was to make the activities of supervisors much more visible to their senior managers. In this case production control data which was previously available only to supervisors was now also available to their superiors. In theory managers could now make decisions on manning levels, for example, which were in the past the prerogative of supervisors alone. Under the new arrangements supervisors feared that an element of their pay would be tied to the performance of their section. They regarded this as unfair since there were many other factors affecting performance which were outside their control. They were also afraid that their many informal practices and deals would become known to their bosses.

In practice, however, managers did not usurp the authority of their supervisors since most viewed day-to-day decisions as the responsibility of the supervisor and asked 'why should we reduce the manager to the level of the supervisor?' Child (1984: 221) has recognized this same problem: 'the question has in any case to be asked to what extent senior managers should take on the burden of additional decisions rather than using any saving of time provided by information technology in order to devote the extra capacity to longer term issues'.

More success was achieved with the rather different approach used in 'Consumer Products'. Here team leaders were expected and willing to be evaluated on their ability to achieve the desired level of output. In examples such as this the increase in visibility is achieved in very simple ways usually by a series of signals ranging from cards, to painted squares on the floor, to coloured golf balls rolling down a tube (Schonberger 1982). But in addition to this considerable attention was paid to their ability to achieve desired quality levels and to seek improvements in quality through their own efforts and the efforts of the members of their team.

Overall, the effect of the changes in MCS was to widen the responsibilities of managers and supervisors and increase their accountability to senior managers. However, the extent to which these aims were achieved varied between organizations. In one case, 'Consumer Products', management enjoyed reasonable success in achieving their aims largely because this was a green-field site allowing adequate time for preparation. In the other three cases there was only limited success, or simply no change. In particular the opportunities presented for putting some of the HRM concepts into practice were simply not taken up. The following section deals in some detail with the reasons which account for these differing experiences.

Human resource management techniques supporting management-control systems

Changes in jobs resulting from new controls systems place great emphasis on the expertise of lower-level managers and supervisors. Increases in responsibilities and accountability make it essential that the required skills and knowledge are present throughout the organization. It is unlikely that the MCS changes will be a success if they take place in a vacuum. They need to be supported by a range of human resources techniques which help managers and supervisors to acquire, and encourage them to use, the necessary skills. It is argued that the variability in success observed earlier can be explained by the extent to which these supporting techniques are present.

This section examines these techniques and considers their potential contribution to the achievement of control system objectives. Managers and supervisors find that they are required not only to practise various human resources techniques but they themselves also need the support of such techniques in order to carry out these activities. For example, a manager who is for the first time required to train his own subordinates will require instruction in how to carry this out if he is to be successful. It is argued that frequently these necessary supportive techniques are absent or are not used successfully and this hampers the achievement of MCS objectives. This lack of support can be traced back to the role of human resource departments in the planning and particularly the implementation of the change process. The potential contribution of these techniques is examined in detail: training and development; remuneration and reward; recruitment and selection.

Training and development

Several authors place a great deal of emphasis on the role of training and development in achieving the kinds of changes described here. Indeed, Schonberger (1986) describes training as the catalyst for such changes and goes on to describe what it should and can achieve. Similarly others have advocated that managers ought to adopt a 'strategic approach' to planning for changes of this kind so that 'the workforce can be trained to operate and maintain the new systems' (Senker 1985: 2). To do this managers must anticipate the training needs ahead of, or in parallel with, the innovation cycle, rather than training being 'plugged in' after the change has taken place. Here the trainer's job is to 'act as a predictor and catalyst ensuring that the skills, knowledge and attitudes the company needs now and the different ones they may need in the future are recognised and developed' (Walters 1983: 206).

Four potential areas for training contributions can be identified. First, technical training is required to allow users to operate new control systems. Managers, for example, will need to learn about new budgetary control systems which they are required to operate, and supervisors will need training in the operations of computerized production control equipment. Second, there is a need for training in the ability to interpret and analyse the information produced by these systems because 'although computer systems may help to diagnose problems and opportunities, decisions and appropriate selection are the responsibility of management' (Buchanan and McCalman 1988: 25). Indeed, managers and supervisors will require training to encourage them to make use of the systems by explaining the benefits. There appears to be a large gap between acquiring competence and actually using the new techniques. Third, managers and supervisors will need training to enable them to cope with their changed relationships with their superiors and subordinates. Supervisors, for instance, will require social skills training if they are, for the first time, required to appraise the performance of their subordinates. Managers will need coaching in bargaining skills if they are required to negotiate with trade union representatives as a result of a change in bargaining structures. Finally, training is needed if roles are changed, for example, from that of a traditional supervisor to a team leader. In addition to the other skills mentioned above, these team leaders are encouraged to adopt a wider perspective and will need to learn more about the company and its products.

The view of training put forward above appears to be optimistic when compared with surveys and case study evidence. This suggests that training is not as widespread as is frequently supposed and there are obstacles to its efficiency when it does take place.

Managerial practice in the cases studied adhered to the wider picture of managerial attitudes towards training put forward by survey data (Mangham and Silver 1986). In general there was little in the way of a systematic attempt to analyse training needs or to carry out training programmes on the basis of this analysis. For example in 'Luxury Goods' and 'Hightech' the training for supervisors, which lasted for between two and three hours and was concerned with the technical aspects of operating the new systems, took place during and after the new systems were installed. In 'Consumer Products' and 'Components' both green-field sites, much more detailed training was carried out prior to installation, although the emphasis here too was on the technical aspects of operation. This tends to confirm the experience of training for new technology. For example, Rajan found that less than 10 per cent of employees in his sample had engaged in retraining (1985: 5). It seems that 'Training for new technology was often talked of in advance as a major aspect of new technology, but tended in practice to continue to be treated as a very subordinate issue' (Rothwell 1985: 46).

There are obstacles to the effectiveness of training even when it does take place. Often there is little thought of what training is required and a tendency to use tried and tested methods and trainers. The training approach which is required is not always immediately apparent and needs to be preceded by analysis. A training needs analysis presents an opportunity for a thorough examination of the areas in which training is necessary. Even this, though, will not overcome the problems presented by the attitudes of managers and supervisors towards training. Managers, when asked, would relate to standard reasons of not being able to spare the supervisors to go on training courses and being unable to bear the costs of such exercises. In a period when staff were being cut it is very difficult for a training department to argue against the logic being put forward by line managers no matter what the strength of their case. In some instances supervisors were not motivated to go on training courses particularly where they perceived them as 'remedial' as something to put 'right' what they had been doing 'wrong' for perhaps twenty years or more. Others have noted that supervisors can regard training as like 'going back to school' (Warr and Bird 1976). The personal characteristics of some supervisors can present their own training obstacles. Many of the supervisors observed were of an age and learning ability which made it difficult for them to be trained successfully in new techniques. When this obstacle is not present supervisors may resent training which they feel is inappropriate to their needs and more akin to what the training department and trainer feels is important. One manager summed up the view of some supervisors neatly: 'our supervisors don't want anything to do with paperwork or computers . . . they see their job as man-management'.

The obstacles standing in the way of effective training programmes assisting the achievement of MCS objectives are numerous. Senior managers may not be aware of, or have little time for the training implications of new control systems. Even where training is carried out it may be difficult to overcome the opposition of lower-level managers and supervisors.

Remuneration and reward

Changes in remuneration and reward techniques have the potential to reinforce the aims and objectives of new MCS. They can be used to motivate and encourage managers and supervisors to deal with their new responsibilities and, at the same time, provide a means for increasing their accountability to senior managers. Opportunities exist for changing payment structures, which are concerned with the levels of payment and the relationships between those levels, and systems of payment which involve the methods by which people are rewarded. The cases discussed demonstrate the possible consequences of missing these opportunities.

Managers' and supervisors' jobs are expanded and reshaped as a result of the control system changes. Some jobs will grow and become more complex, while others will become narrower or more routinized as elements of the job are removed or computerized. Clearly, managers and supervisors are more likely to carry out their new responsibilities when they are adequately compensated for doing so.

These job changes have potentially profound effects for the existing payment structure within organizations. The new control systems will disturb existing relationships between jobs and absolute levels of payment, and the relative value of jobs. Where these changes are sufficiently wide-ranging there will be a need for a re-evaluation of some or all of the jobs involved. Consequently, certain jobs will be more highly evaluated and others more lowly evaluated than previously. Where the changes are very wide ranging there will be a demand for a new job evaluation scheme. It is possible that there is a need to move, for example, from a non-analytical to an analytical method, or that the factors used within an analytical method have to be changed or their weighting changed. Where supervisors are allocated budgets for the first time there may be pressure to move from a job grading scheme to a points based system to reflect more accurately the increased complexity of the job. An increase in the autonomy of junior line managers could mean that factors such as discretion or responsibility are introduced or given a heavier weighting in the job evaluation scheme.

Such changes, however, are unlikely to be without problems. Changing a job-evaluation scheme and payment structures is likely to be a long and costly process. Indeed, it may not be possible to carry out such a change before the MCS are introduced. Managers will find it very difficult to anticipate in detail the changes likely to take place in jobs. It is possible that re-evaluation has to wait until some time after the new control systems have been implemented. A delay of this kind can lead to the kind of problems experienced in 'Hightech'.

Before the change timekeepers in 'Hightech' used a manual system to record data on attendance, operations performed by employees, and the movement of components through the production process. This system was highly labour-intensive, costly, and slow, and line managers frequently complained that 'we can never find the piece we want on the shop floor'. The new system was designed to reduce the manual input involved and speed up the whole process. It also involved a considerable broadening of the skills required of timekeepers as they moved away from manual records and punched cards to data collection terminals and VDUs. The timekeepers claimed that this change of job deserved an immediate re-evaluation and regrading of their job with a consequent pay increase to compensate them for their added responsibilities. Management refused this,

149

arguing that existing job evaluation guidelines, which stated that a job must have existed for three months before a re-evaluation could take place, must be adhered to. The timekeepers demanded re-evaluation to a higher grade arguing that they should not have to wait for a pay increase when they had a clear-cut case. Consequently, the timekeepers took strike action lasting six weeks, during which time management ran a skeleton service. Eventually, a compromise was reached whereby new duties were added to the timekeepers' jobs assuring them of the pay increase they desired and payments were made for the overtime needed to clear the backlog of work which had built up.

There are similar implications for the payment systems employed following the introduction of new control systems. New MCS make it possible to relate the level of pay to the activities and performance of employees in a way which was not previously possible. Some new production control systems will make available a whole mass of data relating not only to the production process but also to employee performance. The facilities for monitoring output will also provide feedback on the productivity of employees in a much more comprehensive way than in the past. For example, a prototype system was being developed in 'Hightech' where employees would not only record their attendance at work but would also book on and off jobs via a computer terminal. This information would then be compared with other data on machine output and capacity. Clearly, the potential exists here for a sophisticated analysis of employee performance based on time taken, machine output and capacity, and quality. This performance could then be related in some way to a bonus system of some kind. These shop-floor data collection systems can therefore create a broader range of information than the existing manually operated payment-by-results systems. This opportunity had not, however, been exploited at the time of the research.

The joint goal-setting process integral to decentralized management can also be supported by changes in human resource techniques. Supervisors, for example, may find that some variable element of their pay is linked to the achievement of the goals which have been set for them. Indeed, there may be some demand from supervisors for this to happen as was illustrated in 'Components'. As noted above, one consequence of the MCS introduced in this organization was that supervisors' performance was more easily monitored by their managers than in the past. Soon after the introduction of the new system the supervisors argued that this improvement in monitoring should lead to some element of their pay being related to their performance. Indeed, they wanted to participate in an efficiency bonus scheme operated for the manual workers, claiming that since their efforts were contributing to the improved performance they should share the benefits alongside the manual workers. Management refused to agree to this arguing that no change had taken place in the supervisors' jobs, only a change in the visibility of their performance. The result was a strike by supervisors lasting two weeks as they pressed management to accept their argument, although the supervisors were ultimately forced to concede.

Recruitment and selection

The problems associated with training and development create the opportunity for recruitment and selection techniques to make a contribution to MCS aims. New employees may be required for a number of reasons. First, in the short term at least, the new MCS actually lead to an increase in the number of people required to operate the system. In some cases, as in 'Luxury Goods', it is necessary to run the old and the new systems in parallel during the commissioning phase. Second, the skills and knowledge required for the new systems often simply do not exist within the organization. New employees are required to operate the new equipment or to train others to do this. Finally, consultants or specialists are needed who have knowledge of similar changes to provide advice and guidance, although they would not be permanent staff and be employed only on a temporary basis.

The experience of the cases again supports the broader findings; little attempt was made to employ more or different staff, the emphasis was on using the new systems to reduce the numbers employed. Indeed, a survey by Rajan (1985: 37) found that employers used external recruitment as the source of new skills for less than 1 per cent of employees.

A number of reasons can be identified to account for the limited take-up of this opportunity. First, concerns over the numbers employed, or 'head count' are likely to loom large. Since the whole aim is to reduce costs and improve efficiency it is very difficult to justify an increase in numbers employed even in the short term. Indeed the situation is likely to be as Rothwell describes (1985: 46) where recruitment was 'frozen' in most of the companies she studied with the only major area of recruitment being programmers and a few technicians.

Second, even where there are funds available to recruit new employees there are difficulties in selecting those who are actually needed, since a thorough job analysis is required to produce an accurate person specification. There are problems involved when trying to predict exactly what kinds of skills are required before the MCS changes are made. Therefore companies often wait until the changes have been made and then attempt to recruit where there is a shortfall of skills. The danger is of recruiting people who match a person specification which does not reflect the skills which are required in practice. Finally, there are problems with attracting new employees even when the person specification can be drawn up accurately. Changes in the skill requirements of jobs are not always adequately matched by changes in the level of payment, perhaps because of the inflexibility of existing pay structures. This can lead to attempts to recruit highly skilled employees who are in demand with an inadequate level of payment. Therefore companies are faced with either coping with the likely shortfall, or making changes to the pay structures to attract the necessary staff. If changes are made to pay structures at the entry point then this suggests that changes should be made at other points along the career path. Without this, organizations are able to attract new employees initially only to lose them after a few years to competitors offering more generous packages.

Conclusion

This discussion has highlighted the potential contribution that the emergence of an HRM approach might make towards the achievement of the goals of new control systems. In particular the analysis has examined the ways in which human resources developments might enable managers and supervisors to widen their responsibilities and become more accountable to senior managers. However, it appears that on the basis of this evidence at least, these opportunities will not always be taken up, largely because of inadequate support from human resources techniques. Managers and supervisors need to be trained, encouraged, and motivated if they are to take on fully their new responsibilities and accountabilities. In the absence of this it is likely that the benefits of these new MCS will not be fully realized.

It appears that the human resources issues of new MCS were either not considered, or dealt with only in so far as they affected the technical aspects of the change. The typical approach tended to be as follows. Often there was what might be described as a managerial imperative for change, almost at any cost. Senior managers, perhaps because of pressure from outside, or the fear that funds might disappear, were extremely anxious to push through changes; or at least to be seen to be doing something. They may have been aware of the wider implications, or a HRM specialist within the organization will have made them aware, but they argued that there was too little time to take these factors into account. The argument commonly was 'let's push through the changes and worry about picking up the pieces later'.

This approach can be traced back to the way in which decisions were made and the changes carried out. Although human resource specialists were often involved in the decisions taken at a senior level, they were commonly not involved in the implementation stages. For example in 'Hightech' HRM specialists were involved in the strategic decisions but the implementation teams were composed virtually entirely of line managers and systems specialists. These managers were either unwilling or unable to give human resources issues more than a passing glance.

However, the examples discussed here show clearly the human resources issues which need to be considered before the advantages of the new MCS can be exploited. As such these examples are therefore consistent with those observed elsewhere where 'experience in most of our companies tended to reinforce the weakness rather than strengthen the role of the personnel function' (Rothwell 1985: 49).

The examples discussed here while highlighting the potential contribution that HRM might make, have tended to concentrate on the reasons why these opportunities are not taken up. Questions must now be posed about the extent to which these examples are typical. There are for example many persuasive accounts (see for example Schonberger 1986) of the apparently successful introduction of new MCS. It would be of particular interest to compare the role played by HRM in these successful companies with that observed in some of the cases described here. Alternatively, there would be much to be gained from studying the extent to which developments in human resources contribute to the aims of new control systems in those companies which have set out to pursue a distinct HRM approach.

Acknowledgements

The empirical research upon which this chapter is based was funded by ESRC award number FO9 22 0077. The author would like to thank Alan Arthurs, Roy Staughton, Cyril Tomkins, Edward Johns and, in particular, John Storey for helpful comments on an earlier draft of this chapter.

Chapter ten

Limits and possibilities for HRM in an age of management accountancy

Peter Armstrong

For many advocates of HRM, an injection of precision into the concept, not to say ambition on behalf of its practitioners, is achieved by linking it with that of strategy. Human resource planning on this model is supposed to be both strategic in itself and to form a key element in the formulation of overall corporate strategy. According to recent research by Sisson and Scullion (1985), there are models for this version of human resource management in some of the less diversified of Britain's large companies. Where the production of specific operational skills and styles of work amongst employees is seen as a major strategic resource, it also tends to form a key element of corporate planning with a correspondingly central role for the personnel function. It may be that this promise of an enhanced role for expertise in the management of the employment relationship lies behind the current interest in human resource management in the pages of personnel journals.

Alongside this promise, however, there is a threat. At a more tactical level, the new centrality of the employment relationship within general management is said to require an end to the functional separation of personnel and line management. Naturally the terms on which this merger is to be achieved have provoked considerable discussion amongst existing personnel managers. This too has entered the debate on human resource management in the journals of the personnel profession.

It is with this debate, with the threat and the promise of human resource management to the personnel profession that this chapter will be concerned. Specifically it will focus on the *context* of the debate and on whether the prescriptions which are emerging from it constitute an adequate response. Thus human resource management is seen in the context of a search for new 'models' of personnel management which has been going on for some time. The chapter begins by sketching out this wider debate.

Personnel management: the nature of the crisis

During the last decade, writings on the personnel profession have been pervaded by a sense of exclusion from the major management decisions. For example, Hunt (1987) reports that human assets are rarely considered in decisions on company acquisition policy and that personnel managers are only involved in relatively peripheral aspects, such as the transfer of pension rights. Daniel (1986) found that personnel managers are normally excluded from decisions on reorganization which follow the introduction of new technology, although they are sometimes involved in other forms of organizational change. In fact even this latter involvement may be of a fairly passive character in view of Evans and Cowling's (1985) finding that personnel managers do not usually take an executive role in company reorganization (see also Fowler's 1985 suggestions, on how the education of personnel managers might be reformed so as to enable them to play a more active part in this respect).

As already noted, additional threats to the profession seem to be posed by the fashion for human resource management where this is interpreted as a move to 'give personnel decisions back to the line' (Guest 1982) and there are parallel developments in the public sector associated with the Financial Management Initiative (Peat Marwick 1984). Rationalized as methods of integrating personnel with business decision-making, these trends also potentially reduce the need for the personnel function to be represented by a specialist department.

When the foregoing developments are coupled with anecdotal evidence of the run-down of personnel departments (e.g. Purcell and Gray 1986), it is easy to see why some of the recent writings on the profession have been preoccupied with a search for new 'models' for the profession.

At first sight, this gloomy picture appears to be contradicted by the major survey findings of Batstone (1984) and Daniel (1986) which report that the personnel function remains undepleted both in numbers and in status, whilst the (self-rated) importance of its work has, if anything, increased. However, even these surveys give cause for concern in their fine print. Daniel reports that much personnel work is now concentrated on the peaceful negotiation of redundancies – scarcely a secure long-term base for the profession – whilst Batstone reveals a narrowing of the range of bargaining issues which bodes ill for the traditional industrial relations component of personnel work. On close examination, it is all too easy to see little for the personnel profession in the Daniel and Batstone surveys beyond survival by institutional inertia and a determined optimism in response to survey questions.

In terms of Tyson and Fell's (1986) typology, what appears to be happening is that the 'contracts manager' model of personnel management, centred on the 'old industrial relations game' is dying out with the diminution of union bargaining power. Its likely replacement is a polarized profession consisting of a mass of 'clerks of works', performing routine administrative work for a newly self-confident line management whilst a few elite 'architects' of strategic human resources policy continue to operate at the corporate headquarters level.

The problem for the profession lies in the fact that, on present trends, the two types of position are not going to be linked by recognizable career paths. Though a small number of personnel executives on the 'architectural' pattern certainly exist, they tend to be confined to that minority of large companies which have expanded around a recognizable 'core' of operational activities (Sisson and Scullion 1985). In the more typical highly diversified company, many of the activities which might go to make up an architectural role for personnel executives are either being performed by managers in other functions or are devalued within the existing managerial culture.

It is worth labouring this point. Management accountancy, just as much as personnel management, can claim to possess a means of motivating and assessing the performance of individuals and groups. Like personnel records, accounting reports can monitor the costs of absenteeism and other lost time and so indicate the need for management action. For the sophistications of manpower planning, it can substitute the cruder but financially effective manpower budget – and so on.

Once this is appreciated, it becomes clear that it is a considerable over-simplification to ascribe the current problems of the personnel profession to the recession. Whilst this can certainly account for a diminution of the collective bargaining side of personnel work and in that sense lies behind the search for new functions, it can throw little light on the difficulties faced by the profession in finding them. To do that, it is necessary to look at who is presently performing the potential components of an 'architectural' role for personnel management or why the need for them to be performed at all fails to be appreciated within presently existing corporate cultures. The first question involves an examination of the competition faced by personnel professionals in establishing the need for their distinctive contribution to the overall process of strategic management (Armstrong 1987a). The second question concerns the cultural consequences of the present outcome of that competition; namely the marked and increasing ascendancy of the accounting profession and its characteristic approach to management in many British companies (Armstrong 1987b).

The purpose of this chapter is to examine the effects of these developments on personnel practice and thought and their implications for human resource management in particular. First, it will be maintained that there is only a limited future for the profession in passively adapting to the demands made upon it by management accounting systems. Second, it will be argued that attempts to isolate the 'people' aspects of the employment relationship as an area of professional expertise – as in some 'strategic' versions of human resource management – are likely to end up by marginalizing the profession within the overall framework of budgetary planning and control. Third, the point will be made that those versions of human resource management which call for a 'return of personnel functions to the line' need to be evaluated, not in vacuo, but in the context of the management accounting controls which now pervade most of Britain's large companies. The chapter will argue that, far from reasserting the centrality of the human aspects of management, this version of human resource management, in its context, is likely to subordinate them still further to the management accounting framework. On the positive side, the chapter concludes by suggesting that human resource management – and the personnel profession – can most usefully come to grips with the organizational politics of Britain's large companies by developing a critique of the human consequences of management accounting practice.

The growth of accounting controls as a feature of British management.

The accounting profession and its general approach to management have long been prominent in British industry. For example, a 1965 survey by *The Director* revealed that about 15 per cent of directors of companies with a share capital exceeding £5 million were chartered accountants, far outnumbering all other professions. Nevertheless, the widespread use of management accounting techniques of any real sophistication is comparatively recent in Britain. Until the merger wave of the 1960s and the increasing adoption of multi-divisional forms of organization (Steer and Cable 1978), most large British firms were organized as holding companies in which headquarters control was largely limited to the periodical inspection of the accounts of constituent companies. Financial controls at lower levels were similarly undeveloped. As late as 1960, a noted authority (Parker 1969: 11) could comment on the rarity of standard costing systems in British firms. By 1980, however, Jones's survey indicated that over 90 per cent of companies were then using some form of budgetary control and financial-performance indicators. Coates *et al.*'s (1983) survey of management accounting practice in multi-divisionals also revealed a very widespread use of accounting ratios as a key management control device. Over the last two decades then, there has been a spectacular increase in the sophistication and prominence of accounting controls in British companies.

The flow of variously qualified accountants into managerial positions is consistent with this picture of growing functional salience. Membership of the (now) Chartered Institute of Management Accountants, most of whom work in industry, has increased from 15,837 in 1977 to 25,639 in 1985. The corresponding increase for the Institute of Chartered Accountants for England and Wales was from 63,494 to 76,419, about 40 per cent of whom are employed in industry. The current output of Chartered Accountants of all kinds is over 5,000 per annum, which is roughly equivalent to the entire national output of business studies graduates.

Both of these trends are intimately linked with the growing diversification of British companies. Where this has progressed to the point at which a 'core' company activity can no longer be identified, the tendency has been for company head offices to concentrate upon such long-range strategic issues as company finance, investment, and acquisition policies, whilst industrial relations and other personnel issues have been decentralized to the level of operating subsidiaries (Hill and Pickering 1986; Sisson and Scullion 1985). Whilst this has been good news for qualified accountants interested in managerial careers, it poses problems for those who believe that the personnel function has a part to play in the formulation of overall company strategies.

The decentralization of company structures, the spread of management–

accounting techniques and the corresponding recruitment of accountants into management positions, then, are all developments which have gathered momentum during the recession. Indeed they may in some ways be responses to it. However, on re-examining the literature of the 'personnel crisis', it will become apparent that the efforts of the profession to come to terms with the 1980s, both at the levels of prescription and practice have been as much attempts to adjust to the accounting ascendancy as responses to the recession itself.

The personnel function and the accounting ascendancy

The recognition of the importance of accounting control systems for industrial relations and, by implication, for the personnel profession began with a prescient article of 1979 in which the late Eric Batstone explored the problems which they posed for the then current issue of workers' participation. Essentially his argument was that management accountancy imposes a system of priorities and a 'vocabulary of motives' which makes it very difficult for workers' representatives to challenge any management action which is grounded in accounting logic. Subsequently this theme has been explored by many accounting writers, though not explicitly in an industrial relations context (e.g. Hopper and Powell 1985).

In fact Batstone's argument implied a fundamental incompatibility between accounting controls and *all* forms of pluralist industrial relations practice. Although unremarked at the time, the implications for the personnel function were profound, since personnel professionals in the late 1970s were frequently the advocates and sometimes the practitioners of industrial relations reform on the 'constitutionalist' model. Batstone's article pointed forward to what Tyson and Fell (1986) have subsequently characterized as the death of the 'old industrial relations' game, not so much by starvation as a result of the recession but by strangulation at the hands of the management accountant.

The previous year, Legge (1978) produced an analysis of the options of 'conformist' and 'deviant' innovation available to the personnel profession as means of increasing its influence in the face of the 'dominant utilitarian values and bureaucratic relationships' of the business organization. Though this diagnosis of the problem made no explicit mention of accounting controls (the 1986 discussion by Gowler and Legge is more explicit in this respect), the clammy hand of the accountant was nevertheless visible, especially in the nature of the remedies proposed.

In the management accounting context, 'conformist innovation' implies the adaptation of personnel practice to the requirements of control and reporting systems, whereas 'deviant innovation' involves some form of challenge to the accounting frame of reference itself. Instances of 'conformist innovation' listed by Legge were the provision of 'hard' data by the personnel department for consumption by management accounting systems, attempts to justify personnel activity itself in cost terms, and the possible development of human-asset accounting as a means of solving both of these problems simultaneously. This list has subsequently proved to be a fair guide to developments both at the intellectual and practitioner levels.

The 'hard data' option

A minimum level of adaptation is probably represented by a case reported by Tyson (1985) as an instance of what he called the 'systems reactive' model of personnel management (roughly equivalent to Legge's 'conformist innovation'). In this instance, training costs were regularly reported and compared to predetermined budgets. Here, the personnel function had evidently done little more than respond to the demands of the accounting department for the kind of cost-control information typically extracted from operations units.

There are obvious dangers for the personnel function if the reaction is to be as passive as this. If the data provided are to be no more nor less than those demanded by the management accountant, what is to become of the distinctive personnel input to the management process?

Even so, adaptation at this level may pose problems for some personnel departments. As early as 1966, a British Institute of Management survey revealed that personnel departments were already becoming isolated from the flows of financial information within Britain's companies – even on personnel matters. Moreover, given that much management information on absenteeism, time-loss analysis and the like is now electronically stored and processed, there is a danger that the apparent reluctance of the personnel profession to engage with computer technology (Torrington, Mackay, and Hall 1985) may lead to managers in other functions (notably accountants) taking over data handling of this type. A loss of control of the spadework may then lead to competition from the management accountant for the actual decision-making element within these traditional personnel-department preserves.

Payment systems are a case in point. In a firm researched ten years ago by the writer, a sophisticated and influential personnel department had ceded the design of profit-related incentive schemes to the accounting department, one of whose efforts came close to provoking a walk-out of white–collar staffs. Presumably the rationale for this takeover by the accounting department was that the data on profitability lay within their province, as did the 'expertise' of attributing responsibility for it.

The fashion for value-added payment schemes which developed in the late 1970s, although less pervasive than popularly supposed (P.K. Edwards 1987), also places a premium on the collection and processing of accounting data, thus reinforcing the grip of management accountants on this area. It also (incidentally) gives considerable discretion over reward structures to those prepared to engage with the accounting minutiae of the calculation of added value, since there exists no agreed standard for this (Bowey and Thorpe 1986).

The justification of personnel work in accounting terms

Adaptation by the profession to the growing accounting ascendancy is also visible in recent academic-prescriptive works which have advocated the justification of personnel activity in cost-effectiveness terms, though the extent to which practitioners have actually adopted such strategies is unknown. Cannon (1979) called for a relatively pro-active form of 'conformist innovation' of this type in which pay-back periods or return-on-investment figures were to be computed in justification of proposals for action by the personnel department. Whilst clearly allowing for initiative on the part of the personnel department, based on a distinctive expertise, such a strategy remains conformist in Legge's sense, in that it depends on, rather than challenges, the existing framework of management accounting.

In that respect the strategy is not without its pitfalls. Firstly, it runs the risk of creating the expectation that *all* personnel department activity must be justified in cost-effectiveness terms – with implications that the profession would do well to ponder. Secondly, it voluntarily hands over the decision on whether or not to proceed with personnel department initiatives to managers outside the function.

Tyson and Fell (1986) were also preoccupied with the question of justifying personnel activity in financial terms. Essentially they proposed a whole series of measures of personnel department effectiveness which depended upon indices of employee productivity. Whilst quite logical in view of Guest's (1982) observation that personnel activity is increasingly focused on, and justifying itself through, productivity improvements, such a strategy displaces the problem rather than solves it. The claims of the personnel department to be the one responsible for productivity increases is more than likely to be disputed by line managers in whose departments any improvements occur (Legge 1978: 60–61), to say nothing of staff managers in other functions.

In some respects, then, the strategy of seeking to justify personnel work in accounting terms may cede too much to the dominant accounting culture and may also, in the end, achieve little security for the personnel function. It may be better to concentrate on the inadequacies of accounting projections as an exclusive basis for managerial decision-making, especially where human resources are concerned. However a debate of this nature cannot be entered unless personnel practitioners have mastered the accounting approach to the point where they can clearly identify its shortcomings.

Human resource accounting as a way forward?

It was, in fact, the shortcomings of the traditional accounting treatment of human resources, especially of investments in training, which provided the original impetus behind human resource accounting (HRA). Unfortunately, the hopes placed in this initiative as a means of coping with the accounting ascendancy do not yet appear to have been realized. An ambitious attempt to integrate the personnel function into management accounting systems on their own terms, HRA, according to one of its principal advocates (Flamholz 1974) thereby 'offers a way out of the limited role of the personnel function'. Based on the intuitively appealing notion that a well-trained and well-motivated workforce represents a considerable business asset, HRA has been the subject of a joint publication of the Institute of Personnel Management and the (then) Institute of Cost and Management Accountants (Giles and Robinson 1972) and it is now covered in approximately five hours of the IPM national syllabus.

Regrettably, the traditional accounting mind is proving inflexible on the question of whether formally free human beings can be regarded as assets in the same way as legally owned property (c.f. Jauch and Skigen 1977). More important, the central and critical question from the point of view of conventional accounting systems – that of placing a monetary value on 'human assets' – has, despite a tendency to obscurantist wriggling on the point, so far defeated even enthusiastic advocates of the approach.

In fact the lack of success of HRA on this front may well tell us more about the deceptions of accounting exactitude as a means of assessing the real worth of business assets as it does about the failings of HRA itself. Research by Hunt (1987) reveals that human asset values are rarely the subject of a professionally informed audit during takeover battles, yet are often a source of disappointment once the dust has settled. Such a sequence of events makes little sense and it clearly indicates a place for some form of HRA in strategic decision-making. The uncertainty involved in valuing human assets is no reason at all for ignoring them – and is a very good reason for treating traditional accounting valuations as only one of a number of inputs into managerial decision-making.

In some respects, then, the HRA initiative points a way forward for the profession. Whilst recognizing that management accountancy and the culture that goes with it are here to stay, it yet advocates a critical practice towards it. That is to say, it pinpoints a defect in conventional accounting systems (that training and other forms of staff development are counted as costs rather than as investments – c.f. Coopers and Lybrand 1985) and attempts to further the cause of the personnel function by offering a remedy.

Management appraisal and development as a core activity for the personnel profession

A concern with human resources is also at the centre of what appears at first sight a purely negative reaction to the supposed diminution of the industrial-relations role of personnel management: proposals such as that of Gowler and Legge (1986) that the salvation of the personnel function lies in cultivating a role as the recruiter, developer, and custodian of a stable 'core' of employees within the fashionably advocated 'flexible firm' (Atkinson 1984). Yet even here the ramifications of accounting controls manifest themselves.

According to Sisson and Scullion (1985) there has been an increased emphasis within personnel work on management development so as to enable managers within this stable core to cope with the pressures of budgetary control. This is scarcely surprising in view of the spread of management appraisal systems which link careers to accounting measures of departmental performance. However the implication – that personnel managers will need a considerable grasp of the actual operation of budgetary controls – has scarcely begun to sink in.

This issue is the more urgent because the task of management appraisal – if not yet that of development – shows signs of becoming a terrain disputed between the accounting and personnel professions. Besides designing performance-linked appraisal methods, accountants both in the public and private sectors are now claiming that the methods of management audit – originally little more than a check on the correct observance of procedures – can be broadened into a means of evaluating the performance of management organizations as a whole (Santocki 1979; Peat Marwick 1984). It seems unlikely that the personnel profession can secure a future within management appraisal and development without coming to terms with these new approaches. On the other hand, even in the minds of advocates of the management audit, there *is* a place for personnel practitioners able to work within multi-disciplinary teams (Santocki op. cit.). Clearly, they will need some acquaintance with accounting procedures.

Gowler and Legge themselves envisage a personnel role within the 'core' workforce which is concerned with devising development and reward systems which foster entrepreneurial values. Though they do not consider the implications of the fact that this intervention must necessarily take place within a management accounting framework, such a proposal meshes well with the critique of bureaucratic financial controls implied in Goldsmith and Clutterbuck's (1984) identification of 'loose–tight' control structures with the 'winning streak'. Where Goldsmith and Clutterbuck saw a kind of neo-paternalistic leadership as the means of injecting entrepreneurial flexibility into financial control systems, the Gowler/Legge proposal amounts to a more systematic, professionalized way of doing the same thing.

In fact there is a tradition of research on the behavioural aspects of accounting on which expertise in this area could be founded. From Argyris (1953) to Hopwood (1974) through to the current debates in *Accounting Organizations and Society*, the motivational and other shortcomings of traditional financial reporting systems and budgetary procedures have been explored and various remedies debated. At the moment it is probably fair to say that this work, like other aspects of accounting research, has not been taken up to any great extent by practitioners (c.f. Scapens 1983). Therein lies a space in which a fruitful intervention by personnel professionals might be made – but only if they thoroughly understand management accounting techniques, especially in their problematic aspects.

Decentralization and its ills

The problems posed for the personnel profession by the increased salience of management accountancy are also visible in recent studies of large, diversified companies. In the case studies of multi-divisional companies reported by Purcell and Gray (1986), the industrial relations functions of the corporate personnel departments had been reduced to that of ensuring that the bargaining activities of divisional personnel remained compatible with predetermined budgets. The implication is that the personnel input into industrial relations in these companies had degenerated into a simulation of devolved collective bargaining, which served only to dissipate trade-union energies so that the process of centralized financial planning could continue unobstructed. Obviously such an outcome is a long way from the ambitions of the profession to become involved with the process of corporate planning itself, for example on the 'business manager' model proposed by Tyson (1985).

Recent evidence from the Warwick University Industrial Relations Research Unit survey of the top 100 private-sector companies in the UK (Sisson and Scullion 1985) has more accurately located the developments reported by Purcell and Gray. These, it appears, are occurring predominantly in the more diversified of Britain's large companies, in which headquarters management acts primarily as a 'banker' for the various operating divisions. In such companies the divorce between strategic and operational management on the classic multi-divisional pattern is more or less complete and it is mainly here that the personnel function has been devolved to divisional or even operating subsidiary level and subordinated to the system of financial control (Hill and Pickering 1986).

However a minority of large companies have diversified around a recognizable 'core' of operational activities. These exhibit a tendency for operational management, including the personnel function, to retain a considerable headquarters presence. Sisson and Scullion (1985) argue that this is because in such companies, the development of a workforce, management, and working relationships appropriate to the core operation is a strategic contingency for the entire company and so warrants representation at the highest policy-making level. Accordingly, it is mainly companies of this type which are likely to employ personnel executives operating at the level of corporate strategy and who approximate to Tyson and Fell's 'architectural' model.

If this line of reasoning is correct, the important conclusion follows that unmodified 'architectural' models of personnel management cannot simply be transplanted into the typical highly diversified company. In these companies, projected futures for the personnel function which ignore the centrality of financial control systems or which seek to locate them in some grandiose vision of company-level human resource policy making are simply unrealistic.

Implications

From the evidence reviewed here, it appears that the problems faced by the personnel profession have as much to do with the increasing dominance of management accounting systems in British companies as with the recession. Unfortunately recognition of this aspect of the problem has been piecemeal even amongst the intellectual leaders of the profession and this has hindered the formulation of a realistic strategy in response.

It is against the background of an increasing domination of business organization by management accountancy that the current spate of prescriptive writing on human resource management needs to be evaluated. The immediate point to make is that most of it is actually quite parochial. Perhaps because of the threats and promises which it implies for personnel work, much of the writing is addressed inwards towards personnel specialists rather than outwards towards general managers or other functional specialists. In other words, the human resource management movement – if it can be called that – shows little awareness of the context in which it must make its way. Assertions that human resource management is essentially strategic and should form a central element of corporate policy rarely confront the fact that, at the moment, decision making on human resources in most of Britain's large companies takes place at levels considerably subordinate to budgetary planning and control (Hill and Pickering 1986), whatever lip-service is paid to the importance of human resources. Advocates of human resource management display little sense of how they are going to go about convincing the present generation of corporate planners that there is something wrong with this procedure. In other words, whilst human resource management contains within itself a claim for corporate centrality, it lacks a critique of present-day management accounting techniques. Why, one is inclined to ask, should those who presently control Britain's large companies – no doubt successfully in their own eyes – pay any attention at all to human resource management?

To look at the matter another way, the ease with which our business leaders are capable of producing platitudes on 'the importance of people as a resource' (see Goldsmith and Clutterbuck 1984 for samples) may well be enough to convince them that they are already in the human resource management game. Where is the critique of present practice – which is largely management accounting practice – which will convince them otherwise?

As for human resource management at the tactical level, the tendency on the part of its advocates to ignore the management accounting framework is more serious still. Beginning with the declared intention of reasserting the centrality of the employment relationship to the overall management process, one influential version of human resource management advocates an end to the functional separation of personnel and line management. The key point missed here is that the 'line manager' in the present-day large company is becoming, before all else, a *budget-holder* (see Storey 1987b). This means that his or her performance is primarily evaluated in terms of budgetary or return-on-investment targets, with short-term bonuses or long-term career progression often linked to these measures of performance with greater or lesser degrees of formality. The delivery of human resource management *practice* into the hands of managers controlled in such a fashion, whatever the rhetoric behind it, promises to turn the treatment of human resources into an instrument for the achievement of short-run accounting targets. Taken in this sense, then, human resource management, far from promoting a strategic treatment of human resources, is actually likely to subordinate it still further to budgetary controls.

In fact this intention is quite explicit in recent developments in the public sector. There, responsibility for personnel decisions has been 'returned to the line' specifically in order to ensure that those who take personnel decisions are held responsible for the financial consequences. In this case, however, the rhetoric is that of 'financial management' and the overt intention has been to 'harden up' decision making on personnel issues (Peat Marwick 1984).

Speaking more broadly, a consideration of the organizational politics surrounding the future of the personnel profession leads us to two conclusions. On the one hand, the evidence currently available indicates that the formulation of corporate planning models of the personnel mission, implicit in some versions of human resource management, is relevant only to those companies which have expanded around a recognizable 'core' of operational activities. In the more typical highly diversified company, it is likely to shatter against the brute reality of corporate management's continuing preoccupation with investment decisions and financial monitoring systems. There are no grounds whatsoever for supposing that the personnel function in these companies, alone amongst managerial specialisms, is going to escape the process of devolution and subordination to financial planning and control procedures. Indeed the discrepancy between such expansive ambitions and the mundane reality of much personnel work is only likely to exacerbate the intellectual gap which Thurley (1981: 26) diagnoses as one of the 'sicknesses' of the profession.

Nor, on the other hand, is it likely that territory for the operation of the personnel function can be claimed by some form of 'deviant innovation' based on a vaguely defined 'people expertise' – supposedly exclusive to personnel practitioners – which can usefully operate independently of the existing routines of management. Fowler (1985) is surely correct in arguing that personnel managers will continue to find it difficult to take an active role in organizational restructuring so long as all they have to offer is a handful of behavioural nostrums which are, in any case, taught to most management accounting students. He concludes that a credible personnel contribution will need to be based on a systematic analysis of functions and procedures in relation to the overall management task. What Fowler does not spell out, in his advocacy of 'organizational analysis', is that many of the functions and procedures of a modern management organization take the form of budgetary controls and financial monitoring systems.

Once this aspect of the problem is confronted, it becomes apparent that the future of the profession, and of human resource management, in most of Britain's large companies lies in a more modest and practical version of 'deviant innovation' which recognizes the enduring fact of accounting controls but also seeks to exploit their problematic aspects as a means of promoting intervention by the personnel profession. In practice, personnel department initiatives of this type will have to take place on the established ground of accounting systems and, in order to engage the issues, personnel practitioners will need to become aware of the substantial research tradition on the problematic aspects of budgetary controls and management accounting.

One wonders whether today's personnel managers are equipped for such a task. Within the current national Institute of Personnel Management syllabus, something under 10 hours is devoted to management accounting and human-asset accounting taken together. Within such a compass, it is reasonable to ask whether the treatment of accounting controls can be sophisticated and critical enough to indicate fruitful points of intervention for the profession. There are further question marks over the knowledge of current practitioners in this area and these, for the immediate future are the people who matter. Finally, the contents of personnel journals and conferences indicate little awareness that today's personnel function operates within a managerial culture which is increasingly dominated by the language and structures of management accountancy.

Chapter eleven

Looking to the future

John Storey and Keith Sisson

It was noted in the Introduction to this book that there was *prima facie* evidence that potentially major changes were taking place, or were being planned, in the way the employment relationship is managed. In their different ways the ensuing chapters each set out to examine the nature and to probe the significance and implications of these developments. These issues have been tackled from a mix of conceptual, theoretical, and empirical approaches.

In this final chapter our aims are four-fold: first, to pull the main strands together; second, to attempt to weigh the evidence and arguments by constructing a 'balance sheet' from which a broad assessment of trends can be made; third, to consider the main implications for practitioners and policy-makers; and fourth and finally, to examine the implications for future research.

Pulling the strands together

Five strands are examined and re-examined in this book. The first centres on whether there is indeed a discernible *qualitative* shift in the approach to the management of the employment relationship in Britain. This issue transcends, in the first instance, whatever particular label may or may not be attached to such a movement. More important is the probing of its essential nature and explorations in the significancies which it may carry.

The second turns on the *extensiveness* of any such shift – in particular whether the possible reorientation in labour management characterizes only a few, perhaps sector-specific 'special cases', or whether it has spilled over so as to influence organizations across the board.

Thirdly, many contributors to this book have tried to assess the *limits and possibilities* for a greater take-up of the ideas and policies associated with HRM in organizations in the future. Most noticeably, a number of the authors have detected 'barriers' which are likely to inhibit the flow of human resource management across the employment scene.

A fourth strand relates to the *interconnections* between developments in the management of human resources and developments on other fronts in work organizations. It has to be remembered that changes in HRM, whether great or small, are not taking place against a static context. On the contrary, as for example Purcell reminds us, corporate strategies and structures are changing dramatically, and, as Kinnie shows, managerial control systems are likewise in a state of transition. Both sets of managerial initiatives are not only far-reaching in themselves but they carry profound implications for the way employees are managed – irrespective of whether there is a putative 'third force' of semi-autonomous ideas labelled HRM.

The search for competitive edge is demanding experimentation in strategies, structures and control systems and these in themselves impel a reappraisal of existing ways of managing labour. The concurrent availability of a pool of ideas which de-emphasize proceduralism but hold out the promise of flexibility, accountability, and commitment, engenders a state of affairs which Max Weber (Weber 1958: 90–92; Giddens 1971: 211) would term 'elective affinity'. In other words, perceived interests are seen to 'fit' with one set of ideas amongst a number of alternatives 'on offer'. Competing definitions of reality, of the reasonable and indeed the possible are made available by spokespersons (Bendix 1963) who themselves may or may not be key practitioners. More important, they are people able to articulate a coherent and convincing *Weltanschauung* – a mix of perspective, observation and ideology. Influential spokespersons such as Tom Peters, Sir John Harvey Jones, or Rosabeth Kanter thus not only point the way at the crossroads of uncertainty but they also furnish a not inconsiderable degree of legitimacy to those who are bold enough to take the new direction. Hence, corporate group-viewings of the Tom Peters' video, 'A passion for excellence' (a common-enough event in a wide range of British organizations over the past few years) are not so much an ideational exercise as an emboldening one.

The fifth and final strand which extends through this book relates to the *actual practices which constitute HRM*. If HRM is to be translated from an ideology into a concrete set of initiatives, then it must find expression through managerial action. As was noted in the introductory chapter, the classic diagram drawn from Devanna, Fombrun, and Tichy identifies 'strategic human resource management' as comprising a coherent interlink between approaches to selection, appraisal, reward, and development. In this book we have tried to subject to close, and indeed critical examination, the realities and contradictions embedded in each of these at the concrete level. In particular, the chapters by Townley, Keep, and Schuller concentrate most directly on these aspects. Townley sees the trend towards systematic selection and appraisal as carrying certain inherent dangers for individual freedom. Whilst systematization in both areas could be welcomed as a move away from highly subjective (and biased) judgements, there are, none the less, fears that the attendant emphasis upon the attitudinal and behavioural characteristics of labour represents a trend towards what Blau and Schoenherr (1971) term 'insidious forms of control'.

Hence, if 'commitment' – a central tenet of most definitions of HRM – is in practice to be regarded as the exercise of discretion within tight boundaries of implicit expectations and in accord with a set of 'norms', then, the negative, 'unfreedom' aspects of these developments will necessitate at least as much scrutiny as the rather more celebratory accounts of HRM and 'excellence' which have so far predominated.

But these are not the only grounds for dubiety. Keep's pessimism stems from an altogether different source. Starting from the base proposition that training must surely constitute a central pillar of almost any conceptualization of human resource management, his research leads him to judge that it is nevertheless a pillar that will simply fail to get built. Most discussions of HRM suggest that it entails the recognition of, investment in, and development of the key human resource. But Keep's review of the evidence on training suggests that, while there is indeed a sign of significant accord with this at the level of rhetoric, there are simply so many institutional and attitudinal obstacles in the British context that the prospects for implementation of this, arguably crucial, aspect of HRM are not good. Hence, while Townley envisages the growth of one particular set of HRM practices and techniques, Keep concludes that another set will probably fail to take root.

Can both be correct? Is it possible that one facet associated with HRM could enjoy take-up, while another facet does not? The answer must surely be in the affirmative. Managers in Britain have often been described as predominantly 'pragmatic' (Purcell and Sisson 1983). If structural impediments such as corporate diversification, accounting controls, and an entrenched take-over/divestment orientation mean that long-term investment in training and an development is crowded-out, this does not necessarily mean that other facets – such as briefing groups, quality circles and new selection and appraisal techniques will also fail to be promoted.

This line of argument begs the question as to the interlink between such initiatives and, by extension, raises the issue of whether a coherent phenomenon is traceable. This brings us therefore to our attempt to provide an overview – that is to try, however schematic it might be at this stage, to marshall the evidence and the arguments so that they can be brought within the same frame. For the purposes of this assessment a 'balance sheet' is drawn up which garners and presents the evidence and the arguments. These are considered therefore under the headings of 'credits' and 'debits' – though we are not here making any normative judgements.

The balance sheet

On the 'credit' side of the case 'for' the view that human resource management has made headway in Britain, one should note that at the very least there is evidence of quite a number of important organizations which have changed the title of their personnel and industrial relations departments, examples would include even reputedly traditional manufacturers such as GKN and TI. And again at the very least there is plentiful anecdotal evidence of major change with stewards back on the job at Austin Rover and personnel managers being put in their place by resurgent production managers. Sir Peter Thompson of National Freight has talked openly of the role of chief executives and chairmen driving major change. There is also evidence of greater attention being paid to the management of employee relations as opposed to industrial relations: British managers, it seems, have rediscovered the individual. Greater attention is being paid to selection testing – including the greater use of psychometric tests; appraisal systems are being looked at not only for managers but also manual workers; merit pay for this group is also under more serious consideration in many companies; for white collar and blue collar alike the talk is increasingly of individualized pay. Some companies have moved to integrated pay scales to embrace all employees and profit sharing has again attracted a lot of attention.

Harmonization and single-status arrangements have been reported in cases such as Mars, Whitbread and Cummins, and on a range of green-field sites. Even Austin Rover, a company more well known for its imposed procedure agreement in the form of the blue newspaper, is now well into a period of negotiation on this front. Whitbread draymen in the south east have relinquished their previous contracts and have been turned into front-line sales representatives for the company. Developments in participation and involvement also suggest a greater focus on the individual. Many British managers seem no longer prepared to communicate solely or perhaps even mainly through the trade-union channel. There has therefore been a growth in face-to-face forms of communication in the style of 'team briefing' – the Industrial Society alone claims to have assisted no fewer than 400 to 500 organizations introduce them (*Industrial Relations Review and Report* 361). A related development has been the growth in direct forms of participation such as quality circles. Here too recent estimates do suggest a growth from a mere handful of organizations having them in the late 1970s to at least 400 in 1985 (IDS Study 353, 1–12). The National Society for Quality Circles (NSQC) has over 100 member companies with an estimated total of 2,500 circles in operation. The growth path of this body would suggest that we may estimate the number of organizations with experience of QCs to have increased to approximately 700 to 800.

Added to all of this, on the traditional IR front of relations with trade unions it seems that while signs of concerted strategic moves to deunionize are so far confined to particular marginal groups there is a more widespread tendency to act as though unions might just go away if ignored for long enough. There is also a change in the 'texture' of joint relations – essentially from joint regulation to joint consultation – or even just the merest communication of intent. In sum, there are at the very least many fragments of evidence of a veritable shift in the approach to employment management. But there is the other side of the balance sheet to consider.

There are grounds for believing that the organizations introducing the above-mentioned initiatives could well be the exceptions rather than the rule. For example, there are only about a dozen companies which have so far introduced integrated pay systems. And while the quality-circle figures may at first sight look impressive, set in the context of 11,000 establishments in manufacturing alone, the coverage is clearly limited. (And this is to leave aside the point that even those organizations which are counted as having circles may in fact only have operated two or three – perhaps with a total of 10 to 20 people involved – and many circles which are established wither away after just a few months (Dale and Lees 1986)).

It is also very uncertain whether the kind of changes catalogued above are being introduced as part of an integrated approach to which senior line and general managers are committed or whether these are instances of piecemeal reaction. It is one thing to introduce team briefing as part of an overall approach such as would appear to be the case at Jaguar and Grattans; it is quite a different matter if it is undertaken in a 'flavour of the month' manner. There is evidence – some of it emerging as part of the IRRU's ongoing research programme – that where team briefings and QCs and the like have been introduced, they face indifference or even hostility from middle line managers; suggestions are all too often not followed up and meetings are not held or are perfunctory affairs. Likewise, to an extent far greater than has been reported, the remaining shop steward union organizations have sometimes been instrumental in effectively boycotting these initiatives. Even in some of the more oft-cited 'successful' cases there are, in fact, continuing problems not only with QCs but also even with the feedback of information from employee attitude surveys.

Finally, on this side of the balance sheet we must enter reservations about the degree of HRM integration with business policy. IRRU's recent company-level survey found that although 80 per cent of large enterprises claimed to have an overall policy or coherent approach to the management of people, subsequent questioning revealed that less than half put it in writing and less than a quarter gave copies to their employees. Most telling of all, very few of the informants (senior corporate-level personnel specialists) could in fact describe the claimed policy in any adequate way. Moreover, subsequent analysis of the data revealed very little correspondence between the accounts of those who could articulate an approach and the data which had been collected about what was happening in practice. For example, when the IRRU researchers tried to correlate statements which carried a 'participative' orientation with the data on briefing groups and the like, the two sets simply failed to add up.

So much then for the broad findings; what implications do they carry for practitioners and policy-makers? It is towards a consideration of this question that we turn in the next section.

Policy and practice

Practitioners looking to the foregoing chapters for solutions to immediate problems will no doubt be disappointed. At first sight, the book does not appear to offer much practical help. Little or no advice has been offered on which technique to adopt. There has also been no attempt to offer the 'answer' to the human resource problem; there have been no sets of 'dos' and 'don'ts' of the kind which practitioners have come to expect from books dealing with the management of people. Indeed, most of the authors have implicitly if not explicitly rejected the idea of 'universal' solutions.

None the less, the kind of approach and analysis pursued throughout this book does carry certain crucial messages for practitioners and policy-makers. The overriding impression to be gained from studying what is happening (as opposed to should be happening) is that, despite the powerful advocacy of the 'excellence' literature – supported massively by the government and its agencies – there is little evidence of a strategic approach to human resource management being adopted in most organizations. If there is anything like a strategic approach, then significantly, it is largely to be found in foreign-owned companies (Purcell, Marginson, Edwards, and Sisson 1987). Many of the developments which, at first sight, appear to herald major departures, in communications, participation and involvement and the like, turn out, on serious analysis, to be no more than piecemeal and *ad hoc* responses to immediate pressures. Perhaps even worse, they reflect, in too many instances, merely a slavish following of the 'fashion' or the 'fad'. With relatively few exceptions, there is little evidence of attempts being made to integrate policies and practices with one another. Similarly, there is little evidence of the integration of these policies and practices with business strategy.

A useful way to begin our observation on the practical implications is to note the telling remarks made by Charles Leadbeater, the industrial correspondent of the *Financial Times*:

> The more flexible working practices introduced in the 1980s were a big step from the demarcation lines of the 1970s. But in many companies it has been at best an uncertain, interim step. They are *clearer what they are moving away from than what they want to move to*. If the flexibility of the 1980s is to be developed into new production methods for the 1990s, companies will have to invest more heavily in the skills of their managers and workers.
>
> (*Financial Times* 5 December 1988, emphasis added)

In our view this is precisely where the real problem begins. A major concern, as Keep's chapter powerfully argues, must be British management's approach to training and development. Yet, despite the massive amount of attention paid to the subject it remains the case that the under-investment in the human resource in Britain remains woefully deficient when contrasted with our major international competitors. Thus, even following a vast array of 'initiatives' such as TVEI, YTS, and a host of other disparate measures, and even following reports from NEDO, the Training Commission and the CBI, and despite governmental exhortation, the picture remains bleak.

A forthcoming report from the Department of Employment's Training Agency, reveals that Britain *still remains* close to the bottom of the international training league table. The survey reveals that half of all employees received no training at all in the year 1986-7 and that less than a third of companies even had a training budget – and this remember was a period when the publicity about the need for training was extensive. It is against this kind of inertia that the question of the implications for practitioners and policy-makers has to be set. Clearly it would be far too easy merely to repeat the call for a step-change in the amount and quality of investment in the human resource to at least meet the levels of our international competitors. Evidently the problem goes far deeper. There would appear to be structural inhibitors which serve to impede progress despite massive pressure of opinion in influential circles. In such circumstances there can be nothing more practical than a clear understanding of the nature of these impediments to action. This will be one of the central aims of this section.

The failure to develop an effective strategy towards training and development is all the more worrying because of the incessant ticking of the demographic time-bomb. In the 1990s the number of 18- and 19-year olds is going to drop by 25 per cent. In some regions it is going to drop by 30 per cent. The skill and person-nel shortages that are already in evidence are going to get far worse. Preliminary evidence from NEDO and elsewhere suggests that few British employing organiza-tions have taken any steps whatsoever to plan for this eventuality. Our discussions with employers too frequently reveal a vague intention to adjust remuneration levels so as to be 'more competitive' at this end of the labour market. But clearly, at a systems level, if a number of companies adopt this 'plan' it will merely result in an upward twist to the pay-bill.

Another concern must be the failure of British management to integrate their approaches to the individual with their policies towards trade unions. As many of the chapters have confirmed, more and more stress is being placed on the individual in the aim of greater cooperation and commitment. Outside of the handful of companies which have introduced so-called 'new style' agreements – and even senior officials in the electricians' union, their most powerful sup-porters, are reported to be having doubts about these (*Financial Times* 2 December 1988) – little seems to be changing. The approach continues to be 'adversarial'. Yet the institutional framework remains more or less intact – despite govern-ment encouragement for a more decisive move away from collective bargaining. The current rather tepid, half in and half out arrangement seems expressive of a managerial stance which rests on a hope that the trade unions may, at some point, simply fade away if they are side-lined for long enough. This would ap-pear to be a vain hope – especially so in Britain given the general lack of serious investment in alternative people–management approaches.

As with training and development, how long management can avoid the issue remains to be seen, for the experience of the USA suggests that it may prove to be counter-productive (Kochan *et al.* 1986). In the USA in the 1970s a number of companies, including Ford, General Motors, Xerox, and some of the major airlines, began to adopt some of the practices of the non-union companies. Managements, much as they have done in the UK, targeted individuals and the trade unions were kept at arm's length. They soon found, however, that they were not getting the maximum: the 'cold war' relations with trade unions were undermining their efforts. In the 1980s therefore there has, at least in the USA, been a considerable about-turn. Attempts have been made to integrate individual and collective policies. In particular, there has been a trend towards the greater involvement of trade unions in the process of change.

As well as drawing attention to the lack of a strategic approach, the chapters also point to a set of explanations which practitioners and policy-makers would do well to take into account. For, piecing together the arguments of Armstrong, Keep, and Purcell, to quote only the most obvious, it can be suggested that this failure to develop a strategic approach is not just a question of will or conviction, but of deep-seated structural features. Thus, Armstrong points to the composition of British management and the domination of the finance function; Keep stresses the significance of the patterns of ownership and the critical role played by institutional investors who are not tied to the long-term development of the business; and Purcell emphasizes the importance of diversification and the implications of the widespread adoption of the multi-divisional pattern of organization. Each one of these factors on its own might justifiably be thought to present a serious obstacle to the development of a strategic approach. The size of the problem becomes even clearer, however, when it is recognized that, together, they constitute a constellation of impediments which are mutually reinforcing.

Even when the key structural obstacles to the adoption of human resource management are clarified it might be argued that this merely presents practitioners with a convenient set of excuses for relative inaction. We would therefore now like to carry the argument a little further by indicating some of the practical implications for managers at both corporate- and business-unit levels. Of course we cannot guarantee that the pointers will be welcome, in fact it may be expected that, on the contrary, many practitioners will be distinctly discomfited by what we have to say at this point.

The overriding implication for us arising out of a reading of the foregoing chapters is that if there is to be the level of investment in human resource issues that most analysts seem to accept as necessary, then there is a fundamental need for head-office managers to reconsider their role. Either they follow the model of the M-form and become more decisively involved in the formulation of strategy: move that is (to paraphrase Goold and Campbell 1987) from being 'financial controllers' to being 'strategic planners'. Or, if this is seen to be inappropriate in the specific circumstances, they will have to ensure that unit managers can and do assume the responsibility for developing the strategy of their units.

Failing both of these, managers in the operating units have a stark choice. Either they continue merely to respond to the financial regimes imposed from above (in which case there is every prospect that their business will eventually become uncompetitive due to lack of investment), or they take on the responsibility for strategic management themselves. Now this latter option we recognize as being perhaps the most problematical because our information suggests that, surprising though it may seem at first sight, the unit manager who 'diverts' resources into medium- and long-term plans may face censure rather than applause from head offices which are expecting total effort expended on maximizing short-term financial performance. Indeed, we have accordingly encountered instances where business-unit chiefs are in effect practising human resource management in a *covert* fashion because they anticipate negative rather than positive reaction to their developmental activities.

For policy-makers in government and governmental agencies, there is one overriding conclusion: exhortation is not going to be enough. Nor does it seem likely that simply continuing with the divulgation of 'best practice' will be anywhere near sufficient to engender a change in prevailing practices – especially if, as is invariably so, the 'best-case' examples are drawn from business structures of the critical function type where the linkages between corporate plans and human resource plans are so much more self-evident than in the more mixed cases which frequently obtain. The time may well now be right for a more radical approach. Again this can be best illustrated using the crucial example of human resource *development*. A package of measures seems to be required which will encourage companies to work in the direction of policy objectives and to, in effect, penalize them if they do not. Examples of measures of this kind would be financial incentives to invest in training and development; a statutory require-ment to publish details of investment in training and development in company annual reports; the establishment of training and development committees based on the model of health and safety committees; enshrining individuals with the right to training and development opportunities perhaps using some form of 'credits' system.

At a broader level, public policy could move towards a clearer set of objec-tives and arrangements for the training of young people so that the present inchoate patchwork of vocational education and training is replaced with a simpler, more coherent and more effective system. The newly-proposed employer-led local training councils may or may not prove to be effectual, whatever institutional arrangements might eventually emerge; what matters is that budgets should be sufficient and that both employers and employees have appropriate incentives to make training a priority.

The arguments about the market being an appropriate or inappropriate mechanism to cope with such questions will undoubtedly continue. But, on any measure, international comparison of Britain's human resource provision produces a dismal profile. Moreover, the insufficiency of the steps currently being taken to upgrade it would suggest that the situation is now sufficiently dire, and the prospects for competitiveness in the undoubtedly more sophisticated markets of the 1990s so dubious, that some measure of action along the kind of lines adumbrated above would now seem to be imperative.

So far, we have drawn implications for practitioners and policy-makers, in each case it has been necessary to emphasize the shortcomings in the amount of knowledge about current practice and trends let alone the ultimate meanings of current developments. This being so, the implications of the analyses in previous chapters for future research effort is clearly a crucial question and it constitutes the subject of the next, our final, section.

Research agenda

The starting point

Although there are signs of change – the study as well as the practice of employment management appears to be in a state of transition – the existing literature is dominated by two main approaches. The first, and by far the most important in terms of the number of contributions, is intended for managers, and students of management, and is largely concerned with the techniques of personnel management. The second, which draws on a very different tradition, is essentially a critique: labour management is seen largely as a set of controls which are imposed on workers in order to maximize the surplus value of their labour power. Each of these has had a profound influence on how employment management is viewed.

Starting with the former approach, it is evident that the empirical grounding of much of the work in this tradition is extremely dubious. Even within its own terms, of seeking to help managers to do the job better, there are major weaknesses. There is usually very little discussion of the problems managers experience in applying the techniques and, perhaps even more important, little or no information given about what actually happens in practice. Although considerable emphasis is placed on the interaction with the environment, attention is rarely given to the wider society in which the organization operates. Trade unions and the law, for example, are seen largely as external constraints on what goes on in the workplace and there is scarcely any appreciation of the interaction between them and management practice. Even the implications of differences in organization structures, which have received considerable attention in business history and economics, following the pioneering work of Chandler (1962 and 1977) and Williamson (1975), are ignored; one organization is assumed to be much like another. Similarly ignored are differences in ownership structures, in the composition of management, and in market structures – all of which, it can be argued, have a profound effect on management practice. In short, the prescription is universal and so is the analysis.

Some of the criticisms levelled at the prescriptive approach also apply paradoxically to the labour process tradition. With a number of notable exceptions empirical underpinning is too often unsatisfactory, and even when data is presented it seems to be in the form of using examples to illustrate theory rather than to test it. Similarly, although there are numerous statements denying it, the impression given is that, allowing for differences in the stages of capitalism, in size, and technology, things are always and everywhere much the same (though there are of course certain significant instances where this criticism would not be valid (such as Burawoy 1985). Management, it is recognized, does not have matters all its own way and workers' opposition is seen as a potential constraint. Even so, too little attention is paid to specific differences in business structures and institutions such as trade unions and collective bargaining; or to the interaction between management and trade unions in specific contexts and the opportunities and constraints this produces. In short, the impression is generated that managers would appear to have little choice in the way they manage people and, even if they do, it is at the margin and makes little material difference.

The pattern of employment management in Britain is deeply rooted in a distinctive set of historical and institutional conditions. In consequence there is no escape from careful and systematic research if the patterns are to be made clear. The evidence which is available about concrete managerial practices (Sisson (ed.) 1989; Marginson *et al*. 1988) suggests that the approach is *ad hoc* (Thurley 1981: 26) or 'opportunistic' (Purcell and Sisson 1983: 116). Certainly according to the survey evidence the prevailing approaches are in the main very different from the impression to be gained from the prescriptive texts. Thus, although the typical large organization in Britain is likely to employ personnel specialists and have a range of personnel policies, there is usually little integration between them; there is also unlikely to be an explicit philosophy or strategy towards the management of people and little integration of personnel policies with business planning more generally.

Early analysis from more detailed case-study based research (Storey 1987b; and forthcoming) suggests that rather more may be happening on the ground than is apparently detected by the survey method. The central point of the argument remains, however: there is considerable variety of practice, and developments are highly contingent on specific contexts.

Overriding needs

The fundamental need then is for more empirical information. There is still too little data about what actually happens. Take planning, for example. There is only one major survey of the incidence of manpower planning in Britain and this was carried out in 1975. Moreover, this was a simple questionnaire about the coverage of manpower planning. Virtually nothing is known about integration of personnel policies with business policies and business planning. The surveys that have been conducted more commonly consider the reported utilization of techniques such as selection and appraisal. The actual processes by which, for example, people acquire knowledge about what is expected of them are more or less a closed book.

The need for more empirical information must be combined with more analysis. Otherwise, as in the early study of industrial relations there will be a danger of merely indulging in 'fact grubbing' (Bugler 1968). There is a need for theories of the 'middle range' which can come from the more rigorous testing of some relatively simple hypotheses relating policies and practice to structural features.

To what extent, for example, is it the case that organizations which have 'stuck to their knitting', are in fact more likely to adopt a strategic HRM approach than those which tend towards conglomeracy? Purcell's chapter in this volume would suggest that this hypothesis has some validity. Is the nature of personnel policy and practice linked to the nature of the planning systems used more generally? Again, Purcell's chapter is suggestive here. How important is the type of technology in the policies that are adopted towards personnel? Similarly, testable propositions can be constructed and researched in connection with other issues raised in this book. For example, to what extent is it the case that the growth of interest in selection and appraisal is to do with the shift in emphasis in control systems brought about by the changing nature of work? And how far is it the case that the view of training as a cost rather than an investment is inextricably bound up with the nature of ownership and the type of accountancy conventions? Each of these is a major research topic in its own right and there are many more like them.

Implicit in these points are several others which deserve emphasis. The focus of attention should be on employment management as a set of *activities*. Clearly, personnel managers are not unimportant and study of them as a group striving for professional status (see Torrington and Armstrong in this book) is especially critical in understanding what Thurley (1981) has termed the 'stunted growth' of personnel management in Britain. Even so, there is a need to recognize that the 'personnel management or human resource management' issue is only one part of a much wider and more important debate.

There is a need to extend the work of Edwards (1987) and Storey (1987) in understanding the role of line managers. Two main areas are involved. One is policymaking – if, as the survey evidence suggests, personnel managers are not generally involved in matters of strategic importance affecting personnel management, it is important to establish the values of, and constraints on, those who are. The second is implementation; even if personnel managers are involved in the process of drawing up personnel policies, it is the line managers who are responsible for their implementation.

At bottom, the point we would make concerning overriding needs is that a good deal of *analytical work of a fairly fundamental character* still has to be done. The obvious example is the one we used in the previous section relating to the continued under-provision of training and development in Britain despite massive exhortation. There is no shortage of books telling British management how it should go about training and development. The steps are set out very clearly. What is interesting is that it does not get done despite all this! The explanation would seem to lie not in British management myopia or ignorance of the techniques of training, but in structures which impel British management to treat training as a cost. Much work remains to be done, however, in unpicking the meaning-systems and mechanisms which translate broad structural constraints into varying sorts of practical responses.

The next steps

Any serious discussion of research needs has to consider not only the general issues but also suggest, perhaps more contentiously, some of the priorities. Three areas are selected as demanding immediate attention: the development of new forms of employment and the attempts to introduce more flexibility into working arrangements; the balance of emphasis between individualism and collectivism and the associated issue, which Guest raised in Chapter 3, of the tension between IR and HRM; and thirdly, the question of impact and durability of recent innovations, including the issue of what changes have actually been wrought on various workforces. This last is perhaps the crucial issue for it also raises the question of what significance HRM carries for employers; is it really related to productivity and on what grounds does employer interest in the phenomenon rest? Each of these areas will be considered in turn.

The first area, the form and status of employment, has already occasioned considerable controversy in recent years. The debate over whether or not British management is seeking to introduce 'core' and 'peripheral' workforces has become especially heated. Clearly, there has been a considerable increase in what might be termed 'less conventional' forms of employment – to use a more appropriate and less value-laden way of describing such practices as part-time and temporary working, sub-contracting, and franchising. (The alternative term which is sometimes used – 'non-traditional' – is itself misleading in that many of these forms of employment have in fact a lengthy history.) The explanation for these developments, together with the implications, remain unclear. In particular, it is not at all apparent whether the balance of pressures rests with 'demand-side' or 'supply-side' considerations. In other words, does the growth of these forms of employment represent a conscious and changing strategy to the employment relationship on the part of British management, much as advocates of the 'core-periphery' model would seem to imply, or does it represent a largely *ad hoc* reaction to changes in the supply of labour – including, for example, the greater proportion of married women who are economically active, and the acute labour shortages in London and the South East? And how is the move towards 'harmonization' and 'single status' to be interpreted? Clearly there is scope for more than just one explanation.

Flexibility of working arrangements has so far elicited less controversy, but it also raises problems of interpretation. On the face of it, for example, there have been considerable changes in working practices. In the case of functional or task flexibility, a wide range of initiatives are reported: the 'combination' of jobs – with the elimination of differences within and between crafts; 'team' working involving interchangeability and flexibility between jobs; 'balanced labour force' techniques designed to deal with shortages and surpluses by having workers in one craft or occupation supplement those in another; the ending of 'trade' supervision under which craftsmen would only accept instructions from a supervisor who had completed an apprenticeship in the same trade; and a breakdown of the

distinction between blue- and white-collar jobs – especially craftsmen and technicians (IRRR 1984: 2–9). Yet Cross's (IRRR 1988: 2–10) study of manufacturing
suggests that relatively little by way of major changes has in fact taken place in
this area. The precise nature and extent of these changes is open to question as
are the more radical claims for changes in job structures and job descriptions.

The second area, the shift in emphasis from 'collectivism' to 'individualism'
or, to put it more appropriately, from management–trade union relations to
management–employee relations, goes to the very heart of the debate over the
move towards the human resource management approach. At the present time,
we think it fair to isolate this as one of the most interesting issues. Having looked
fairly closely at a whole range of different organizations over the past couple
of years, we have reasonably established, to our own satisfaction at least, that
many non-avant-garde, middle-of-the-road, organizations have indeed been under-
taking a quite considerable array of initiatives. These are on a scale totally different,
for example, from that existing in the early 1970s when the literature was full
of references to QWL, job enrichment and the like.

Now, although even mainstream organizations have clearly been affected by
talk of, and action on, issues pertaining to commitment, and devices designed
to reorient individual behaviours, one senses that a critical point has now been
reached. So far, initiatives have largely been taken separate from and parallel
with the ongoing IR machinery (either because the company has chosen to keep
things separate or because the unions rebuffed earlier advances). But managers
now seem to recognize that the not inconsiderable ground won so far is nevertheless
still essentially in the nature of a bridgehead. If organizational 'transformation'
is to be taken much further, then somehow the relationship between the two parallel
approaches to employment management will have to be faced up to and resolved.
If the declared aspirations towards openness, trust, flexibility, commitment and
so on are to take root across the organization, then issues such as sharing the
proceeds will have to be confronted. A fundamental issue which many management teams have skirted is the question of the relative costs of managing with
and without unions. The argument that the representative machinery offers a convenient and available channel through which to come to understandings with a
disparate range of individuals and factions is in part recognized. But, at the same
time, there is an increasing fascination in some circles with the alternative and
previously 'unthinkable' option (and it might be added the largely unthought-
through option) of not only by-passing the unions but at some point completely
ignoring them. A matter for investigation, meanwhile, is the operation of those
cases where the attempt is being made to sustain parallel systems – one collective
and adversarial, the other individual and collaborative. The third issue concerns
the durability and impact of the kind of managed change so far brought about.
The question is frequently asked whether this or that apparent change is durable.
The pendulum metaphor looks less and less apt as time goes by and the question
as normally posed is probably unanswerable. But what ought to be considered
is a more systematic study than has been attempted so far, on the way in which new

employment practices have impacted upon the people who are deemed to be the recipients of the array of 'messages' and initiatives. On this aspect the available evidence to date even about such supposedly well-known cases such as BA and Jaguar, is, on reflection, very slight. Too much of the present literature is restricted to descriptions of formal systems (e.g. the impressive interlacing of multiple communication devices; or the outline of the new training programme). At best this tends to be supplemented with anecdote.

Where some evidence of company turnaround is available it is, at best, usually ambiguous on the question of the contribution made by attitudinal and behavioural changes which may, or may not, have resulted from the array of initiatives which normally accompany such revitalization. Even managers in those organizations which have undergone a productivity and profit transformation tend to be sceptical about the extent to which this has derived from 'hearts and minds' campaigns as opposed to new manufacturing techniques. Yet, if measures designed to win commitment are judged to have made little real impact, how then do we explain the intense interest in them in the past three or four years? Issues pertaining to managerial ideology plainly come to the fore. Is the talk of HRM a cover for old-fashioned work intensification? If it is something more than this, are there none the less grounds for other concerns about the erosion of autonomy?

Clearly, there is scope for many critical questions of this sort under this broad heading. The analysis can even be switched around: what's in it for employers? If the research evidence continues to suggest little connection between job satisfaction and productivity, are proponents of HRM pursuing a chimera or is the project less a question of satisfaction and enrichment as these were previously conceived and rather more to do with a restructuring of attitudes and ideologies?

Concluding remarks

Potentially, then, there are rich opportunities for researchers who are prepared to take the issues seriously. The task, however, is going to be a formidable one. Simply gathering the empirical information is going to take considerable time and resourcefulness. It is one thing to seek out data on fairly bread-and-butter techniques but the difficulty in correcting for underprovision in areas as elusive as which organizations really do pursue an integrated HRM approach suggests that different and more imaginative research techniques will be required. Even with regard to the apparently 'straightforward' topics, it should be remembered that personnel managers and other similar survey respondents are usually assumed to know far more than they actually do (and are prepared to reveal) about their organizations. Investigations in many of the areas we have identified in this chapter are likely to demand the same kind of methodological sophistication which John Kotter argued would be required in advancing the study of general managers. He described this research approach as depending upon:

more longitudinal, historical and multiple-method field research, and it will require less emphasis upon the single most popular research method in use today – the single questionnaire. Unfortunately, shifting our emphasis from research based on a single questionnaire to work based on longitudinal, historical and multi-method field-based studies will not be easy.

(Kotter 1982: 150)

Kotter describes the obstacles as deriving from the sheer time-consuming nature of such work. Young academics face the temptation to produce output which is measurable in the short run in order to meet the pressures deriving from lack of tenure and/or from the promotion system. (Ironically the human resource characteristics of academia relating to recruitment, retention, and 'flow' of its manpower therefore affect the very study of the phenomenon!) Research students may have the time but lack the experience and standing which may be required in order to gain long-term, close access to senior management. Older, tenured academics may have the credibility but Kotter implies they may not have the stamina which this kind of research can demand. Moreover, they may in fact not have the time either if other commitments they have accumulated crowd out research of this kind.

Although Kotter is addressing himself to the academic employment conditions in the United States the points seem to have an increasing bearing on the developing situation in Britain.

The kind of 'basic' or 'fundamental' research which is being advocated here, and which emphasizes structures rather than techniques, can also have policy implications which may be uncomfortable; the prescriptions that very often flow from the logic of the research findings may conflict with the prevailing philosophy or approach of the policymakers of the day. To suggest, for example, that the widespread adoption of financial control systems associated with the M form structure of organization – many of which, in any event, rest on extremely dubious accountancy conventions – is at odds with seeing expenditure on people as an investment, is unlikely to be well received by those senior managers who have introduced such systems. Similarly, to conclude, even on the basis of exhaustive case study and survey work, that some form of remissible training tax is going to be necessary to help overcome the structural problems preventing most British managements investing in training is hardly likely to win friends in present government circles; intervention of this sort is likely to be viewed as a major departure from their preferred stance on industrial policy issues.

Clearly, these are formidable obstacles and there are no simple answers. However, not all is gloom and doom. This book itself exemplifies the fact that there are researchers able to look at the issues in a fresh and stimulating way. And a final observation should also help to rekindle optimism. The experience of our involvement in a wide range of teaching, research, and conference activities suggests that there may also be unsuspected allies among managers themselves:

managers who, occupying senior positions which carry heavy responsibilities, have shown themselves eager to take a fresh and critical look at the whole range of practices and assumptions which together constitute human resource management.

Bibliography

ACAS (1988) *Annual Report, 1987*, London: ACAS.

Aggarwal, S.C. (1985) 'MRP, JIT, OPT, FMS? Making sense of production operations systems', *Harvard Business Review*, September/October.

Ahlstrand, B. and Purcell, J. (1988) 'Employee relations strategy in the multi-divisional company', *Personnel Review*, vol. 17, no. 3.

Allen, D. (1985) 'Strategic management accounting', *Management Accounting*, March.

Andrews, K.R. (1980) *The Concept of Corporate Strategy*, Homewood, Ill.: Irwin.

Angle, H.L. and Perry, J.L. (1986) 'Dual commitment and the labor-management relationship climate', *Academy of Management Journal*, no. 29.

Anthony, R.N. and Dearden, J. (1980) *Management Control Systems*, (4th edn), Homewood, Ill.: Richard D. Irwin.

Argyris, C. (1953) *The Impact of Budgets on People*, New York: The Controllership Foundation.

Armstrong, M. (1987) 'Human resource management: a case of the emperor's new clothes?', *Personnel Management*, vol. 19, no. 8.

Armstrong, M. (1988) *A Handbook of Human Resource Management*, London: Kogan Page.

Armstrong, P. (1987a) 'The personnel profession in the age of management accountancy', *Personnel Review*, vol. 17, no. 1.

Armstrong, P. (1987b) 'The rise of accounting controls in British capitalist enterprises', *Accounting, Organisations and Society*, vol. 12, no. 5.

Armstrong, P. and Goodman, J. (1979) 'Managerial and supervisory custom and practice', *Industrial Relations Journal*, vol. 10, no. 3.

Arthurs, A. and Kinnie, N. (1984) 'Time up for clocking?', *Employee Relations*, no. 3.

Atkinson, J. (1984) 'Manpower strategies for the flexible firm', *Personnel Management*, August.

Atkinson, J. and Meager, N. (1986) *Changing Patterns of Work – How Companies Introduce Flexibility to Meet New Needs*, Falmer: IMS/OECD.

Bain, G. (ed.) (1983) *Industrial Relations in Britain*, Oxford: Blackwell.

Bain, G.S. and Clegg, H.A. (1974) 'A strategy for industrial relations research in Great Britain', *British Journal of Industrial Relations*, vol. 12, March.

Baird, L. and Meshoulam, I. (1988) 'Managing the two fits of strategic human resource management', *Academy of Management Review*, vol. 13, no. 1.

Ballin, M. (1986) 'How British Steel tempered the job cuts', *Transition*, January.

Barham, K., Fraser, J. and Heath, L. (1988) *Management for the Future*, Berkhamsted and London: Ashridge Management College and Foundation for Management Education.

Barnett, C. (1986) *The Audit of War*, London: Macmillan.

Bartram, D. and Bayliss,R. (1984) 'Automated testing: Past, present and future', *Journal of Occupational Psychology*, vol. 57.

Bassett, P. (1986) *Strike Free*, London: Macmillan.

Bassett, P. (1988) Non-unionism's growing ranks', *Personnel Management*, March.

Batstone, E. (1979) 'Systems of domination, accommodation and industrial democracy', in Burns, T. (ed.), *Work and Power*, London: Sage Publications.

Batstone, E. (1984) *Working Order*, Oxford: Blackwell.

Batstone, E., Ferner, A. and Terry, M. (1984) *Consent and Efficiency*, Oxford: Blackwell.

Beattie, D. (1987) 'Integrating human resource and business plans at ICL', Institute of Personnel Management, National Conference Paper, *mimeo*.

Beer, M., Spector, B., Lawrence, P., Mills, D. and Walton, R. (1985) *Human Resources Management: A General Manager's Perspective*, New York: Free Press.

Beer, M. and Spector, B. (1985) 'Corporatewide transformations in human resource management', in Walton, R.E. and Lawrence, P.R. (eds), *Human Resource Management, Trends and Challenges*, Boston: Harvard Business School Press.

Bell, D. and Hanson, D. (1984) *Profit-sharing and Employee Shareholding*, London: Industrial Participation Association.

Bendix, R. (1963) *Work and Authority in Industry*, New York: Harper and Row.

Benjamin, A. and Benson, N. (1986), 'Why ignore the value of people?', *Accountancy*, February.

Bessant, J. (1983) 'Management and manufacturing innovation: the case of information technology', in Winch, G. (ed.), *Information Technology in Manufacturing Processes*, London: Rossendale.

BIM (1963) *A Survey of Selection Methods in British Industry*, London: British Institute of Management.

Blackburn, R.M. and Mann, M. (1979) *The Working Class in the Labour Market*, Cambridge: Cambridge University Press.

Blau, P.M. and Schoenherr, R.A. (1971) *The Structure of Organisations*, New York: Basic Books.

Boddy, D., McCalman, J. and Buchanan, D.A. (eds), (1988), *The New Management Challenge: Information Systems for Improved Performance*, London: Croom Helm.

Boston Consulting Group, (1970) *The Product Portfolio Concept*, Perspective No. 66, Boston Consulting Group, Inc.

Bowen, P.(1987) 'High performance management', *Focus on Adult Training*, no. 12.

Bowey, A. (1973) 'The changing status of the supervisor', *British Journal of Industrial Relations*, XI.

Bowey, A.M. and Thorpe, R. (1986) *Payment Systems and Productivity*, Basingstoke: Macmillan.

Boyatzis, R. (1982) *The Competent Manager*, New York: Wiley.

Bradley, K. and Gelb, A.(1986) *Share Ownership for Employees*, London: Public Policy Centre.

Bradley, K. and Hill, S. (1987), 'Quality circles and managerial interests', *Industrial Relations*, vol. 26, no. 1.

Brady, T. (1987) *Education and Training in Lucas Industries*, London: National Economic Development Office.

Brandes, S. (1976) *American Welfare Capitalism 1880–1940*, Chicago: University of Chicago.

Braverman, H. (1974) *Labor and Monopoly Capital*, New York: Monthly Review Press.
Briggs, A. (1961) *Social Thought and Social Action: a Study of the Work of Seebohm Rowntree*, London: Longman.
British Institute of Management (1966) *Budgetary Control in the Small and Medium Size Company*, Information summary no. 126, London: British Institute of Management.
Brown, G.F. and Read, A.R. (1984) 'Personnel and training policies – some lessons for western companies', *Long Range Planning*, vol. 17, no. 2.
Brown, J.K. and O'Connor, R. (1974) *Planning and the Corporate Director*, Report no. 627, New York: Conference Board.
Brown, W. (ed.) (1981) *The Changing Contours of British Industrial Relations*, Oxford: Basil Blackwell.
Brunsson, N. (1982) 'The irrationality of action and action rationality: decisions, ideologies and organizational actions', *Journal of Management Studies*, vol. 19, no. 1.
Buchanan, D. (1983) 'Technological imperatives and strategic choice', in Winch, G. (ed.), (1983), *Information Technology in Manufacturing Processes*, London: Rossendale.
Buchanan, D. and Boddy, D. (1983) *Organisations in the Computer Age: Technological Imperatives and Strategic Choice*, Aldershot: Gower.
Buchanan, D. and McCalman, J. (1988) 'Confidence, visibility and performance: the effects of shared information in computer-aided hotel management', in Boddy, D. *et al.* (eds) *The New Management Challenge: Information Systems for Improved Performance*, London: Croom Helm.
Bugler, J. (1968) 'The new Oxford group', *New Society*, 15 February.
Bullock, Lord, (1977) *Report of the Committee of Inquiry on Industrial Democracy*, Cmnd 6706, London: HMSO.
Burawoy, M. (1979) *Manufacturing Consent*, Chicago: University of Chicago Press.
Bureau of National Affairs, (1983) *Performance Appraisal Programs*, Washington DC: ENA.
Cannon, J. (1979) *Cost-effective Personnel Decisions*, London: Institute of Personnel Management.
Cassels, J.S. (1985) 'Learning, work and the future', *Royal Society of Arts Journal*, June.
Chandler, A.D. (1962) *Strategy and Structure*, Cambridge, Mass: MIT Press.
Chandler, A.D. (1977) *The Visible Hand: The Managerial Revolution in American Business*, Cambridge, Mass: Harvard University Press.
Channon, D. (1982) 'Industrial structure', *Long Range Planning*, vol. 15, no. 5.
Child, J. (1964) 'Quaker employers and industrial relations', *Sociological Review*, vol. 12, no. 3.
Child, J. (1972) 'Organization structure, environment and performance: the role of strategic choice', *Sociology*, no. 6.
Child, J. (1980) 'Factors associated with the managerial rating of supervisory performance', *Journal of Management Studies*, October.
Child, J. (1984) 'New technology and developments in management organisation', *Omega*, vol. 12, no. 3.
Child, J. and Partridge, B. (1982) *Lost Managers*, Cambridge: Cambridge University Press.
Christiansen, H., Cooper, A.C. and Dekluyver, C.A. (1982) 'The dog business: a re-examination', *Business Horizons*, November/December.
Church, R. (1971) 'Profit sharing and labour relations in England in the nineteenth century', *International Review of Social History*, no. 14.
Coates, J.B., Smith, J.E., and Stacey, R.J. (1983) 'Results of a preliminary survey

into the structure of divisionalised companies, divisionalised performance appraisal, and the associated role of management accounting', in Cooper, D., Scapens, R., and Arnold, J. *Management Accounting Research and Practice*, London: Institute of Cost and Management Accounts.

Cockburn, C. (1983) *Brothers: Male Dominance and Technological Change*, London: Pluto Press.

Collinson, D. (1987) 'Who controls selection', *Personnel Management*, May.

Collinson, D. (1988) *Barriers to Fair Selection: A multi-sector study of recruitment practices*, London: HMSO.

Constable, J. and McCormick, R. (1987) *The Making of British Managers*, London: British Institute of Management.

Coopers and Lybrand (1985) *A Challenge to Complacency: Changing Attitudes to Training*, London: Manpower Services Commission.

Courtney, G. and Hedges, B. (1977) *A Survey of Employers' Recruitment Practices*, London: Social and Community Planning Research.

Cowling, A.G. and Mailer, C.J.B. (1981) *Managing Human Resources*, London: Edward Arnold.

Cressey, P., Eldridge, J., and MacInnes, J. (1985) *Just Managing*, Milton Keynes: Open University Press.

Cressey, P. and MacInnes, J. (1980) 'Voting for Ford', *Capital and Class*, no. 11.

CRIDP, (1987) *Developments in Profit-sharing and Employee Share Ownership*, Glasgow University Centre for Research in Industrial Democracy and Participation.

Crowther, S. (1988) 'Invitation to Sunderland: corporate power and the local economy', *Industrial Relations Journal*, Spring.

Cuming, M.W. (1975) *The Theory and Practice of Personnel Management*, (3rd edn), London: Heinemann.

Cuthbert, W.H. and Hawkins, K.H. (eds), (1973) *Company Industrial Relations Policies: the Management of Industrial Relations in the 1970s*, Harlow: Longmans.

Dale, B.G. and Lees, J. (1986) *The Development of Quality Circles*, Sheffield: Manpower Services Commission.

Daly, A., Hitchens, D.M.W.N. and Wagner, K. (1985) 'Productivity, machinery and skills in a sample of British and German manufacturing plants', *National Institute Economic Review*, February.

Daniel, W.W. (1986) 'Four years of change for personnel', *Personnel Management*, December.

Daniel, W.W. (1987) *Workplace Industrial Relations and Technical Change*, London: Frances Pinter/Policy Studies Institute.

Daniel, W.W. and Millward, N. (1983) *Workplace Industrial Relations in Britain*, London: Heinemann.

Davis, L.E. and Taylor, I.C. (1976) 'Technology, organization and job structure' in Dubin, R. (ed.), *Handbook of Work, Organization and Society*, Chicago: Rand McNally.

Dawson, P. and McLoughlin, I. (1986) 'Computer technology and the redefinition of supervision: a study of the effects of computerization on railway freight supervisors', *Journal of Management Studies*, no. 23.

Dawson, P. and McLoughlin, I. (1988) 'Organisational choice in the redesign of supervisory systems' in Boddy, D. *et al.* (eds), *The New Management Challenge: Information Systems for Improved Performance*, London: Croom Helm.

Devanna, M.A., Fombrun, C.J. and Tichy, N.M. (1984) 'A framework for strategic human resource management', in C.J. Fombrun *et al.*, *op. cit.*

Director, The (1965) 'Survey of the qualifications of British directors', January.

Dobson, G. (1986) 'Working patterns in the north of England', London: BIM, 1986.

Donaldson, B. (1986) 'Customer service – the missing dimension in marketing management', *Journal of Marketing Management*, winter vol 2, no. 2.

Donovan, Lord, (1968) *Report of the Royal Commission on Trade Unions and Employers Associations*, London: HMSO.

Dore, R.P. (1985) 'Financial structures and the long-term view', *Policy Studies*, vol. 6, part 1, July.

Drucker, P.F. (1968) *The Practice of Management*, London: Pan Books.

Dulewicz, V. (1984) 'Uses and abuses of selection tests', *Personnel Management*, January.

Dunkerley, D. (1975) *The Foreman*, London: Routledge and Kegan Paul.

Edwards, P.K. (1987) *Managing the Factory: a Survey of General Managers*, Oxford: Blackwell.

Edwards, R. (1979) *Contested Terrain*, London: Heinemann.

Equal Opportunities Review, (1985), 'Discrimination law: the American example', May–June.

Evans, E. and Cowling, A. (1985) 'Personnel's part in organisational restructuring', *Personnel Management*, January.

Fayol, H. (1949) General and Industrial Management, London: Pitman.

Fifield, D.M. (1987) 'The implications and expectations of ownership', *Business Graduate Journal*, vol. 17, no. 1, January.

Financial Times (1988) 'New town looks to the young and skilled', 18 January.

Flamholz, E. (1974) *Human Resource Accounting*, Encino, Calif: Dickenson Publishing Co.

Flanders, A. (1965) *Industrial Relations: What is Wrong with the System?*, London: Faber.

Fletcher, C. (1984) 'What's new in performance appraisal', *Personnel Management*, February.

Fletcher, C. and Williams, R. (1985) *Performance Appraisal and Career Development*. London: Hutchinson.

Fombrun, C., Tichy, N.M., and Devanna, M.A. (1984) *Strategic Human Resource Management*, Chichester, Sussex: John Wiley.

Fortune, (1988) 'Corporate strategy for the 1990s', 29 February.

Foulkes, F. (1980) *Personnel Policies in Large Non-Union Companies*, Englewood Cliffs, N.J.: Prentice Hall.

Foulkes, F.K. (ed.), (1986), *Strategic Human Resource Management. A Guide for Effective Practice*, Englewood Cliffs, New Jersey: Prentice Hall.

Fowler, A. (1985) 'Getting into organisational restructuring', *Personnel Management*, February.

Fowler, A. (1987) 'When chief executives discover HRM', *Personnel Management*, vol. 19, no. 3.

Fox, A. (1974), *Beyond Contract: Work, Power and Trust Relations*, London: Faber and Faber.

Fox, J. (1988) 'Norsk Hydro's new approach takes root', *Personnel Management*, January.

Freedman, A. (1985) *Changes in Managing Employee Relations*, New York: The Conference Board.

Friedman, A. (1977) *Industry and Labour*, London: Macmillan.

Fudge, C. (1986) 'Retraining for new technology: six success stories', *Personnel Management*, February.

George, K.D. and Ward, T.S. (1975) *The Structure of Industry in the EEC*, Cambridge: Cambridge University Press.

Giddens, A. (1971) *Capitalism and Modern Social Theory*, Cambridge: Cambridge University Press.

Giles, W.J. and Robinson, D.F. (1972) *Human Asset Accounting*, London: Institute of Personnel Management and Institute of Cost and Management Accountants.

Gill, C. (1984) 'Swedish wage-earner funds: the road to economic democracy?', *Journal of General Management*, vol. 9, no. 3.

Gill, D. (1977) *Appraising Performance: Present Trends and the Next Decade*, London: Institute of Personnel Management.

Gill, D., Ungerson, B. and Thakur, M. (1973) *Performance Appraisal in Perspective*, London: Institute of Personnel Management.

Glueck, W.F. (1974) *Personnel. A Diagnostic Approach*, Dallas, Texas: Business Publications.

Goldsmith, W. and Clutterbuck, D. (1984) *The Winning Streak*, London: Weidenfeld and Nicholson.

Golzen, G. (1988) 'How "company cultures" can block innovation', *Financial Times*, 24 January.

Goold, M. and Campbell, A. (1986) *Strategies and Styles: The Role of the Centre in Managing Diversified Corporations*, Oxford: Blackwell.

Gouldner, A. (1954) *Wild Cat Strike*, New York: Harper and Row.

Grant, D. (1987) 'Automating the selection procedure', *Personnel Management*, July.

Grieco, M. and Whipp, R. (1986) 'Women and the workplace: gender and control in the labour process, *Gender and the Labour Process*, D. Knights and H. Willmott, (eds), Aldershot: Gower.

Grinyer, P., Mayes, D. and McKiernan, P. (1987) 'Sharpbenders: the process of marked and sustained improvement in performance in selected UK companies', paper presented to British Academy of Management, University of Warwick, September.

Gowler, D. and Legge, K. (1986) 'Personnel and paradigms: four perspectives on the future', *Industrial Relations Journal*, vol. 17, no. 3.

Guest, D. (1982) 'Has the recession really hit personnel management?', *Personnel Management*, vol. 14, no. 10.

Guest, D. (1987) 'Human resource management and industrial relations', *Journal of Management Studies*, vol. 24, no. 5.

Guest, D. (1988) 'Human resource management; a new opportunity for psychologists or another passing fad?', *The Occupational Psychologist*, no. 2.

Hakim, K. (1988) 'Seminar presentation', LSE, January, 1988.

Hall, D.T. and Goodale, J.G. (1986) *Human Resource Management Strategy, Design and Implementation*, Glenview, Ill.: Scott Foresman and Company.

Hall, L. and Torrington, D. (1986) 'Why not use the computer? The use and lack of use of computers in personnel', *Personnel Review*, vol. 15, no. 1.

Hamermesh, R.G. (1986) *Making Strategy Work: How Senior Managers Produce Results*, New York: Wiley.

Handy, C. (1987) *The Making of Managers: a Report on Management Education, Training and Development in the United States, West Germany, France, Japan, and the UK*, London: National Economic Development Office.

Hannah, L. (1986) *Inventing Retirement*, Cambridge University Press.

Harrigan, K.R. (1980) *Strategies for Declining Businesses*, Lexington, Mass.: DC Heath.

Haspeslagh, P. (1982) 'Portfolio planning: uses and limits', *Harvard Business Review*, January–February.

Hax, A.C. and Majlup, N.S. (1983) 'The use of the industry attractiveness –
business strength matrix in strategic planning', *Interfaces*, April.

Hayes, R.H. and Garvin, D.A. (1983) 'Managing as if tomorrow mattered', *The
McKinsey Quarterly*, Spring.

Hedley, B. (1977) 'Strategy and the business portfolio'. *Long Range Planning*, vol.
10, no. i.

Hegarty, W.H. and Hoffman, R.G. (1987) 'Who influences strategic decisions?',
Long Range Planning, vol. 20, no. 2.

Hendry, C. and Pettigrew, A. (1986) The practice of strategic human resource
Management', *Personnel Review*, vol. 15, no. 3.

Hendry, C. and Pettigrew, A. (1987) 'Banking on HRM to respond to change',
Personnel Management, November.

Hendry, C. and Pettigrew, A. (1988) 'Multiskilling in the round', *Personnel
Management*, vol. 20, no. 4.

Hickson, D.J., Butler, R.J., Cray, D., Mallory, G.R. and Wilson, D.G. (1986) *Top
Decisions: Strategic Decision Making in Organisations*, Oxford: Blackwell.

Hill, C.W.L, and Hoskisson, R.E. (1987) 'Strategy and structure in the multiproduct
firm', *Academy of Management Review*, vol. 12, no 2.

Hill, C.W.L. and Pickering, J.F. (1986) 'Divisionalisation, decentralisation and
performance of large United Kingdom companies', *Journal of Management
Studies*, vol. 23, no. 1.

Hirsh, W. and Bevan, S. (1988) *What Makes a Manager?* Brighton, Institute of
Manpower Studies, University of Sussex.

Hollway, W. (1984) 'Fitting work: psychological assessment in organisations', in J.
Henriques, *et al. Changing the Subject*, London: Methuen.

Hopper, T. and Powell, A. (1985) 'Making sense of research into the organisational
and social aspects of management accounting: a review of its underlying
assumptions', *Journal of Management Studies*, vol. 22, no. 5.

Hopwood, A. (1974) *Accounting and Human Behaviour*, London: Haymarket.

Hough, L., Keyes, M. and Dunnette, M. (1988), 'An evaluation of three alternative
selection procedures', *Personnel Psychology*, vol. 36.

Hunt, J. (1987), 'Hidden extras: how people get overlooked in takeovers', *Personnel
Management*, July.

Hyman, J. and Schuller, T. (1983) *Employee Participation in the Management of
Pension Schemes*, Glasgow University, Centre for Research in Industrial
Democracy and Participation.

Hyman, J. and Schuller, T. (1984) 'Occupational pension schemes and collective
bargaining', *British Journal of Industrial Relations*, vol. 22, no. 3.

Hyman, R. (1987) 'Strategy or structure? Capital, labour and control', *Work,
Employment and Society*, vol. 1, no. 1, March.

Incomes Data Services, (1986) 'YTS: The two year scheme', IDS Study, no. 353, January.

Incomes Data Services (1987) 'Performance Appraisal of Manual Workers', Study
no. 390, July.

Incomes Data Services, (1988a) 'A slow start for profit-related pay', *IDS Report*,
532, London.

Incomes Data Services, (1988b) *Flexible Working*, Study 407. London: IDS.

Industrial Relations Review and Report (1984) 'Flexibility agreements: the end of
who does what?', March, no. 316.

Industrial Relations Review and Report (1984) 'Merit pay for manual workers', May,
no, 319.

Industrial Relations Review and Report (1986) 'Nissan: a catalyst for change',
November, no. 379.

Industrial Relations Review and Report, (1987) 'Manual workers' appraisal – a growing trend surveyed', August, no. 398.

Institute of Personnel Management (1963) 'Statement on personnel management and personnel policies', *Personnel Management*, March.

Jauch, R. and Skigen, M. (1977) 'Human resource accounting: a critical evaluation', in Benston, G.J. (ed.), *Contemporary Cost Accounting and Control*, Boston: CBI Publishing Co.

Jenkins, R. (1986) *Racism and Recruitment. Managers, Organisations and Equal Opportunity in the Labour Market*, Cambridge: Cambridge University Press.

Jewson, N. and Mason, D. (1986) 'Modes of discrimination in the recruitment process: formalisation, fairness and efficiency', Sociology vol. 20, no. 1, February.

Johnson, G. (1987) *Strategic Change and the Management Process*, Oxford: Blackwell.

Jones, C.J. (1980) *Financial Planning and Control: a Survey of Practices by U.K. Companies*, London: Institute of Cost and Management Accountants, Occasional Paper.

Jucius, M.J. (1975) *Personnel Management*, (8th edn,), Homewood, Ill.: Irwin.

Kanter, R.(1984) *The Change Masters*, London: Allen & Unwin.

Kaplan, R.S. (1985) 'Yesterday's accounting undermines production', *The McKinsey Quarterly*, Summer.

Keep, E. (1987) 'Britain's attempt to create a national vocational, educational and training system: a review of progress', *Warwick Papers in Industrial Relations*, number 16, Coventry: University of Warwick.

Kelly, J.(1988) *Trade Unions and Socialist Politics*, London: Verso.

Kennedy, G.(1987) *Tioxide UK Limited: The Introduction of Staff Status*, London: Daily Telegraph.

Kinnie, N.(1986) *Introducing Information Technology into British Industry – The Case of Time Recording Equipment*, End of Contract Report to the ESRC.

Kinnie, N. and Arthurs, A. (1986) 'Clock, clock – who's there?', *Personnel Management*, August.

Kinnie, N. and Arthurs, A.(1988) 'New techniques for recording time at work: their implications for supervisory training and development', in D. Boddy *et al.* (eds) *The New Management Challenge: Information Systems for Improved Performance*, London: Croom Helm.

Klein, K. and Rosen, C. (1986) 'Employee stock ownership in the United States', in Stern, R. and McCarthy, S. (eds), *The Organizational Practice of Democracy*, New York: John Wiley.

Klock, H.S. (1986) 'Decentralization: the key to the growth of the human resources function' in Foulkes, F.K. (ed.), *Strategic Human Resource Management. A Guide for Effective Practice*, Englewood Cliffs, New Jersey: Prentice Hall.

Knights, D. and Willmott, H. (eds) (1987) *Managing the Labour Process*, Gower: Aldershot.

Kochan, T.A. (ed.), (1985) *Challenges and Choices Facing American Labour*, Cambridge, Mass: MIT Press.

Kochan, T.A. and Barocci, T.A. (1985) *Human Resource Management and Industrial Relations*, Boston: Little Brown and Company.

Kochan, T.A., and Chalykoff, J.B. (1987) 'Human resource management and business life cycles: some preliminary propositions' in Kleingartner, A. and Anderson, C.S. (eds) *Human Resource Management in High Technology Firms*, Lexington Mass., Lexington Books.

Kochan, T.A. Katz, H., and McKersie, R.B. (1986) *The Transformation of American Industrial Relations*, New York: Basic Books.

Kotter, J.P. *The General Managers*, New York: The Free Press, 1982.

Labour Research Department, (1988), *Labour Research*, vol. 77, no. 4, April.

Leadbeater, C. (1987) 'The YTS: positive effects but improvements needed', *Financial Times*, 18 November.

Leavitt, N.J. and Whisler, T.L. (1988) 'Management in the 80s', *Harvard Business Review*, no. 36.

Lee, R.A. and Piper, J.A. (1987) 'Towards a conceptual framework for analysing managerial promotion processes', Loughborough, Department of Management Studies, Loughborough University of Technology, mimeo.

Legge, K. (1978) *Power, Innovation and Problem Solving in Personnel Management*, Maidenhead: McGraw-Hill.

Legge, K. (1988) 'Personnel management in recession and recovery: a comparative analysis of what the surveys say', *Personnel Review*, vol. 17, no. 2.

Lessom, R. (1986) *The Roots of Excellence*, Harmondsworth: Penguin.

Lewis, C. (1984) 'What's new in selection', *Personnel Management*, January.

Lewis, C. (1985) *Employee Selection*, London: Hutchinson.

Lindopp, E. and Haslett, P. (1988) 'Long-term pay deals: an interim verdict', *Personnel Management*, April.

Lockyer, K. (1983) *Production Management*, London: Pitman.

Long, P. (1986) *Performance Appraisal Revisited*, London: Institute of Personnel Management.

MacBeth, D. (1988) 'Manufacturing information systems at the crossroads' in Boddy, D., McCalman, J. and Buchanan, D. (eds) *The New Management Challenge: Information Systems for Improved Performance*, London: Croom Helm.

MacInnes, J. (1987) *Thatcherism at Work*, Milton Keynes: Open University Press.

MacKay, L. (1987) 'The future – with consultants', *Personnel Review*, vol. 16, no. 4.

MacKay, L. and Torrington, D. (1986) *The Changing Nature of Personnel Management*, London: Institute of Personnel Management.

McMillan, I.C., Hambrick, D.C. and Day, D.L. (1982) 'The product portfolio and profitability – a PIMS based analysis of industrial-product businesses', *Academy of Management Journal*, 25 (4).

McRae, H. (1988) 'Managements will buy but firms won't yet sell', *Guardian*, 11 April, London.

Maguire, M. (1986) 'Recruitment as a means of control', *The Changing Experience of Employment*, (eds), Purcell, K., Wood, S., Watson, A., and Allen, S., London: Macmillan.

Mangham, I.L. and Silver, M.S. (1986) *Management Training: Context and Practice*, School of Management, University of Bath, ESRC/DTI Report.

Manpower Services Commission (1983) *MSC Corporate Plan 1983/87*, Sheffield: MSC.

Manpower Services Commission (1985) *Adult Training in Britain*, Sheffield: MSC.

Manpower Services Commission/National Economic Development Office (1986) *Challenge to Complacency*, Sheffield: MSC.

Manpower Services Commission/National Economic Development Office (1987) *People: The Key to Success*, prepared by Peat Marwick McLintock: HMSO.

Manwaring, A. (1983) 'The extended internal labour market', *Cambridge Journal of Economics*, vol. 8, no. 2.

Manwaring, A. and Wood, S. (1985) 'The ghost in the labour process', in D. Knight *et al.* (eds) *Job Redesign: Critical Perspectives on the Labour Process*, London: Heinemann.

Marchington, M. and Armstrong, P. (1985) 'Involving employees through the recession', *Employee Relations*, vol. 7, no. 5.

Marginson, P., Edwards, P., Martin, R., Purcell, J., and Sisson, K. (1988) *Beyond the Workplace*, Oxford: Blackwell.

Martin, P. and Nicholls, J. (1987) *Creating a Committed Workforce*, London: IPM.

Mayo, E. (1933) *The Human Problems of an Industrial Civilization*, New York: Macmillan.

Megginson, L.C.C. (1972) *Personnel – A Behavioral Approach to Administration*, (revised edn), Homewood, Ill.: Irwin.

Mercer, D. (1987) *IBM: How the World's Most Successful Company is Managed*, London: Kogan Page.

Metcalf, D. (1988) 'Water notes dry up', mimeo: LSE, June.

Miles, R.E. and Snow, C.C. (1984) 'Designing strategic human resources systems', *Organizational Dynamics*, Summer.

Miller, K.M. and Hydes, J. (1971) *The Use of Psychological Tests in Personnel Work*, vol. 1, London: Independent Assessment and Research Centre.

Miller, P. (1987) 'Strategic industrial relations and human resource management – distinction, definition and recognition', *Journal of Management Studies*, no. 24.

Millward, N. and Stevens, M. (1986) *British Workplace Industrial Relations 1980–84*, Aldershot: Gower.

Mintzberg, J. (1979) *The Structuring of Organisations*, Englewood Cliffs, New Jersey: Prentice Hall.

Morgan, G. (1986) *Images of Organization*, Beverley Hills: Sage.

Morgan, K. and Sayers, A. (1984) 'A modern industry in a mature region: the remaking of management and labour relations', University of Sussex, Urban and Regional Studies, working paper no. 39.

Morris, T. and Wood, S. (1988) 'Change and continuity in British industrial relations', mimeo: London Business School, May.

Mowday, R., Porter, L., and Steers, R. (1982) *Employee–Organization Linkages: The Psychology of Commitment, Absenteeism and Turnover*, New York: Academic Press.

Mumford, E. (1972) 'Job satisfaction: a method of analysis', in *Personnel Review*, vol. 1, no. 3.

Munchus, G. (1985) 'The status of pre-employment enquiry restrictions on the employment and hiring function', *Employee Relations*, vol. 7, no. 3.

National Economic Development Office, (1965) *Management Recruitment and Development*, London: NEDO.

National Economic Development Office/Manpower Services Commission, (1984) *Competence and Competition*, London, NEDO.

National Economic Development Office, (1987) *Education and Training in Lucas Industries*, London: NEDO/MSC/DTI.

Nichols, T. (1980) 'Management, ideology and practice', in Esland, G. and Salaman, G. (eds) *The Politics of Work and Occupations*, Milton Keynes: Open University Press.

Niven, M.M. *Personnel Management 1913–63*, London: Institute of Personnel Management.

Norburn, D. and Miller, P. (1981) 'Strategy and executive reward: the mismatch in the strategy process', *Journal of General Management*, vol. 63, no. 4.

Odiorne, G.S. (1984) *Strategic Management of Human Resources*, Chicago: Joossey Bass.

Offe, C. (1976) *Industry and Inequality*, London: Edward Arnold.

Oliver, J.M. and Turton, J.R. (1982) 'Is there a shortage of skilled labour?', *British Journal of Industrial Relations*, vol. 20, no. 2.

Ouchi, W. (1981) *Theory Z*, Reading, Mass: Addison-Wesley.

Oversight Hearings Before the Sub-committee on Labor Management Relations of the Committee on Education and Labour, House of Representatives, 96th Congress, First Session (1979) *Pressures in Today's Workplace*, Washington: US Government Printing.

Owens, W.A. and Schoenfeldt, L.F. (1979) 'Towards a classification of persons', *Journal of Applied Psychology*.

Ozanne, R. (1967) *A Century of Labour-Management Relations at McCormick and International Harvester*, Madison: University of Wisconsin Press.

Parker, P. (1986) 'Can we learn from Japan?', *The Guardian*, 3 March.

Parker, R.H. (1969) *Management Accounting: an Historical Perspective*, London: MacMillan.

Pay and Benefits Bulletin (1988) 'Performance pay – new moves, new proposals', January, no. 199.

Peat Marwick (1984) *Financial Management in the Public Sector: a Review 1979–84*, London: Peat Marwick.

Peters, T. and Waterman, R. (1982) *In Search of Excellence*, New York: Harper and Row.

Pettigrew, A.M. (1985) *Awakening Giant*, Oxford: Blackwell.

Piercy, N. (ed.) (1984) *The Management Implications of New Information Technology*, London: Croom Helm.

Pigors, P. and Myers, C.A. (1969) *Personnel Administration* (6th edn), New York: McGraw-Hill.

Pigors, P., Myers, C.A. and Malm, F.T. (1973) *Management of Human Resources*, (3rd edn), New York: McGraw-Hill.

Piore, M.J. and Sabel, C.F. (1984) *The Second Industrial Divide: Possibilities for Prosperity*, New York: Basic Books.

Pointing, D. (1986) 'Retail training in West Germany', *MSC Youth Training News*, April.

Pollert, A. (1988) 'The flexible firm: A model in search of reality, or a policy in search of a practice', *Warwick Papers in Industrial Relations*, no. 19, University of Warwick.

Poole, M. (1988) 'Factors affecting the development of employee financial participation in contemporary Britain', *British Journal of Industrial Relations*, vol. 26, no. 1.

Porter, M.E. (1987a) 'From competitive advantage to corporate strategy', *Harvard Business Review*, May–June.

Prais, S.J. (1985) 'What can we learn from the German system of education and vocational training?', in G.D.N. Worswick (ed.) *Education and Economic Performance*, Aldershot: Gower.

Prais, S.J. and Wagner, K. (1981) 'Some practical aspects of human capital investment: training standards in five occupations in Britain and Germany', *National Institute Economic Review*, November.

Prais, S.J. and Wagner, K. (1988) 'Productivity and management: the training of foremen in Britain and Germany', *National Institute Economic Review*, February.

Purcell, J. (1985) 'Is anybody listening to the corporate personnel department?', *Personnel Management*, September.

Purcell, J. (1987) 'Mapping management styles in employee relations', *Journal of Management Studies*, vol. 24, no. 5.

Purcell, J. and Ahlstrand, B. (1987) 'Business strategy and employee relations structures in the multi-divisional firm', paper presented to the *British Academy of Management*, University of Warwick, September.

Purcell, J. and Gray, A. (1986) 'Corporate personnel departments and the management of industrial relations: two case studies in ambiguity', *Journal of Management Studies*, vol. 23, no. 2.

Purcell, J. and Sisson, K. (1983) 'Strategies and practice in the management of industrial relations', in G. Bain (ed.), *op cit.*

Purcell, J., Marginson, P., Edwards, P., and Sisson, K. (1987) 'The industrial relations practices of multi-plant foreign owned firms', *Industrial Relations Journal*, vol. 18, Summer.

Rajan, A. (1985) *Training and Recruitment Implications of Technical Change*, Aldershot: Gower.

Randell, G., Packard, P., and Slater, J. (1984) *Staff Appraisal*, London: Institute of Personnel Management.

Reichers, A. (1985) 'A review and reconceptualization of organizational commitment', *Academy of Management Review*, vol. 10, no. 3.

Reilly, R. and Chao, G.T. (1982) 'Validity and fairness of some alternative employee selection procedures', *Personnel Psychology*, vol. 35.

Richards, M. (1986) 'Crash courses', *Times Higher Educational Supplement*, 5 July.

Roberts, B. (1987) *Mr Hammond's Cherry Tree: The Morphology of Union Survival*, London: Institute of Economic Affairs.

Robertson, I.T. and Makin, P.J. (1986) 'Management selection in Britain: a survey and critique', *Journal of Occupational Psychology*, vol. 59, no. 1.

Rodgers, P. and Tran, M. (1988) 'US feathers ruffled at British invasion', *The Guardian*, 26 April.

Rothwell, S. (1984) 'Supervisors and new technology', *Employment Gazette*, January.

Rothwell, S. (1985) 'Company employment policies and new technology', *Industrial Relations Journal*, vol. 16, no. 3.

Rothwell, S. and Davidson, D. (1983) 'Training for new technology', in G. Winch, (ed.) *Information Technology in Manufacturing Processes*, London: Rossendale.

Rowe, K. (1964) 'An appraisal of appraisals', *Journal of Management Studies*, vol. 1.

Russell, R. (1985) *Sharing Ownership in the Workplace*, Albany, State University of New York Press.

Santocki, J. (1979) *Auditing: a Conceptual and Systems Approach*, Stockport: Polytechnic Publishers.

Scapens, R. (1983) 'Management accounting research – a change of emphasis', paper 1 in Cooper, D., Scapens, R., and Arnold, J. *Management Accounting Research and Practice*, London: Institute of Cost and Management Accountants.

Schonberger, R. (1982) *Japanese Manufacturing Techniques: Nine Lessons of Simplicity*, London: Collier Macmillan.

Schonberger, R. (1986) *World Class Manufacturing: The Lessons of Simplicity Applied*, London: Collier Macmillan.

Schuler, R.S. and Jackson, S.E. (1987) 'Organizational strategy and organizational level as determinants of human resource management practices', *Human Resource Planning*, vol. 10, no. 3.

Schuller, T. (1985) *Democracy at Work*, Oxford: Oxford University Press.

Schuller, T. (1986) *Age, Capital and Democracy: Member Participation in Pension Scheme Management*, Aldershot: Gower.

Senker, P. (1984) 'Training for automation' in M. Warner (ed.) *Microprocessors, Manpower and Society*, Aldershot: Gower.

Senker, P. (ed.) (1985) *Planning for Microelectronics in the Workplace*, Aldershot: Gower.

Senker, P. and Beesley, M. (1985) 'Computerized production and inventory control systems: some skill and employment implications', *Industrial Relations Journal*, vol. 16, no. 3.

Silverman, D. and Jones, J. (1973) 'Getting in: the managed accomplishment of "correct" selection outcomes', in J. Child (ed.) *Man and Organisation*, London: Allen & Unwin.

Simpson, D. (1986) 'Where hearts and mind are in the front seat', *The Guardian*, 1 August.

Sisson, K. (1988) *The Management of Collective Bargaining*, Oxford: Blackwell.

Sisson, K. (ed.) (1989), *Personnel Management in Britain*, Oxford: Blackwell.

Sisson, K. and Scullion, H. (1985) 'Putting the corporate personnel department in its place', *Personnel Management*, December.

Sisson, K. and Storey, J. (1988) 'Developing effective managers', *Personnel Review*, vol. 17, no. 4.

Smith, E.C. (1982) 'Strategic business planning and human resources: parts I and II', *Personnel Journal*, August.

Smith, G. (1986) 'Profit sharing and employee share ownership in Britain', *Employment Gazette*, September, London.

Smith, M. and Robertson, I.T. (1986) *The Theory and Practice of Systematic Selection*, London: Macmillan.

Sneath, F., Thakur, M., and Medjuck, B. (1976) *Testing People At Work*, London: Institute of Personnel Management.

Sorge, A. and Warner, M. (1980) 'Manufacturing organization and workplace relations in Great Britain and West Germany', *British Journal of Industrial Relations*, XVIII.

Sparrow, P. and Pettigrew, A. (1988) 'Contrasting HRM responses in the changing world of computing', *Personnel Management*, vol. 20.

Steedman, H. (1987) *Vocational Training in France and Britain: Office Work*, discussion paper no. 14, London: National Institute of Economic and Social Research.

Steedman, H. and Wagner, K. (1987) 'A second look at productivity, machinery and skills in Britain and Germany', *National Institute Economic Review*, November.

Steer, P. and Cable, J. (1978) 'International organization and profit: an empirical analysis of large UK companies', *Journal of Industrial Economics*, vol. 27.

Storey, J. (forthcoming), *Developments in the Management of Human Resources*, Oxford: Blackwell.

Storey, J. (1987a) 'Locating the line', University of Warwick, mimeo.

Storey, J. (1987b) 'Developments in the management of human resources: an interim report', *Warwick Papers in Industrial Relations* no. 17, IRRU, School of Industrial and Business Studies, University of Warwick, November.

Streeck, W. (1988) 'The uncertainties of management in the management of uncertainty: employers, labour relations and industrial adjustment in the 1980s', *Work, Employment and Society*, vol. 1, no. 3.

Taylor, F.W. (1911) *Scientific Management*, New York: Harper and Row.

Terry, M. (1977) 'The inevitable growth of informality', *British Journal of Industrial Relations*, vol. 15, no. 1, March.

Thomason, G.F. (1976) *A Textbook of Personnel Management*, (2nd edn), London: IPM.

Thompson, R.S. (1981) 'Internal organization and profit: a note', *Journal of Industrial Economics*, no. 30.

Thurley, K. (1981) 'Personnel management in the UK: a case for urgent treatment', *Personnel Management*, August.

Thurley, K. and Wirdenius, H. (1973) *Supervision: a Reappraisal*, London: Heinemann.

Thurley, K. and Wood, S. (1983) 'Business strategy and industrial relations strategy' in Thurley, K. and Wood, S. (eds) *Industrial Relations and Management Strategy* Cambridge: Cambridge University Press.

Tichy, N.M., Fombrun, C.J., and Devanna, M.A. (1982) 'Strategic human resource management', *Sloan Management Review*, vol. 23, no. 2, winter.

Toner, B. (1985) 'The unionization and productivity debate: an employee opinion survey in Ireland', *British Journal of Industrial Relations*, vol. 22, no. 2.

Torrington, D. and Hall, L. (1987) *Personnel Management, A New Approach*, London: Prentice Hall.

Torrington, D. and MacKay, L. (1986) 'Will consultants take over the personnel function?', *Personnel Management*, February.

Torrington, D., MacKay, I., and Hall, L. (1985) 'The changing nature of personnel management', *Employee Relations*, vol. 7, no. 5.

Tyson, S. (1985) 'Is this the very model of a modern personnel manager?', *Personnel Management*, April.

Tyson, S. (1987) 'Management of the personnel function', *Journal of Management Studies*, September.

Tyson, S. and Fell, A. (1986) *Evaluating the Personnel Function*, London: Hutchinson.

Upton, R. (1987) 'The bottom line: Bejam's ingredients for success', *Personnel Management*, March.

Vollman, T.E. *et al.* (1984) *Manufacturing Planning and Control Systems*, Homewood, Ill.: Richard D. Irwin.

Walker, D.A. (1985) 'Capital markets and industry', *Bank of England Quarterly Bulletin*, December.

Walters, B. (1983) 'Identifying training needs', in Guest, D. and Kenny, T. (eds), *A Textbook of Techniques and Strategies in Personnel Management*, London: IPM.

Walton, R.E. (1985) 'From control to commitment in the workplace', *Harvard Business Review*, vol. 63, no. 2, March–April.

Walton, R.E. (1985) 'Toward a strategy of eliciting employee commitment based on policies of mutuality', in R.E. Walton and P.R. Lawrence (eds) *Human Resource Management, Trends and Challenges*, Boston: Harvard Business School Press.

Walton, R.E. and Lawrence, P.R. (1985) (eds) *Human Resource Management. Trends and Challenges*, Boston: Harvard Business School Press.

Warr, P.B. and Bird, M. (1976) *Identifying Supervisory Training Needs*, London: HMSO.

Watson, T.J. (1977) *The Personnel Managers: A Study in the Sociology of Work and Employment*, London: Routledge and Kegan Paul.

Watson, T.J. (1983) 'Towards a general theory of personnel and industrial relations management', *Occasional Paper Series*, no. 2, Trent Business School, Nottingham.

Weber, M. (1958) *The Protestant Ethic*, New York: Bedminster.

White, M. and Trevor, M. (1983) *Under Japanese Management*, London: Heinemann.

Wickens, P. (1987) *The Road to Nissan*, London: Macmillan.

Wickham, J. (1976) 'Translator's introduction', in C. Offe, *Industry and Inequality*, London: Edward Arnold.

Wilkinson, B. (1983) *The Shop Floor Politics of New Technology*, Aldershot: Gower.

Williamson, O.E. (1975) *Markets and Hierarchies*, New York: Free Press.

Winch, G. (ed.) (1983) *Information Technology in Manufacturing Processes*, London: Rossendale.

Windolf, P. and Wood, S. (1988) *Recruitment and Selection in the Labour Market*, Aldershot: Gower.

Winkler, J. (1974) 'The ghost at the bargaining table: directors and industrial relations', *British Journal of Industrial Relations*, vol. 12, no. 2.

Wood, D. (1983) 'Uses and abuses of personnel consultants', in *Personnel Management*, October.

Wood, S. (1985) 'Recruitment systems and the recession', *British Journal of Industrial Relations*, vol. 24, no. 1.

Wood, S. (1986a) 'The cooperative labour strategy in the US auto industry', *Economic and Industrial Democracy*, vol. 7.

Wood, S. (1986b) 'Personnel management and recruitment', *Personnel Review*, vol. 15, no. 2.

Woodward, J. (1980) *Industrial Organisation: Theory and Practice*, (2nd edn), London: Oxford University Press.

Index

DATE DUE